THE
WORLD ATLAS
OF
ARCHEOLOGY

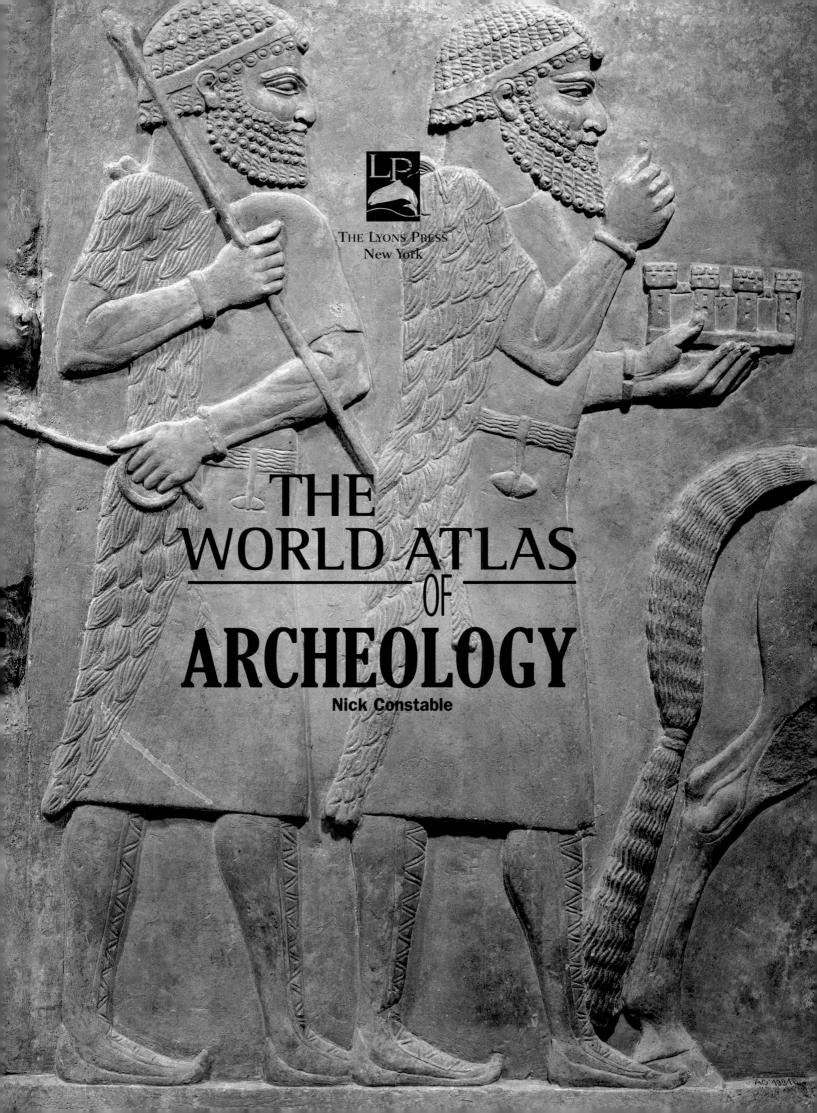

LP

THE LYONS PRESS
New York

THE
WORLD ATLAS
OF
ARCHEOLOGY

Nick Constable

The World Atlas of Archeology

Copyright © The Lyons Press 2000

Original text and design copyright © Thalamus Publishing 1999

Printed and bound in Spain by Graficomo S.A.

ISBN: 1-58574-091-8

Illustrations and reconstructions: Oliver Frey
Maps: Keith Williams and Roger Kean
Design: Joanne Dovey

Picture Acknowledgments
Picture Research by Image Select International Limited.

Frontispiece: *The "Calendar Stone" from the Great Pyramid at Tenochtitlán, depicts the mask of Tonatiuh, surrounded by symbols depicting the earthquake which will end the world. Around this are all the signs of the days of the Aztec year. It now stands in the National Museum of Anthropology in Mexico City.*

Previous pages: *An 8th century BC bas-relief from the palace of Sargon II in Khorsabad, Iraq depicting triumphant Medes with horses.*

INTRODUCTION

In July, 1893, a young Englishman named Austen Henry Layard set out to ride from England to India. Nine months later, he stood on the banks of the Tigris River in northern Mesopotamia and gazed on the dusty mounds of Biblical Nineveh. He was entranced. Layard wrote: "Desolation meets desolation; a feeling of awe succeeds to wonder; for there is nothing to relive the mind, to lead to hope, or to tell of what has gone by."[1] Three years later, the young adventurer tunneled into Nimrud and Nineveh and discovered the shadowy Assyrians of the Second Book of Kings.

Layard was the epitome of the 19th-century adventurer-archeologist. He supervised small armies of laborers, searched assiduously for large and spectacular antiquities and found two Assyrian royal palaces in a month. His magnificent finds were the stuff of legend: lion-headed bulls, bas-reliefs of kings strutting to war and hunting lions, thousands of cuneiform-inscribed clay tablets.

So were the archeological adventures of American traveler John Lloyd Stephens, who explored the rainforests of Central America in search of the ancient Maya while Layard as in Mesopotamia. Stephens wandered through the ruined city of Copín, overgrown with clinging forest, marveling at intricately carved stelae and finely crafted stone walls. All he could hear were troops of monkeys moving through the dry branches overhead. The romance of archeological discovery, of swashbuckling adventure in search of the past, stems from the heady days of Victorian times when you could find a hitherto unknown civilization in a month.

Victorian archeology seems larger than life. Heinreich Schliemann, businessman turned archeologist, who believed in the literal historical truth of Homer's Iliad, found both Troy and a heavily fortified Mycenae. Englishman Flinders Petrie revolutionized excavation in Egypt and found el-Amarna, capital of the heretic pharaoh Akhenaten. Another Englishman, General Augustus Lane Fox Pitt-Rivers, inherited an enormous fortune and devoted himself to developing highly precise methods of archeological excavation. The list of heroic discoverers continues in to the twentieth century: Arthur Evans, discoverer of the Palace of Minos and the Minoan civilization of Crete, Gertrude Bell, desert archeologist in Mesopotamia and, of course, Lord Carnarvon and Howard Carter, who found the Tomb of the young pharaoh Tutankhamun in 1922. The popular image of archeologists as romantic adventurers comes from these, and many other, great discoveries of yesteryear.

Our early predecessors did indeed bear some resemblance to the fictional Hollywood archeologist, Indiana Jones, himself an amalgam of several famous, near legendary excavators. They were as much adventurers as archeologists, at home in remote lands, hundreds of kilometers from their own kind. Henry Layard knew how they felt: "The great tide of civilization has long since ebbed, leaving these scattered wrecks on the solitary shore... We wanderers were seeking what they had left behind, as children gather up the colored shells on the deserted sands."[2]

Archeology has come a long way since Layard floated Assyrian bulls down the Tigris river on goatskin-supported rafts and Schliemann hired engineers from the Suez Canal to trench into ancient Troy. The scientific study of the past was a child of the twentieth century—ten decades which turned archeological discovery from an adventure and an amateur pastime into a precise science. Pollen analysis, sophisticated survey and excavation methods, radiocarbon dating and aerial photography, computers and plant flotation—these are but a few of the scientific advances that have transformed the study of the past. Today archeologists focus not on spectacular finds, but on the minutest of clues studied in the laboratory: tiny seeds, ancient beetles, broken animal bones, and the trace elements in prehistoric copper and volcanic glass. Today, they can tell the direction of the wind on the day of an 8,000-year-old hunt, establish whether Stone Age artisans were left-handed, and date the beams of Indian pueblos to within a year. Today's archeologist is not an adventurer but a time detective—and usually a specialist in a small segment of the past. But these small segments make up the pageant of human history over two-and-a-half million years.

The World Atlas of Archeology celebrates archeological discoveries from every continent and from every chapter of the human past, from the first hominids of two-and-a-half million years ago to the Anglo-Saxons, Vikings, and Chinese empires of the past two millennia. Some of these finds, like the Olduvai Gorge hominids found by Louis and Mary Leakey, were made after years of diligent search and on shoestring budgets. Others like Maya village at El Cerén in San Salvador, came to light by accident and have been excavated with all the panoply of modern archeology. Still others, like the Abu Simbel temple in Egypt, are triumphs of conservation over the inexorable onslaught of modern industrial society. They are part of our collective cultural heritage, a priceless legacy that we must preserve for future generations.

We marvel at the achievement of the ancient Egyptians in building the Pyramids of Giza, gasp in amazement at the magnificent wealth of the Lord Pacal of Maya Tikal, walk the winding contours of Hadrian's Wall, the outermost frontier of the mighty Roman Empire. But all too often we wonder about what has vanished. Sometimes we feel like Hernán

1 Austen Henry Layard, *Nineveh and its Remains.* John Murray, London, 1849, p.155.

2 Layard, op. cit (1849), p.166.

With all the scientific advances in archeology, laborers digging ditches are probably still the best bet when it comes to rewriting history.

Cortés and his Spanish conquistadors as they gazed at the gleaming Aztec capital in the midst of the Valley of Mexico in 1519 and likened it to an enchanted vision. A half century after the Conquest of Mexico, conquistador Bernal Diaz remarked that "all we saw is now vanished." This book teaches us how we owe it to future generations to ensure that the glories of the past which we now enjoy are also theirs to enjoy, not only because of their beauty and ingenuity, but because they offer lessons for today and the future.

As I stand before the Temple of the Feathered Serpent at Teotihuacán, explore the chambers of Minoan Knossos, or admire the sunken court at Chavín de Huantar high in the Andes, I marvel not only at the genius of those who built them, but at the archeological skills which led to their discovery. Our science allows us to identify ancient food remains and trace copper ingots to their source hundreds of kilometers away, but these skills are no substitute for the greatest archeological qualities of all: the sheer common sense and instinct that led Austen Henry Layard to the Assyrians and Mary Leakey to the cranium of Zinjanthropus at Olduvai Gorge. Nick Constable's Atlas is a celebration of the unique qualities of a disciplined search for the past that is one of the great scientific achievements of modern times.

I am often asked whether all the most spectacular archeological finds have been made. The answer is, of course, a resounding no, for we have barely scratched the surface of many continents. A century from now, a book like this will be double the size and an even more lavish celebration of that most priceless of all scientific skills: the archeologist's instinct for discovery.

BRIAN FAGAN
Santa Barbara, California
February, 2000

AFRICA

The richness and diversity of archeological sites in Africa has only come to light within the last hundred years. This is partly attributable to the difficult and dangerous terrain facing expeditions, but also because academic interest inevitably focused on the Ancient Egyptians and the breathtaking array of treasures emerging from graves in the Nile Valley.

While Egypt is rightly regarded as one of the truly great classical civilizations, its history has overshadowed far deeper questions about the continent's role in the origins of humanity. Until the mid-20th century, many anthropologists believed Asia would provide the

Nok figurine

answers to man's evolutionary progress. It was not until this shibboleth was challenged by palæoanthropologists such as Raymond Dart, Louis and Mary Leakey, and the team of Wymer and Singer that attention shifted to Africa as the first realm of humankind.

In more recent times evidence has emerged that complex African civilizations evolved comparatively quickly from the Stone Age to embrace copper, bronze, and even iron-working as early as 450 BC. The Nok people of Nigeria were transformed from "primitive" hunter-gathers to farmers and followers of a fertility religion within the span of a few centuries. Their fascinating terracotta figurines probably inspired later

bronzes of the highest craftsmanship. Meanwhile, in central southern Africa, the arrival of the Shona founded a powerful dynasty that built extraordinary stone fortresses (the zimbabwes), courthouses of god-like rulers.

With such a background, there is only one archeological certainty: Africa has not yet yielded all of her secrets.

A 16th/17th century Nigerian Benin sculpture, probably influenced by the achievements of the much earlier Nok culture, which flourished between 900BC and 200 AD.

Nok
Igbo Ukwu

Sabratha
Leptis Magna

The ruins of Leptis Magna.

Australopithecus
boisei, or
Nutcracker Man.

River
Congo

Lake
Victoria

Olduvai Gorge

Laetoli

Great Rift Valley

Soapstone bird
figure (one of
seven) from Great
Zimbabwe.

Great Zimbabwe

Skull of
Australopithecus
africanus, 2.8m BC.

Apollo II cave

Taung

Klasies river mouth

ANCESTORS OF HUMANITY
The Laetoli Footprints and the Olduvai Gorge

On September 15, 1976, a group of high-spirited young scientists were taking a break from studies at an excavation site at Laetoli, on the northern Tanzania plains. The excavation was run by Mary Leakey, a world-renowned British palæoanthropologist whose previous fossil discoveries were regarded as crucial to the understanding of human evolution.

Despite the weighty reputation of their mentor, the scientists felt in need of some diversionary relaxation and decided on a dried elephant-dung fight—hurling large handfuls at each other amid loud shrieks and laughter. As the battle intensified, one of the group, Andrew Hill, slipped and sprawled head-first onto some hard earth; opening his eyes, he discovered a set of curious imprints. He couldn't have known it, but he had just taken a glimpse three million years back in time.

The marks, Leakey later established, were made by some prehistoric creature that had walked over damp, volcanic earth. Intrigued, she realized that more could lie in the surrounding landscape, and continued her work apace. Within three years she had unearthed the Laetoli Footprints—3.6 million-year-old sets of fossilized footprints from the *Australopithecus* hominid, generally

thought to be the common ancestor of man and apes.

Intriguingly, the prints appeared to be from two separate individuals. One was about 4' 7" (1.4m) tall, the other 4' 5" (1.36m). They had walked side by side in a manner that suggested companionship. Their footmarks were not wildly dissimilar to those a human might make today by strolling along a wet, sandy beach.

Big toes were set close to the others, not jutting outward or demonstrably longer, as is the case in apes. Even more remarkably, close analysis showed the prints of a third *Australopithecus* superimposed on those of the larger set. The unscientific conclusion was that a young *Australopithecus* had deliberately, even playfully, stepped in the footprints of its parent.

Nutcracker caught on film

While there is no evidence to support such speculation, Leakey's discovery of the first marks made by a human ancestor on earth helped to reinforce a transformation in anthropological theory. Up until the early 1970s it had always been thought that walking on two legs was a feature that emerged at about the same time as the development of larger brains and use of stone tools. The discovery by American anthropologist Don C. Johanson of Lucy, a partial australopithecine skeleton, in Ethiopia's Afar depression in 1974, showed that small-brained ape-type creatures were moving on two legs by

above: *Palæoanthropologist Mary Leakey analyzing a trail of hominid footprints fossilized in volcanic ash at Laetoli, Tanzania 1978.*

c.3,600,000 BC	c.3,500,000 BC	c.2,400,000 BC	c.1,800,000 BC	c.1,790,000 BC	c.1,600,000 BC	c.1,000,000 BC	c.400,000 BC
Australopithecus hominid prints from this era found in Tanzania, 1976.	Partial *Australopithecus* skeleton from this period found in Ethiopia, 1974.	Date of oldest stone tools discovered.	*Homo erectus* spreads to south and southeast Asia.	*Australopithecus boisei* or "Nutcracker" man found in Olduvai Gorge, Tanzania, 1959.	Earliest known use of fire, in South Africa.	*Homo erectus* spreads to Europe. Modern Ice Age begins.	Spear found in Germany is oldest wooden weapon discovered.

Evidence was unearthed to smash orthodox doctrines on the origins of man. Africa was the actual cradle of humanity.

above: *A composite photograph of the skull of Australopithecus boisei, or Nutcracker man, found in Tanzania's Olduvai Gorge by Mary Leakey in 1959.*

right: *The Olduvai Gorge, a canyon cut into the Serengeti Plains of Northern Tanzania, remains crucial to our understanding of early human development.*

around 3.5 million years ago—at least a million years before the first stone tools. Laetoli provided further, overwhelming evidence that it was the emergence of upright walking, rather than larger brains, that helped humankind to branch away from its ape cousins.

For Mary Leakey, who died in 1996, it was the final triumph of a glittering career—and another example of the role fate had played in her work. In 1959 she was working with her husband, the outstanding Anglo-Kenyan palæoanthropologist Louis Leakey, at Olduvai Gorge, a ravine up to 330 feet (100m) deep that stretches for 40 miles (100km) across Northern Tanzania. Mary had planned a small trial dig, but as a favor to some filmmakers who wanted to record her hunt for stone tools, she got up early one morning to explore a gully called Frida Leakey Korongo (named after Louis's first wife).

With her Dalmatian dogs Victoria and Sally at her side, she casually began probing some earth washed away by heavy rain and spotted a tiny fragment of skull bone—the first of 400 she was to gather. Months later she had assembled much of the skull of *Australopithecus boisei*, better known as Nutcracker Man on account of his massive back teeth, and dated it to 1.79 million years old. The filming of the operation grabbed the attention of the world and unleashed a wave of funding for similar human origins research, shifting the emphasis away from Asia and into the arid wastes of East Africa.

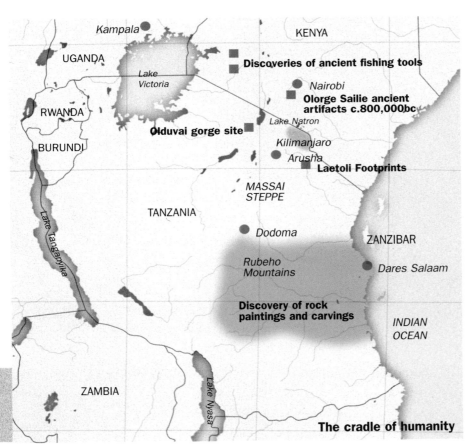

The cradle of humanity

THE SEARCH FOR HOMO SAPIENS

The Taung child, Sterkfontein cave, and the Klasies river mouth excavation

The Leakeys' discoveries at Olduvai, though hugely important, were not the first australopithecine finds. That credit goes to an Australian anatomist called Raymond Dart, Professor of Anatomy at Witwatersrand University, Johannesburg. In 1924 he was handed two wooden boxes of "relics" that had been discovered in the spoil heaps of a lime quarry at Taung (literal meaning: Place of the Lion) in the western Kalahari Desert.

From the second box Dart pulled out a chunk of limestone containing the fossilized skull, face, and lower jaw of a child, now thought to be the prehistoric equivalent of a six-year-old. It took Dart weeks to gently chisel the skull free of its setting, but by the end he was convinced, in his words, of "one of the most significant finds ever made in the history of anthropology".

It was Dart who named the Taung child *Australopithecus africanus*—the "southern ape of Africa"—logging a "type find" that would become common usage among anthropologists. He believed it was one of the missing links between apes and humans, but initially the scientific establishment wasn't so sure.

A dismissed link

For years an intense debate was conducted in academic journals about

Taung's role in the evolutionary scheme of things, with many experts clinging to the idea that the "missing link" should have a much larger brain—a school of thought based on the hoaxed Piltdown Man skull discovered in England around 1913. However, it is now generally accepted that the two-million-year-old Taung, with its human-like jaws and ape-like brain, was an intermediary in the emergence of the human family and

was among at least two types of australopithecines (one heavily built, the other much lighter) roaming southern Africa between one and three million years ago.

Arguments over the arrival of our own genus, *Homo sapiens*, have raged equally fiercely in the corridors of academia. Until the early 1970s the received wisdom was that modern or "near modern" humans appeared in Europe and Africa at

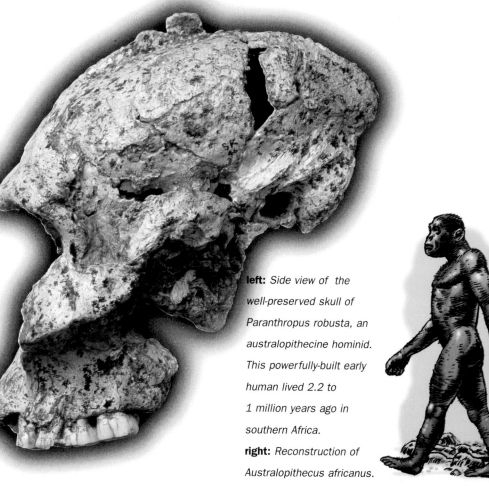

left: *Side view of the well-preserved skull of Paranthropus robusta, an australopithecine hominid. This powerfully-built early human lived 2.2 to 1 million years ago in southern Africa.*

right: *Reconstruction of Australopithecus africanus.*

c.3,500,000 BC	c.300,000 BC	c.2,500,000	c.2,000,000 BC	c.1,600,000 BC	c.1,500,000 BC	c.1,000,000 BC	c.300,000 BC
Australopithecus skeleton nicknamed "Little Foot" discovered in Sterkfontain, South Africa, 1998.	Elephants hunted in Spain. Hunters build temporary shelters in Nice, France.	Crude tools of volcanic stone used in Ethiopia. *Homo* species established in Western Europe.	*Australopithecus africanus* child found at Taung in the Kalahari Desert, c.1924.	Earliest known use of fire, in South Africa.	European hominids live in caves; communities develop in Yugoslavia, France, and Jersey.	*Homo erectus* spreads to Europe. Modern Ice Age begins.	Date of a hut in France, the oldest discovered manmade structure.

The discovery of the Taung child, or "missing link," between the apes and modern man caused intense debate among anthropologists looking for mankind's origins.

about the same time, 35,000 years ago. Then excavations at the Klasies river mouth, South Africa—first by John Wymer and Ronald Singer in 1966, then the University of Stellenbosch in 1984—recovered the fossils of humans over 100,000 years old. This suggests modern humans were living in Africa at a time when Europe and Asia were populated only by archaic peoples, although this hypothesis is still unproven.

The problem with the Klasies community is that although they may have looked like us, they did not behave like humans of the Stone Age. They were poor hunters who seemed to shy away from stalking

Little Foot—Big Discovery

The continuing search for humankind's origins was boosted in December 1998 when researchers announced the discovery of the most complete man-ape skeleton ever found— the 3.5 million-year-old *Australopithecus* known as Little Foot. Little Foot was unearthed in a cave at Sterkfontein, South Africa, one of the richest sources of early animal fossils, in 1980, but the bones were wrongly identified as the remains of a monkey and left in a storeroom at Witwatersrand University's medical school. They were re-discovered by British palæoanthropologist Ron Clarke in May 1997 and matched with other foot bones he found there. The Sterkfontein site was reexamined by Dr Clarke's team and by September 1998 they confirmed they had found the complete skeleton of a 4-foot tall hominid encased in limestone. Little Foot had fallen down a shaft, an accident that protected his remains from wild animals. The bone structure should eventually give anatomists an insight into how *Australopithecus* moved, its walking posture, body shape, and the amount of time it spent in the trees.

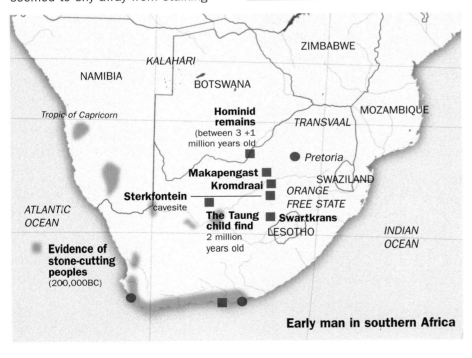

Early man in southern Africa

large, dangerous animals in favor of easier meat. They had no discernible ground-breaking technology, no interest in art or religion, and little or no desire to bury their dead. There are even indications that the scratches and burn marks on some of the recovered bones are the result of cannibalistic feasting. This does not suggest a culture in the way we understand it, and it is likely that these people had key anatomical differences in their brains which marked them out from more "conventional" Stone Age races.

c.128,000 BC	c.100,000 BC	c.50–30,000 BC	c.45,000 BC	c.35,000 BC	c.32,000 BC	c.30,000 BC
Sea temperatures and levels rise as an Ice Age ends	Suggested origin date of *Homo sapiens*, after excavations at Klasies river, 1966.	European and Asian climate grows colder again. Humans arrive in Australia from southeast Asia.	A flute from this time found in Africa.	Traditional age of modern *Homo sapiens*.	Cave art begins to appear across Europe.	Neanderthals die out, replaced by *Homo sapiens sapiens*.

THE GREAT ZIMBABWE
Riches of a 12th century courthouse

left: *A view of Great Zimbabwe. During the 12th and 13th centuries AD its rulers amassed huge fortunes through control of trade routes.*

In 1872 the German geologist Carl Mauch returned from an expedition in southern Africa to announce that he had discovered a mythical land, mentioned in the folk stories of old Portuguese explorers as Ophir, the source of King Solomon's fabulous wealth. Interest in the existence of this land had been boosted by one of Mauch's countrymen, the African missionary Reverend A. Merensky, and the romantic idea of an unknown civilization existing in the heart of the continent inspired some western historians. Moreover, Mauch revealed that he had found the ruins of a lost city supposedly built by the Queen of Sheba herself: Great Zimbabwe.

Among those who jumped on the Mauch bandwagon was the British-born South African financier and politician Cecil Rhodes, a man whose diamond and gold mining companies drove Britain's territorial ambition in the region. Rhodes' British South Africa Company occupied the area of Mauch's investigations and the suggestion that a great northern civilization had once "uplifted" native culture suited his argument that Africa needed the support of superior colonizing powers. Rhodes sponsored detailed archeological investigations of the site but it was not until 1929, 27 years after his death, that the truth emerged. Great Zimbabwe was built by Africans in the country to which it later gave its name (Zimbabwe).

A "zimbabwe" is the term used by the region's Shona people to describe the courthouse of royalty or a spirit medium. There are more than 150 scattered across Zimbabwe's central plains, but the Great Zimbabwe is by far the most impressive. It was built of skillfully-crafted granite blocks, without mortar, and is set partly on a granite hill, partly in the valley below. One of two high-walled enclosures on the hill was occupied by a small, elite

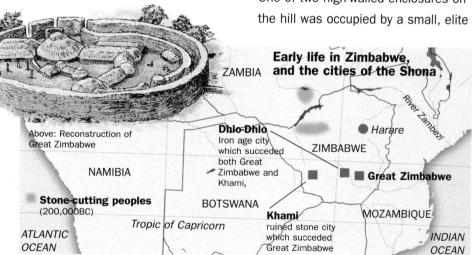

Above: Reconstruction of Great Zimbabwe

Early life in Zimbabwe, and the cities of the Shona

ZAMBIA

NAMIBIA

Stone-cutting peoples (200,000BC)

ATLANTIC OCEAN

BOTSWANA

Tropic of Capricorn

Dhlo-Dhlo Iron age city which succeeded both Great Zimbabwe and Khami.

Khami ruined stone city which succeeded Great Zimbabwe

ZIMBABWE

• *Harare*

■ ■ **Great Zimbabwe**

River Zambezi

MOZAMBIQUE

INDIAN OCEAN

745 AD	c.960 AD	960–1279 AD	974 AD	c.1000 AD	1052 AD	1076 AD	12th century AD
The Uighur Empire of Mongolia begins.	Star of David used as Jewish symbol.	China ruled by Song dynasty.	Earliest earthquake recorded in UK.	Vikings settle on Newfoundland.	Construction of Westminster Abbey, London, begins.	Kingdom of Ghana destroyed by Almoravids.	The city of Great Zimbabwe built, capital of the Shona Empire.

ruling class, the other was a more general residential area. In the valley was a building reserved for royal wives, grain bins—themselves symbols of wealth and power for the king—and the Great Enclosure, a complex structure still not fully understood. Around these was scattered the mud and thatch homes of more than 10,000 commoners.

Lucrative local materials

Great Zimbabwe was built in the 12th century AD and flourished for around 300 years. It was the capital of an important Shona empire extending from the banks of the Zambezi river to the boundaries of South Africa's Northern Province and east Botswana. During that time Shona kings amassed huge fortunes through their control of

gold and ivory exports to Arab merchants, who had set up a trading outpost on the East African coast, and the import of glass beads and Chinese ceramics. Great Zimbabwe was well situated to exploit local resources such as tin, iron, copper, and salt, and in the early years cattle, grain, and timber were plentiful. That said, the expanding population must have taken its toll on the city's ability to be self-supporting. By 1450 it had been abandoned and the capital shifted to Khami in the west.

The tradition of zimbabwe-building seems to have spread across much of central southern Africa. One of the best outlying examples is at Mapungubwe, or "Hill Of The Jackals," in South Africa's Northern Province, close to the Botswana border.

above: *The conical tower of Great Zimbabwe —built from shaped granite blocks without the need for mortar.*

Mapungubwe is a superb natural fortification with one approach route and sheer sides. It was another Shona capital with particularly lucrative trade links—evidence for which has been found in the beautifully fashioned gold recovered from graves. One gold model of a rhinoceros is particularly impressive and there are several other artifacts in which carved wooden figures have been covered with gold plate, held in place by gold tacks. The impression is of a culture with a highly organized class structure—a phenomenon that contrasts sharply with the more egalitarian communities elsewhere in Iron Age southern Africa.

The home of a ruling elite,
Great Zimbabwe was a complex structure of
the Shona empire which lasted for 300 years.

1176 AD	1193 AD	1232 AD	c.1254 AD	1282 AD	1325 AD	c.1450 AD	1498 AD
Construction of London Bridge begins; completed 1209.	Zen Buddhism founded in Japan.	Chinese use rockets in war.	Marco Polo born in Venice.	English King Edward I conquers Wales.	Rise of the Aztecs.	Great Zimbabwe abandoned; Khami becomes new Shona capital.	Vasco de Gama is first European to travel to India and back by sea.

NIGERIAN NOK CULTURE AND THE IGBO UKWU GRAVE

From the Iron Age to bronze vessels

In most parts of the world the transition between Stone, Copper, Bronze, and Iron ages was a gradual process taking many thousands of years. In Africa, advances in metallurgy were telescoped into a few centuries as craftsmen moved from Stone Age tools to those fashioned from iron. The secret was in finding furnaces capable of reaching 2,000° F, the temperature required for iron smelting operations. Special dome-shaped stone structures were built and fired with huge quantities of charcoal.

As knowledge of iron-working increased, so the range of tools available for metalwork, jewelry, and sculpture became more widespread. The first of the native West Africans

to embrace the new technologies were the Nok people of north-central Nigeria. One of their iron-smelters, at Taruga, dates to the fourth century BC, and it's possible that they were working iron in crude forms a hundred years before this.

Nok culture seems to have flourished between roughly the sixth century BC and 300 AD. Its main contribution to Africa's art history are terra-cotta (porous clay) figurines, especially human heads with exaggerated features, such as extravagant hairstyles and large, triangular eyes. Any unusual physical characteristics or deformities were faithfully reproduced and some of the figures wore beads or clutched weapons. Their purpose is unclear, but some experts believe they were linked to an earth fertility cult.

Nok design was not recognized until the early years of this century, when tin miners working on the southern and western slopes of the Jos Plateau discovered fragments of terra-cotta figurines. Painstaking reconstructions showed that they were originally models of animals and human heads,

left and above right: *These Nok terracotta faces, distinguished by their large eyes and strong features, were produced between 900 BC and 200 AD. It is thought they may have been linked to fertility cults.*

but as there were no professional archeologists working in Nigeria at the time, it fell to art historians to place them in context. They were described as "vestiges of Nok culture," with no estimate of their age or origin.

A lavish burial chamber

It wasn't until later excavations at Taruga and Samun Dukiya that the extent of Nok influence became apparent. Iron knives and arrow heads, domestic pottery, and bangles were found in settings that suggested an agrarian society of permanent settlements and comparatively sophisticated religious beliefs. More importantly, these digs gave an insight into later art traditions such as the brass, bronze, and terra-cotta heads from the Nigerian cities of Ife and Benin.

776 BC	753 BC	6th century BC	551 BC	539 BC	c.500 BC	c.490 BC	486 BC
First Olympic Games, held in Greece.	Rome established on the River Tiber.	Beginning of the peak of Nok culture.	Confucius is born.	The Persians conquer Babylon.	The Sinhalese Aryan people reach Sri Lanka.	Persians defeated at Athens in the Battle of Marathon.	Siddhartha Gautama, founder of Buddhism, dies.

Social structures in West Africa evolved at great speed.

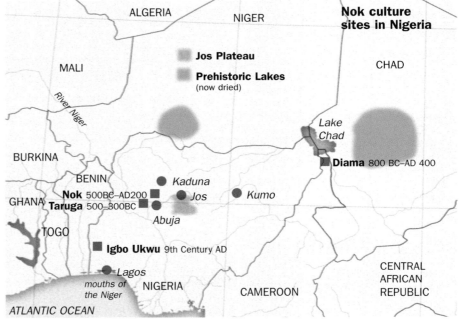

The speed at which social structures evolved in West Africa are well illustrated by the discovery of the Igbo Ukwu grave in the forests of southern Nigeria. Intrigued by the discovery of a hoard of bronzes on the site in 1938, the British archeologist Thurstan Shaw led an exhaustive dig between 1959 and 1960. The grave he found ranks among the most important archeological discoveries ever—a wood-lined and roofed burial chamber in which the royal incumbent was seated on a stool beside three ivory tusks. A further chamber directly above contained the bodies of five servants. Among the grave goods were a bronze staff and whisk, a copper ornament, a crown, and more than 100,000 beads made of glass and semi-precious quartz stones. These beads probably originated from India and would have been imported by Arab traders.

The workmanship, particularly of the bronzes, showed just how quickly African culture had advanced by the ninth century AD. Bronzes were cast by the *cire perdue* or "lost wax" method, in which a wax design was covered in a clay mold, holed at the base, and fired. Once the melted wax had run out, the empty mold was placed in sand and molten metal poured inside. After cooling, the clay was chiseled off and the bronze piece filed and polished into a finished article.

above: *A shell-shaped bronze drinking vessel surmounted by a leopard. It was made using the "lost wax" method of casting.*

Such treasures helped to reinforce the social superiority of their owners and concentrated religious and political control among a small minority. From embracing a Stone Age, hunter-gatherer existence dating back thousands of years, in which small communities lived uncomplicated lives, West Africans had rapidly entered an industrial, technologically advanced culture dominated by kings revered as spirit gods.

above: *This ornate Nok staff head was once encrusted with colored beads.*

Nok culture sites in Nigeria

Map labels:
- ALGERIA
- NIGER
- MALI
- Jos Plateau
- Prehistoric Lakes (now dried)
- CHAD
- River Niger
- Lake Chad
- BURKINA
- **Diama** 800 BC–AD 400
- BENIN
- Kaduna
- **Nok** 500BC–AD200
- Jos
- Kumo
- GHANA
- **Taruga** 500–800BC
- Abuja
- TOGO
- **Igbo Ukwu** 9th Century AD
- Lagos
- mouths of the Niger
- NIGERIA
- CAMEROON
- CENTRAL AFRICAN REPUBLIC
- ATLANTIC OCEAN

4th century BC	334 BC	c.138 BC	220 AD	c.250 AD	c.300 AD	449 AD	9th century AD
An iron-smelting furnace was in use in Taruga, Nigeria.	Alexander the Great invades Asia Minor.	Central Asia explored by Chang Chien.	China splits into three states at the end of the Han dynasty.	Red Sea trade controlled by the Axum kingdom of Ethiopia.	Nok culture recedes.	Saxons, Angles, and Jutes conquer Britain.	Advanced metal-working processes in use in Africa.

IMAGES OF STONE AGE WILDLIFE
Rock art from the Apollo 11 cave, Namibia

above: *Animal rock art enlivens a hillside at Twyfelfontein, South Africa.*

To the ancient bushmen or "San" of southern Africa, the sight of a shaman entering a state of trance was an awe-inspiring glimpse of the spirit world. The shaman—a kind of witch doctor—would begin his preparation amid loud music, rhythmic drumming, chanting, and singing, moving into an elaborate ritualistic dance around a blazing open fire.

As the ceremony unfolded, rapid breathing and immense concentration would herald the onset of trance—at which point the shaman would lean forward, sweating and trembling, and bleed from the nose. According to tradition, this was the moment he metaphorically died, entered the spirit world, and invoked whatever supernatural powers were necessary for the good of his people. Such powers might be used for healing the sick, summoning rains, conquering enemies, or improving the prospects of hunting.

Trance is a feature of numerous ancient cultures and is still practiced in many areas of the world. Typically, someone entering this state (or even experiencing a severe migraine) goes through a series of hallucinations produced by their nervous system. These begin with geometric shapes, spirals, grids, and zigzags and evolve into images of specific living things or objects. In the final, mind-gyrating stage, people reportedly see themselves as part of the hallucination and feel they are changing into an animal or spirit.

It is against this mystical background that some of the world's richest cave and rock art has been produced. Although its interpretation is an inexact science, many experts believe there are close parallels between shamanic magic and southern Africa's prehistoric art. An oft-quoted theory is that paintings of

above: *Basic forms of wall art show natives on the hunt. Bambata cave, Matopos Hills, Zimbabwe.*

Rock art depicts the close relationship between animals and their hunters.

c.27,000 BC	c.25,000–17,000 BC	c.18,000 BC	c.15,000 BC	c.12,000 BC	c.10,000 BC	c.9000 BC	c.8000 BC
Cave habitation in Brazil.	Stone Age cave paintings from this era found in Namibia, 1969.	Earliest example of human sculpture, Asia.	Paintings made on walls of Lascaux Cave, France.	Crude pottery techniques used in Japan.	Cave paintings from this time found in Northern Cape Province, Africa.	Hunters spread across the Americas.	European hunters use the bow and arrow.

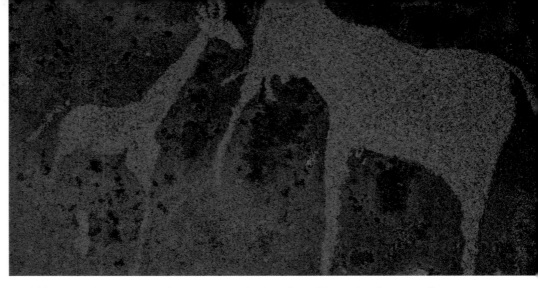

dying antelope symbolize the entry into trance, because the animal's mannerisms at the point of death are similar to that of the shaman. Bushmen have long believed that the eland—one of the largest and spiritually most important antelopes—released great power when killed. This could be harnessed by a tribal shaman for his own purposes.

Space Age rock art

To date, the oldest rock art in the south of the continent has been found on seven slabs in the Apollo 11 cave of Namibia, so-called because the archeologist who found them, Eric Wendt, listened to radio commentary on the 1969 moonshot while working there. The slabs showed various images, including the body of an antelope beneath a red line, a black rhino, a striped animal, and a cat-like beast with apparently human legs. There were also more abstract designs, such as black lines beside a red patch. All of the paintings were ascribed to the middle of the Stone Age—roughly between 25,000 and 17,000 BC—based on radiocarbon dating of charcoal found alongside them.

Elsewhere in Africa there are similarly impressive examples. The Wonderwerk cave in Northern Cape Province contains pictures dating back 10,000 years, Sahara massifs like Hoggar, Adrar des Iforas, and Tibesti have yielded painted engravings of animals produced around 5,000 BC, and the Nswatugi Cave, in Zimbabwe's Matopos Hills, clearly shows the religious importance of wild animals to the indigenous people.

Some of the rock art found is much later—images of domesticated cattle, horses, chariots, and even 19th century British soldiers are proof of this—but certain themes have survived over thousands of years. Pictures of antelope, reflecting San mythology, were still being drawn in South Africa's Drakensburg Mountains between the 16th and 19th centuries AD.

Since the existence of prehistoric cave drawings was formally recognized by mainstream archeologists in the early 1900s, a huge wealth of knowledge has been developed. It is now clear that Stone Age artists did not confine themselves to caves; rather that caves are where their work has best survived the effects of erosion. Cliffs and rock shelters were decorated, and examples of portable art include engraved stones and bones, shaped teeth, and shell pendants.

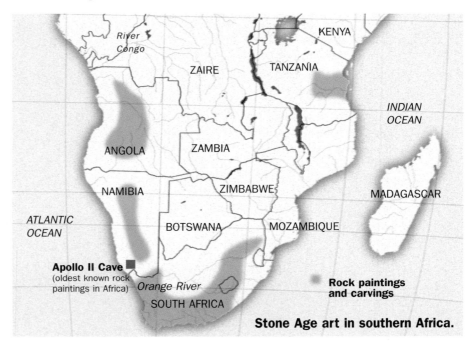

Stone Age art in southern Africa.

c.7000 BC	c.6500 BC	c.6000 BC	c.5000 BC	c.3300 BC	c.3000 BC	16–19th century AD
Domestication of the pig in New Guinea.	Farming begins in Greece and the Aegean.	Rice cultivated in Thailand.	Cave paintings and engravings from this time found in the Sahara and Zimbabwe regions.	Sumerians exchange goods for clay tokens.	Copper knives and axes made in Palestine.	New cave paintings still being created in the Drakensburg Mountains, South Africa.

THE ROMANS IN AFRICA
The cities of Leptis Magna and Sabratha

The city of Leptis Magna, 80 miles (125km) east of Tripoli in Libya, was founded by the Phoenicians around 650 BC. For several hundred years it was a modest port on a minor river estuary, but as the Roman Empire spread across North Africa during the first century AD it increasingly took on new significance. In AD 1–2 a theater was built by local benefactor Annobal Rufus, and the market, originally constructed in 8 BC, was enhanced in AD 31 and 37 by the addition of porticoes surrounding its two octagonal pavilions. By the end of the second century AD, Leptis had become a key trading post between Europe and Africa and the birthplace of the emperor Septimius Severus—a man who heaped patronage upon his home town.

Determined that it should rank alongside other great Roman cities, Septimius commissioned an urban development plan which is today hailed by architects as a model of efficiency and forethought. His grand scheme involved diverting the course of the river—no mean feat, even by modern engineering standards—and enlarging the estuary to create a deeper harbor. Septimius then had an impressive avenue constructed along the dry riverbed, leading to an administrative center with a majestic basilica, or meeting hall.

Sadly, this pride of the city did not last for long. As the Roman empire faltered in Africa two centuries later, dogged by constant attacks from desert tribesmen, a massive flood crashed through the banking that confined the river. The water flowed back down its old course, heavily laden with silt and sand, and buried the walls and columns of Septimius's city. Curiously, this natural disaster helped ensure that Leptis Magna remained among the best preserved of all Roman communities in Africa. In later years, there were comparatively few building materials available for plunder and many features of the buried avenue have since been excavated almost intact.

Olive-processing industry

Another of the city's exceptional landmarks are the Hunting Baths, probably completed in the early years of Septimius's reign, which retain much of their original vaulting and an interior mural of a leopard hunt (hence their name). Burial by sand protected much of the concrete roof. A magnificent triumphal arch features stone reliefs in which the Emperor is pictured riding in a chariot with his sons, Caracalla and Geta. This may have been erected as a memorial to mark the visit of Septimius to the city in 207.

The grandeur of Leptis cannot be attributed purely to the convenience of inherited wealth. Its economy was driven by complex and far-reaching

Lighthouse

Beacon

Old forum, basilica, and curia

Temple

Harbor

Forum of Severus

Old market

Colonnaded avenue

Theater   Chalcidicum

Arch of Severus

Baths of Hadrian

left: Plan of the excavated areas of Leptis Magna. The birthplace of the emperor Septimius Severus, the town was developed by him at great cost to match the splendor of other great cities.

0   300m
0   900 ft

c.550 BC	509 BC	c.500 BC	c.480 BC	323 BC	44 BC	1st century AD	1–2 AD
Arab settlements appear in Ethiopia.	Roman Republic is founded.	Iron first used in Africa.	A quarter of Athens' population dies in a plague.	Death of Alexander the Great.	Julius Caesar assassinated.	Forum constructed at Sabratha at center of caravan trade in west Africa.	Theater built at Leptis Magna by benefactor Annobal Rufus.

Leptis Magna rose from obscure trading post to be one of the finest examples of Roman town planning in North Africa.

trading links, hence the import of marble from what is now Turkey to decorate its public buildings. This stone was probably accompanied by highly specialized craftsmen, to ensure the quality of the finished product.

It is likely that the industrialists behind a thriving olive growing and pressing industry at Leptis would have helped foot the bills. Large "processing plants" have been identified on the edge of the city and

olive oil was almost certainly exported back to Italy. Such was the success of the local olive industry that when Julius Caesar decided to impose a fine on the people of Leptis, he ruled that it should be paid in the form of oil—three million Roman pounds' worth.

below: *North Africa's largest Roman theater, dating from 180 AD and now restored, at the site of the city of Sabratha.*

Sabratha

Sabratha, further west along the coast, is another well-preserved Roman outpost. Originally a Carthaginian colony, its fortunes were boosted by its important geographical position at the hub of caravan trade across the Sahara. Particularly noteworthy buildings are the first century AD forum and the late second century AD theater, one of the grandest and largest anywhere in Roman Africa. There are also impressive remains of a baths, the old harbor, various temples, fountains, and a catacomb. The strategic importance of both Sabratha and Leptis Magna was reflected in the high level of protection provided by the Roman Army, whose Third Legion was based at Lambaesis.

Key Roman sites in North Africa.

Extent of Roman Empire in North Africa c.AD 135

Rome

TURKEY

IRAN

Lixus Roman temple
Rabat
Algiers
Lambaesis
Volubilis Roman Colony
legionary camp
Tunis
IRAQ

MEDITERRANEAN

TUNISIA Tripoli
Sabratha
Roman City
Leptis Magna
Roman City
Alexandria

ALGERIA
LIBYA
EGYPT
SAUDI ARABIA

27 AD	31 & 37 AD	43 AD	58 AD	c.200 AD	c.207 AD	375 AD	c.400 AD
Jesus is baptized.	Leptis Magna's market, established in 8 BC, is enhanced.	Romans invade Britain.	Buddhism introduced to China by Emperor Ming Ti.	Roman Emperor Septimius Severus redevelops Leptis Magna, Africa.	Elaborate Hunting Baths created in Leptis Magna, perhaps to commemorate a visit by Septimius Severus.	The Huns of central Asia attack east Europe.	Septimius Severus' river diversion breaks its banks as Roman Empire falters.

CHAPTER TWO

EGYPT AND THE NILE VALLEY

Few great civilizations embrace mysticism, power, ingenuity, and romance in quite the same way as Ancient Egypt. Although this great royal dynasty emerged later than comparable cultures in the Near East, once established it continued on stable lines for more than 3000 years—dominating African history in the process. From the awe-inspiring pyramids at Giza, to the curse-laden Valley of the Kings and the glorious temples at Karnak and Abu Simbel, here was a land bursting with engineering prowess and captivating mythology. No wonder it became a magnet for explorers and treasure-hunters for centuries.

The origin and royal lineage of the pharaohs is a complicated business, at best, but for the general reader, a brief guide to the key periods in Egyptian history is useful background. Broadly speaking, Egyptologists have divided

The pyramids at Giza.

the various rulers into 34 dynasties (royal families) that extend from the pre- and early dynastic periods (5000–2625 BC), through the Old Kingdom (2625–2130), Middle Kingdom (1980–1630), and the New Kingdom (1539–1075 BC). The gaps in-between and following the end of the New Kingdom are filled by the First, Second, and Third Intermediate Periods and, for good measure, the Late Period (664–332 BC). After this the Hellenistic Period, centered on the old port of Alexandria, takes Egypt up to 30 BC and the final conquest by Rome.

Serene and benign, the face of pharaoh Tuthmosis III, who reigned from 1490–1436 BC, gazes from the dark with the gentle smile of one born to rule.

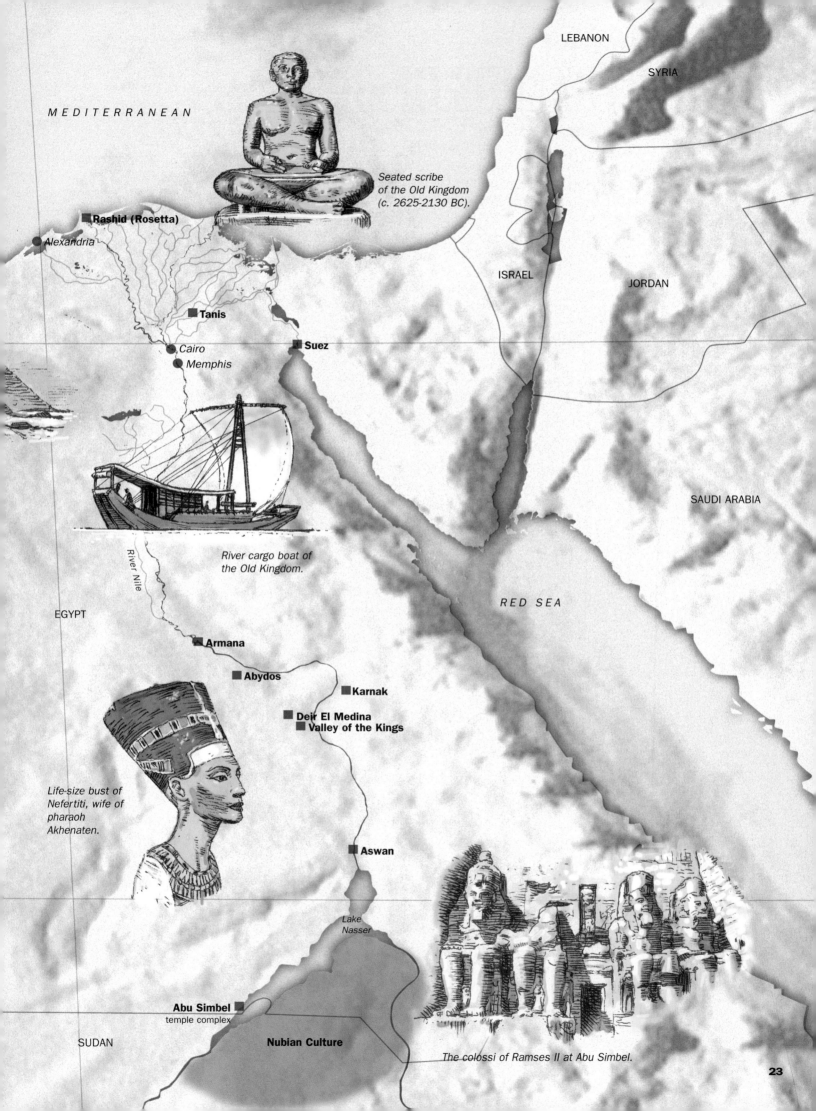

MEDITERRANEAN

Seated scribe
of the Old Kingdom
(c. 2625-2130 BC).

LEBANON

SYRIA

Rashid (Rosetta)

Alexandria

ISRAEL

JORDAN

Tanis

Cairo

Suez

Memphis

River Nile

SAUDI ARABIA

River cargo boat of
the Old Kingdom.

EGYPT

RED SEA

Armana

Abydos

Karnak

Deir El Medina
Valley of the Kings

Life-size bust of
Nefertiti, wife of
pharaoh
Akhenaten.

Aswan

Lake
Nasser

Abu Simbel
temple complex

SUDAN

Nubian Culture

The colossi of Ramses II at Abu Simbel.

THE PYRAMIDS OF GIZA
Stairways to heaven

Ancient Egypt is symbolized by its pyramids and there are none to rival those at Giza, the point where the Nile delta begins. Here stands Khufu, or Cheops, perhaps the most famous of all Egyptian buildings and the structure

above: The Sphinx at Giza with the pyramid of Khaefre towering in the background.

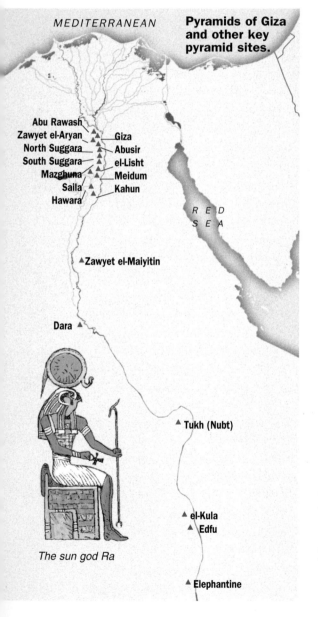

Pyramids of Giza and other key pyramid sites.

MEDITERRANEAN

Abu Rawash
Zawyet el-Aryan
North Suggara
South Suggara
Mazghuna
Saila
Hawara

Giza
Abusir
el-Lisht
Meidum
Kahun

RED SEA

Zawyet el-Maiyitin

Dara

Tukh (Nubt)

el-Kula
Edfu

Elephantine

The sun god Ra

often referred to as the Great Pyramid. With a height of 480 feet (146m) and a base width of 755 feet (230m), it's composed of some 2.3 million limestone blocks and employed 18,000 laborers throughout much of King Khufu's fourth dynasty reign (2585–2560 BC). Beside it are the lesser pyramids of Khaefre, comprising massive chunks of red granite, and Menkaure, hurriedly completed in mudbrick.

The construction of Cheops and the hundred or so lesser royal pyramids remains a thorny problem for archeologists. Most now believe that the huge blocks were man-hauled along a structure of exterior ramps, giving the overseer a sufficient view to make regular surveys. Given that all this happened more than 4,000 years ago, the surveying was almost unbelievably exact. Cheops, for instance, has sides which rise at an angle of precisely 51° 52', with a base oriented to true north. The sides of the 13.5-acre (5.4 ha) base fail to be precisely parallel by the margin of just one inch (2.5 cm).

The design of the pyramid was rooted in worship of the sun god Ra. According to the Pyramid Texts (invocations and spells inscribed on the internal walls of tombs), the death of a pharaoh would result in the sun strengthening its beams to create a gleaming ramp, up which the deceased ruler would climb to achieve immortality. Pyramids were seen as the earthly base for this ramp and the external "step" design, particularly of the earlier types, reinforced the idea of a stairway to heaven. Perhaps the huge dimensions of Khufu are in part due to the king's status as the sun god in earthly form.

c.3000 BC	c.2750 BC	c.2700 BC	2686–2160 BC	2585–2560 BC	c.2500 BC	c.2300 BC	c.2200 BC
First stone temple constructed, in Malta.	Civilizations develop in Indus Valley, Asia.	Silk weaved in China.	Egyptian Old Kingdom.	Fourth dynasty reign of King Khufu; Great Pyramid constructed in this period.	First libraries established in Mesopotamia.	First Central American ceramics created.	A form of hieroglyphics first used in Far East.

There were rumors of terrible curses which would bedevil intruders.

above: *A view of the Khaefre and Khufu pyramids. Their purpose was to help dead pharaohs ascend to heaven.*

Baffling the thieves

The Giza site also contains the remains of a major mortuary complex—funerary structures, temples for the deliverance of offerings and numerous (though simpler) graves of other royal household members. A builders' city was constructed, in which skilled craftsman were billeted separately from manual workers, complete with bakery, grain silos, shops, and a cemetery—particularly useful, given the number of laborers crushed to death. Interestingly, commoners also had pyramids for tombs, albeit smaller and invariably composed of mudbrick.

Religion aside, the pyramids were supposed to fulfill the far more practical purpose of deterring grave-robbers. Given that they were such obvious targets, successive pharaohs ordered elaborate defenses, such as internal mazes *en route* to the burial chamber. There were also rumors of terrible curses that would bedevil intruders. This tactic was soon adopted by commoners. One tomb, occupied by a man who helped construct the Great Pyramid, bore a curse composed by his wife which read: "O all people who enter this tomb who will make evil against this tomb and destroy it; may the crocodile be against them on water, and snakes be against them on land; may the hippopotamus be against them on water, the scorpion against them on land."

Unfortunately for the royals, such deterrents were often unsuccessful. The activities of robbers so horrified rulers of the Middle and New kingdoms (c.1980–1075 BC) that they switched their burial ground to the Valley of the Kings—solid rock vaults beneath the pyramid-shaped Theban Peak, on the west bank of the Nile.

One secret that deceived the tomb-raiders was unearthed in May 1954, when Egyptian archeologist Kamal el-Mallakh was carrying out clearance work on the south side of the Great Pyramid. By chance he uncovered a rectangular chamber concealed by 41 limestone blocks, some weighing 15 tons (15,240 kg). At the bottom of the 102-foot (31m) deep pit lay a cedar funerary boat, 141 feet (43m) long and neatly dismantled into its component parts, ready for reassembly. It is thought this boat may have been used to transport the king's body and was buried with him to help him cross the sky with Ra, the sun god.

right: *The cedar funerary boat of King Khufu was found hidden in a deep chamber concealed by limestone blocks.*

c.2040–1980 BC	c.2000 BC	c.1894-1595 BC	c.1760 BC	c.1620 BC	c.1550–1075 BC	c.1500 BC	c.1250 BC
Egyptian Middle Kingcom.	Sailing vessels used on Aegean Sea.	Babylon's first dynasty.	King of Babylon, Hammurabi, engraves laws on a stone slab.	Rise of Hittites in Anatolia.	Egyptian New Kingdom.	Widespread use of iron weaponry in Near East.	Height of Mycenean civilization.

THE LOST TOMB OF KING TUT
Carter's infamous discovery

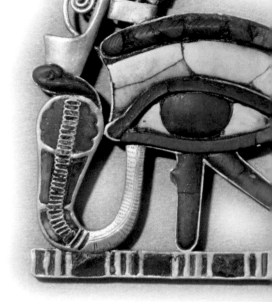

It was Thutmose I who founded the Valley of the Kings burial ground in a dried riverbed near Thebes, on the west bank of the Nile. From his death in 1482 BC until the beginning of the first millennium BC, some 70 royal tombs were sited in solid rock vaults, all beneath the conveniently pyramid-shaped Theban Peak. They contained staircases, corridors, store chambers, and shafts, as well as lavishly furnished burial rooms. Some of the larger tombs penetrated 300 feet (91m) into the cliffs and needed an army of laborers and skilled craftsmen to hew and decorate them. There was even a specially trained necropolis guard to protect the valley from raiders.

Housing all tombs under one roof, so to speak, offered security advantages but didn't stop the robbers gathering like vultures. There is evidence that some graves were raided within days of being sealed, and that guards were bribed to give information on entrances and internal passageways.

Those that survived this early plunder faced the ravages of European "explorers" such as Giovanni Belzoni, whose excavation tools included a battering ram. Little wonder that by the early 20th century there seemed few sites left to discover. Apart, that is, from the lost tomb of the boy king Tutankhamen—the monarch who ruled for less than a decade and died before his 19th birthday, c.1323 BC.

Since 1907 British archeologist Howard Carter had been on the payroll of amateur Egyptologist Lord Carnarvon, a man obsessed with discovering hitherto unknown tombs at Thebes. They had enjoyed some success in locating the graves of minor noblemen near the Theban mountain, but from 1917 onward Carter concentrated his efforts on the

above: A finely-wrought eye-symbol pendant from the tomb. Treasures like these took Howard Carter's team months to catalog.

below: Tutankhamen's death mask—one of the most famous archeological artifacts ever discovered.

left: The decorated lid sealing the casket of Tutankhamen. The young king died before his 19th birthday.

c.1600 BC	c.1500 BC	1482 BC	c.1450 BC	c.1400-100 BC	c.1350 BC	c.1330 BC	c.1323 BC
Bronze Age urban civilization in China.	Symbolic script used in China (ideographic), Crete, Greece (Linear B), and Anatolia (cuneiform).	Death of Thutmose I, founder of Valley of the Kings burial ground.	Minoan Crete destroyed.	Height of Mycenean civilization.	Syrians become multi-lingual, learning Hittite and Babylonian languages.	King Kurigalzu II leaves Babylon and establishes new capital, Dur-Kurigalzu (Aqarquf), 100 miles away.	Death of boy king Tutankhamen.

search for Tutankhamen. When, four years later, there had still been no breakthrough, Carnarvon ordered a halt to the excavation, only to be persuaded by Carter to finance just one more season in what was the only feasible site remaining—a triangle of land near the tomb of Ramesses VI.

The infamous tomb

Just three days into the dig, on November 21, 1922, workmen discovered rock steps leading to a plaster-covered doorway apparently marked with the seals of necropolis administrators. Carter informed his employer and called a halt on work until Carnarvon could arrive to lead an entry into the tomb on November 23.

What he saw within an interior sealed chamber almost defied description; a sumptuous treasure trove of Ancient Egyptian goods, including gilded chests, stools and beds, and life-sized statues of the king

marking the entrance to his burial room. Inside here was an ornate gilded shrine, one of four that nestled within each other, like Russian dolls. Behind the last of these lay the sarcophagus; beneath its granite top was a coffin swathed in gilded foil. Only now did Carter know for sure that he had found the undisturbed tomb of the king.

It took months to catalog Tutankhamen's treasures and it wasn't until February 1925 that Carter was finally able to turn his attention to the coffin. Beneath the granite lid he found two further "Russian doll coffins," one decorated with faience, obsidian, and lapis lazuli, the other fashioned in solid gold one inch (25mm) thick and weighing 243 pounds (110.4 kg).

Even this was not the end of the lavish surprises. As the body of the

king was at last exposed, Carter saw that the head and shoulders were covered in gold, lapis lazuli, and blue glass—the death mask of Tutankhamen, a face destined to be the most famous of any ancient civilization.

For Carnarvon, the story ended in tragedy. He never saw the mask, dying of pneumonia brought on by an infected flea bite in April 1923. A more imaginative view of his demise was adopted by Sir Arthur Conan Doyle, creator of Sherlock Holmes, who suggested Carnarvon had breathed in deadly spores placed in the tomb by priests to punish grave-robbers. Research published in 1998 suggested it was theoretically possible for a virus to survive in a tomb for thousands of years, becoming increasingly potent in the process.

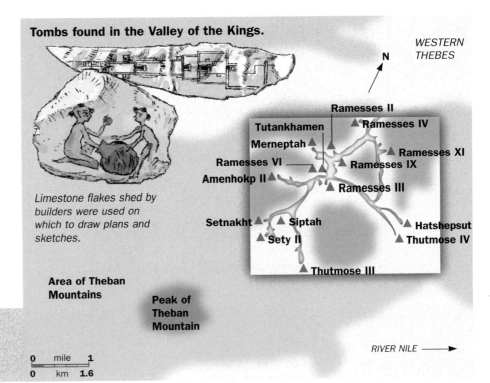

Tombs found in the Valley of the Kings.

WESTERN THEBES

N

Ramesses II
Tutankhamen
Ramesses IV
Merneptah
Ramesses XI
Ramesses VI
Ramesses IX
Amenhokp II
Ramesses III
Setnakht
Siptah
Hatshepsut
Sety II
Thutmose IV
Thutmose III

Limestone flakes shed by builders were used on which to draw plans and sketches.

Area of Theban Mountains

Peak of Theban Mountain

RIVER NILE ⟶

0   mile   1
0   km   1.6

c.1300 BC	c.1200 BC
Settlers arrive in Tonga, Fiji, and Samoa.	End of Hittite Empire; end of Mycenean civilization in Greece.

27

TEMPLES OF THE NILE
Shrines to cult worship

The Egyptians built two main types of temple, one dedicated to the gods of their mythology, the other to their deceased pharaohs (the mortuary cult). In neither case were these sacred places accessible to ordinary people, although the outer precincts would sometimes be busy, noisy places as worshippers bearing offerings mingled with temple administrative and manual workers. For most Egyptians a visit to the temple would be reserved for festival days to watch processions and ceremonies conducted in the courtyards. Only the highest of priests were permitted to enter the dark, silent inner sanctuary, where the statue of the appropriate god or pharaoh was waited upon.

The magnificent temple complex of Karnak, on the east bank of the Nile at Thebes, is probably the best example of the inter-linked complexity of Ancient Egyptian religion. Karnak is a series of temples built by successive kings of the Middle and New kingdoms and includes a number of north-south and east-west alignments marked by monumental gates known as pylons, avenues of sphinxes, and sacred lakes.

The most important temple, dedicated to the "official" state god Amon, was founded by Sesostris I around 1900 BC but wasn't completed until the reign of Ramses II (c.1200 BC). Amon is set in an enclosure measuring 1,500 square feet (140 sq m); the roof of the central hall rests on 122 columns standing more than 70 feet (21m) tall. The walls are covered in reliefs, historical texts, prayers, hymns, and inscriptions, information that has given historians a valuable insight into the Ancient Egyptian lifestyle following the end of the Old Kingdom.

Pharaoh's spiritual meals

As well as the state gods, Egyptians would regularly visit the shrines of lesser deities. These would be offered prayers relating to matters of local importance, such as ensuring a good harvest or banishing sickness. A further complication was that all gods, even state gods, would drift in and out of fashion. Until Amon achieved prominence, Ra had the most status. And the rise of Osiris, the god of the dead said to be buried at Abydos,

coincided with the falling star of his predecessor, Khenty-amentiu.

The rituals of the mortuary temples have become clearer since 1982 AD, when Czech archeologists discovered 2,000 fragments of administrative

Statues would be sprinkled
with perfume, painted,
dressed, and fed.

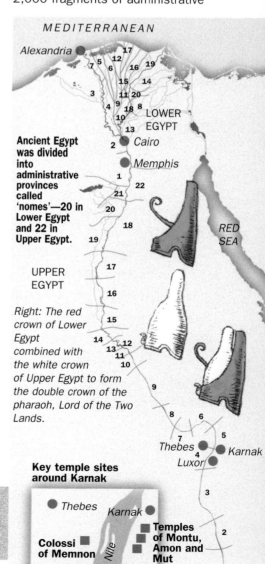

Ancient Egypt was divided into administrative provinces called 'nomes'—20 in Lower Egypt and 22 in Upper Egypt.

Right: The red crown of Lower Egypt combined with the white crown of Upper Egypt to form the double crown of the pharaoh, Lord of the Two Lands.

MEDITERRANEAN

Alexandria

LOWER EGYPT

Cairo

Memphis

RED SEA

UPPER EGYPT

Thebes   Karnak
Luxor

Key temple sites around Karnak

- Thebes   Karnak
- Colossi of Memnon
- Temples of Montu, Amon and Mut
- Temple of Luxor

c.2800 BC	c.2700 BC	c.2500 BC	c.2455 BC	2371–2230 BC
Farming cultures develop in Amazon area.	Bronze made in China.	Horse domesticated in central Asia.	Death of Egyptian minor Fifth-dynasty king Reneferef.	First empire: founded by Sargon I of Agade.

opposite: *A path through the pillars at the Temple of Luxor*

right: *The pylon (gateway structure) and colossi of Ramesses II at Luxor. The temple occupied the southern part of the ancient city of Thebes.*

records linked to the temple of the minor Fifth Dynasty king Reneferef, who died c.2455 BC. These told how every day a solemn procession of priests would troop around the pharaoh's pyramid while his cult statue nearby would be sprinkled with aromatic oil, painted, dressed, and "fed." Feeding involved placing a meal offering beside the statue, after which the high priest would rule that it been spiritually "eaten" and share it among attendants. The mortuary temples linked to royal burials in the Valley of the Kings were sited mostly on the west bank south of Thebes. Here the famous statues known as the Colossi of Memnon once marked the entrance to Amenophis III's mortuary temple.

Lesser statues sometimes became so common within a temple that the priests would order a clear-out, gathering many of the older ones for burial. One of the most intriguing caches was found in 1903 on the north-south axis within Karnak. It contained 800 statues and 17,000 smaller religious artifacts.

left: *Egyptian monumental masonry was both grand and technically accomplished.*

The Gold Dust Palace

Early in 1999 the German Egyptologist Edgar Pusch announced that he had discovered the ruins of a golden palace beneath two feet of Nile silt at a location believed to be Piramesse, the lost capital of Ramses II. The excavation's early finds included gold statues, rare ceramics, and detailed bronzes, suggesting that the pharaohs were far wealthier and more advanced than even the pyramids suggested. Pusch said that the unearthed riches gave credence to ancient tales of gold dust on the streets of Piramesse. "There is hardly one cubic centimeter in the palace that does not have some gold," he said. "When you walk across the floor, you stir up tiny flakes of gold dust."

c.2300 BC	c.2000 BC	c.1900 BC	c.1894–1595 BC	c.1800 BC	c.1240 BC	c.1200 BC	c.1150 BC
Sumeria united by King Sargon's empire.	Immigrants from Indonesia settle in Melanesia.	Work begins on Amon temple in Karnak.	First Babylonian dynasty.	State of Assyria established by Shamshi-Adad.	Moses delivers Ten Commandments.	Amon temple completed during reign of Ramses II.	Israel united by King David.

ARMANA
City of the sun god

When Akhenaten became king in 1353 BC, he began a fundamental shake-up of Egyptian religious, cultural, and artistic life. The most far-reaching change concerned an order that the god Amon, whose following centered on the Karnak temple at Thebes, should no longer be the patron of the Egyptian empire. Instead this honor should go to the sun god Aten, of whom his wife, Queen Nefertiti, was a devoted disciple. Akhenaten may even have appointed her to the priestly office, a position normally the exclusive domain of kings.

To hammer home this change, Akhenaten abandoned the ancient capital of Thebes and announced that his capital city would be built from scratch in the middle of Egypt and named Akhetaten (today known as el-Armana). The new city was planned to the finest detail by royal architects and comprised a central administrative center, including the royal palace and Temple of Aten, a villa "estate" for noblemen, and housing suburbs for ordinary inhabitants. An area to the east of the city was set aside for tomb chapels, while the immediate boundaries were marked by 14 stelae, pillars hewn out of the cliffs.

Archives among the fertilizer

Much of our knowledge of the their day-to-day life is owed to a peasant woman who, in 1887, set out to dig at the center of the old metropolis to find sebbakh, a type of fertilizer composed of rotted mudbrick. She suddenly struck a buried hoard of clay tablets etched with an ancient cuneiform script that was later recognized as Akkadian, a language used by Near East diplomats during the late Bronze Age. The 300-plus tablets, now known as the Armana Letters, were an archive of diplomatic activity revealing Egypt's foreign policy

MEDITERRANEAN

River Euphrates

Memphis

Ancient city of Armana

Village of Deir El Medina

Thebes

Elephantine

Egyptian Empire during the new kingdom
14th–13th Centuries BC

RED SEA

Deir El-Medina—City of the Tomb-makers

The unceasing job of building and decorating royal tombs in the Valley of the Kings demanded that a large, highly skilled, and accessible workforce be constantly available. The Egyptian pharaoh Tuthmosis I seems to have tackled this problem by founding the workers' village of Deir el-Medina sometime around 1550 BC. Situated in a secluded cleft of the Theban mountain, its terraced streets of some 70 houses were occupied for 500 years, despite the problems inherent in its lack of water and food supply. Excavations have revealed the tombs of the tomb-makers—scaled down, modest versions of royal sites—containing thousands of ostraka, or crude writing tablets, and detailed documentation referring to the everyday affairs of the residents.

c.1600 BC	c.1595 BC	c.1550 BC	c.1500 BC	c.1500 BC	c.1450 BC	c.1390 BC	1353 BC
Bronze Age urban civilization in China.	End of Hammurabi's dynasty in Babylon, taken by Hittite king Mursilis.	Tomb workers' village of Deir el-Medina founded by Pharaoh Tuthmosis I.	Volcano engulfs island of Santorini in Aegean Sea.	People living near the Great Lakes of North America discover metallurgy.	Minoan Crete destroyed.	Writing begins in China.	Akhenaten king of Egypt.

toward her less-powerful neighbors in the eastern Mediterranean, as well as the kingdoms that regarded themselves as equally influential.

In 1891 the great British Egyptologist Sir Flinders Petrie began work at Armana, exposing part of the Temple of Aten, royal palace, king's house, and the record office. He discovered more cuneiform tablets and established that Armana's central

buildings had been speedily constructed using talatat. Some of these distinctive small stone blocks were re-used across the Nile at Hermopolis Magna, following the abandonment of Akhenaten City on the king's death (c.1334 BC).

But perhaps the greatest find was made by Ludwig Borchardt during digs between 1908 and 1914 in an area that comprised large private

left: *Stone relief showing Akhenaten and his family making sacrifices to the sun god Aten.*

residencies. He came across one of the true masterpieces of Egyptian sculpture, the painted limestone head of Queen Nefertiti, probably a trial piece by the master sculptor Thutmose. It is now held by the Staatliche Museum in Berlin.

As to Nefertiti herself, her influence appears to have been short lived. By the 12th year of Akhenaten's reign she had fallen into the king's bad books and suffered the ignominy of being supplanted by one of her six daughters, Meritaten.

The job of decorating royal tombs demanded a large, skilled workforce close to the Valley of the Kings.

1341 BC	c.1334 BC	c.1300 BC	c.1200 BC	c.1150 BC	c.1100 BC	c.1050 BC	c.1027 BC
Queen Nefertiti supplanted by daughter, Meritaten.	Death of King Akhenaten.	Settlers arrive in Melanesia.	Jews leave Egypt and settle in Palestine.	Olmec civilization established in Mexico.	Phoenicians spread into Mediterranean area.	Village of Deir el-Medina abandoned.	Chou overthrows Chinese Shang dynasty.

SECRETS OF TANIS
Historical theme park

The collapse of Egypt's New Kingdom in 1075 BC resulted in a new dynasty emerging across parts of the northern kingdom. These Tanitic kings looked to build their capital in the northeast of the Nile delta and set about transporting statues, temples, monuments, and buildings from other ancient capitals, particularly Piramesse. As a result, Tanis became a kind of historical theme park for 19th and 20th century archeologists—mainly because of the huge range of artifacts that were unearthed. It had first been described in biblical times as the city of Zoan and was easily distinguishable by its massive central earth mound. As Egyptologists grew bolder and more determined in their search for interesting material, Tanis became their number one target.

The French archeologist Pierre Montet had been running digs there for ten years when, in February 1939, he found himself working inside the Great Temple Enclosure. This area had long been one of the most popular hunting grounds—his countryman Auguste Mariette had studied it as far back as 1860—and Montet was not expecting a headline-making breakthrough. However, when a group of workmen discovered a secret underground

above: *The head of the coffin of Psuennes I. Jars containing the dead king's vital organs were found beside it.*

below: *The Nile Delta is an archeological treasure trove*

room sealed by a limestone block, he quickly changed his mind.

Tanitic royals regarded attempts to protect royal graves in pyramids or hidden valleys as hopelessly flawed. Besides, the geological make-up of the Nile delta meant it was not practical to construct the necessary huge

Tanitic royals regarded attempts to protect royal graves as hopelessly flawed.

c.1700 BC	c.1600 BC	c.1550 BC	c.1500 BC	c.1450 BC	c.1400 BC	c.1400–1100 BC	c.1200 BC
Tribal leader Abraham settles his people at Hebron, Canaan, after abandoning Ur, Sumer.	Bronze Age urban civilization in China.	Beginning of Egyptian New Kingdom.	Traders cross Aegean Sea to reach Sicily.	The birth of Indian literature (Vedas).	Hittites learn to smelt and forge iron.	Acropolis's ramparts are constructed in Athens.	Jews leave Egypt and settle in Palestine.

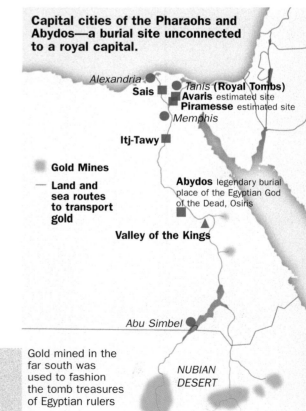

foundations or underground tunnels.
Instead, the Tanitic rulers sited their
burial rooms within the main temples
of their capital, defended by high walls
and an alert guard. Montet's man had
stumbled upon one of these burial
chambers, which would stand
alongside Tutankhamen's tomb in its
overall importance.

A concealed chamber

The room contained four decorated
limestone chambers with the
sarcophagi (decorated coffins) of
Orsorkon III, Prince Hornakht, and the
burial remains of Takelot II and
Orsorkon I. Slightly further north was
another tomb, containing five rooms
that Montet established were dedicated
primarily to Psusennes I. Oddly, the
only coffin was discovered in an
anteroom and belonged to Shoshenq II.

For a time Pierre Montet was
stumped by this enigma, until he
discovered that the western side of the
antechamber cleverly concealed two
doors, one leading to the burial vault of
Psusennes, the other the vault of his
successor, Amenemope. When Montet
pulled back a massive granite sealing
block, still moving easily on its ancient
bronze rollers, he gazed down a narrow
room containing a pink granite coffin on
which the image of Psusennes was
sculpted as the "God Of The Dead",
Osiris. Next to it were jars containing
the dead king's vital organs, together
with gold and silverware, and inside it
was a second coffin, fashioned in black
granite, and a third, made of silver
and bearing a gold face mask. This
was less detailed than Tutankhamen's
but still bore outstanding material
quality and workmanship.

Amenemope's chamber and hoard of
burial artifacts presented a number of
problems. Firstly, it seemed that the
site may not have been intended for
him, but for Queen Mutnodjmet instead.
It seems to have been pressed into
service early, when Amenemope died

only nine years into his reign.
Secondly, when the French team drew
up their scale plan of the tomb, they
realized that the numbers failed to
add up—there was a hidden void at
the center that no one had spotted.
Further excavations revealed yet
another chamber, this time of General
Wendjebaendjed, a friend of Psusennes.

So far the number of intact royal
burials at Tanis outnumber those in
the Valley of the Kings. It seems
certain that this vast sacred site will
produce further remarkable finds in
years to come.

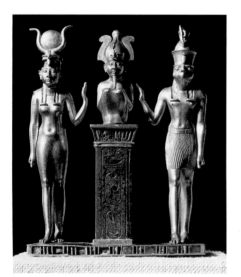

left: Osiris, God of the Dead, crouches on a
pedestal flanked by his wife and sister.

**Capital cities of the Pharaohs and
Abydos—a burial site unconnected
to a royal capital.**

Alexandria
Sais
Tanis (Royal Tombs)
Avaris estimated site
Piramesse estimated site
Memphis

Itj-Tawy

Gold Mines

— Land and
sea routes
to transport
gold

Abydos legendary burial
place of the Egyptian God
of the Dead, Osiris

Valley of the Kings

Abu Simbel

Gold mined in the
far south was
used to fashion
the tomb treasures
of Egyptian rulers

NUBIAN
DESERT

c.1184 BC	c.1100 BC	1075 BC	c.1027 BC	c.1000 BC
Estimated date of the destruction of Troy.	Alphabetic script created by Phoenicians.	Collapse of Egypt's New Kingdom; beginning of Tanitic Kings' reign.	In India, Aryans spread eastward.	Etruscans reach Italy.

THE ROSETTA STONE
The key to understanding ancient Egyptian

For centuries, the barrier to greater understanding of Ancient Egypt lay in its unfathomable texts. Many antiquaries of the 17th and 18th centuries had studied them and concluded that hieroglyphics amounted to a symbolic language used to record an overall repository of philosophy and knowledge. It was not thought that they were in everyday usage for such mundane tasks as detailing food stores and writing diaries.

Like all of the best accidents in history, the breakthrough came from a totally unexpected source—the territorial ambitions of Napoleon Bonaparte. His forces conquered Egypt in 1798 and immediately set about strengthening strategic fortifications along the coast to repel the anticipated response of the British Royal Navy.

One port given such a make-over was Rashid, or Rosetta as Europeans called it, on the western arm of the Nile that ran through to the Mediterranean. As building work started on Fort St. Julien in 1799, the French overseeing officer, Captain Bouchard, saw that workmen had dug out a black basalt slab inscribed bearing intricate texts. This in itself was hardly earth-shattering news—old artifacts often emerged from Egyptian building sites—but the difference here was that the 3' 10" (1.18m) slab carried three different languages, one of which was a decipherable form of Greek.

The Royal Navy's victory over the French fleet at Aboukir Bay and the surrender of Napoleon's forces at

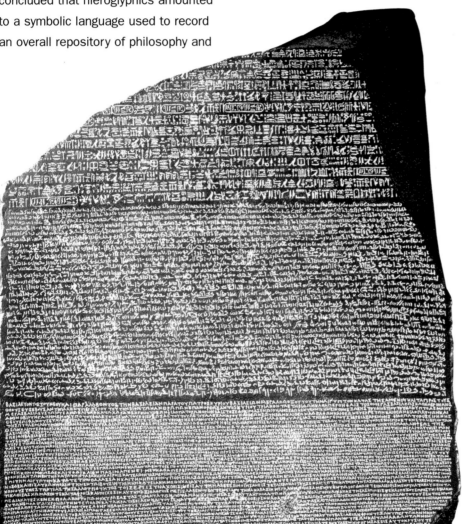

left: *The Rosetta Stone. The same inscription was repeated in three scripts, giving scholars the break-through needed to understand the cipher of hieroglyphics.*

332 BC	322 BC	290 BC	247 BC	243 BC	241 BC	225 BC	224 BC
Alexander the Great conquers Egypt.	Mauryan Empire founded.	Roman conquest of central Italy.	Kingdom of Parthia founded by Arsaces I.	Peloponnese liberated from Macedonians by Aratus of Sicyon.	Rome defeats Carthage in Punic War.	Gallic tribes beaten by Romans at Lake Telemon, northern Italy.	Colossus of Rhodes, one of the Seven Wonders of the Ancient World, destroyed in earthquake.

European scholars realized
the stone was effectively a crib sheet.

Alexandria gave the British control of Egypt. The Rosetta stone, together with hundreds of other items amassed by French academics who had joined the North Africa expedition, was considered spoils of war, taken to London, and exhibited at the British Museum (its present home) to be investigated by a succession of European scholars, most notably the Swedish diplomat Johan Akerblad and British physicist Thomas Young. They realized that Rosetta was effectively a crib sheet, because the same inscription in honor of King Ptolemy V was repeated in all three scripts. By comparing the Greek words with the hieroglyphic and demotic writing, they identified some phonetic letters in the demotic version, along with proper names. It became clear that the stone was dated to the ninth year of Ptolemy's reign (196 BC) and that it had been inscribed by the high priests of Memphis.

Secrets unlocked

The biggest advance came from the work of the brilliant French Egyptologist Jean François Champollion, a man who had mastered six old Oriental languages by the age of 16. In 1821 he started work on the Rosetta Stone and effectively "broke the code," later compiling a guide to Egyptian grammar and a dictionary of the language. Champollion showed Egyptian hieroglyphics comprised two basic types. Ideograms signified a specific object (a sun picture could mean "the sun" or "day," for example), while phonograms were sound signs that had no particular relationship to the word they represented.

To complicate matters, some pictures described a word with a similar sound but different meaning and most sentences involved a combination of pictures and sound signs. Therefore a picture showing the floor of a house translated simply as "house," but the same picture followed by sound signs and a pair of walking legs meant "to go out."

An aid to translation was that certain words were enclosed in oval rings known as "cartouches." From studying the Greek text, Champollion knew that these referred to rulers such as Ptolemy and Cleopatra and was able to apply the signs they contained to other royal names. Within the space of a few years, the mysteries of five millennia of Egyptian writings on stone and papyri had finally been solved.

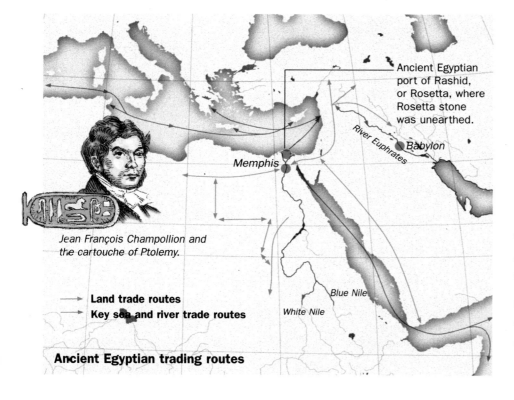

Ancient Egyptian port of Rashid, or Rosetta, where Rosetta stone was unearthed.

River Euphrates

Babylon

Memphis

Jean François Champollion and the cartouche of Ptolemy.

Blue Nile

White Nile

→ **Land trade routes**
→ **Key sea and river trade routes**

Ancient Egyptian trading routes

SAVED FROM THE FLOOD
The glories of Nubia

The pharaohs of the Middle Kingdom (1991–1786 BC) enjoyed prosperous times. Trade links with Asia were at their most lucrative and a desire to further extend the kingdom resulted in the successful conquest of Nubia, a separate civilization centered on the upper reaches of the Nile.

The Nubians were essentially self-sufficient farmers with a strong warrior-race background. Even so, they were no match for a neighbor who could easily mount an invasion force of 20,000. One Egyptian government minister of the 20th century BC, Antefoker, wrote: "I slaughtered the Nubians on several occasions. I came north, uprooting the harvest and cutting the remainder of the trees and torching their houses...." He described this aggression as "setting the fear of Horus [the king] among the southern foreign lands to pacify [them]."

The attraction of Nubia lay in its mineral resources, especially gold. The region's name may even be derived from the Egyptian nbw, meaning "gold," and translated as "Goldland." There were also highly prized items to be had from trading expeditions further south, such as ivory, incense, myrrh, ebony, aromatic timber, and leopard and giraffe skins. Oddly, Egyptian merchants and military raiding parties seemed to avoid using the Nile as a transport route. They preferred to follow the "Oasis Road" which swung away from the river in the middle of Egypt and followed a chain of oases, including Farafra, Dakhleh, and Dush.

below: *The facade of the Temple of Ramses was carved from sandstone.*

Racing to beat the Nile

There are many important archeological legacies of Nubian Egypt, but the Abu Simbel temples on the Nile,

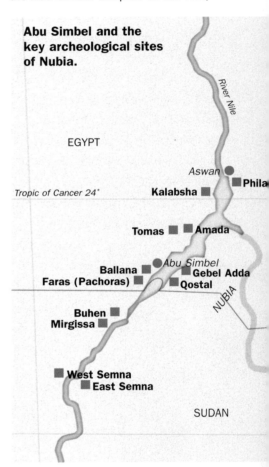

Abu Simbel and the key archeological sites of Nubia.

EGYPT

River Nile

Aswan
Phila[e]

Tropic of Cancer 24°   Kalabsha

Tomas   Amada

Ballana   Abu Simbel
Faras (Pachoras)   Gebel Adda
    Qostal

Buhen
Mirgissa

NUBIA

West Semna
East Semna

SUDAN

just south of the Aswan Dam, are the most spectacular. These two temples were carved out of sandstone cliffs in about 1250 BC under the orders of King Ramses II. The larger one, 180 feet (55m) in depth, was a network of halls and chambers leading to a central sanctuary dedicated to the most favored gods of Thebes, Memphis and

2000 BC	1991 BC	1786 BC
Neolithic culture begins in southern Siberia.	Egypt's Middle Kingdom begins.	End of Middle Kingdom.

Saving Nubian architecture was the greatest archeological rescue operation in history.

left: *Detail from the Ramses temple statues.*

was dedicated to Ramses' Queen Nefertari, and royal children are portrayed on its façade.

One of the most remarkable archeological rescue operations in history began in 1964 with a desperate race to save the greatest Nubian structures from the rising waters of the Nile, a result of the construction of the Aswan High Dam. Egypt and Sudan offered 50 percent of finds to any international team who agreed to work in the threatened area; the 22 countries that responded identified hundreds of new sites. There were thousands of surveys, detailed diaries of excavations, and photographs that showed relics in their original settings. After this, several of the temples, including those at Abu Simbel, were cut apart and re-assembled on sites high enough to avoid the Nile inundation.

Heliopolis. It was positioned so that the rays of the rising sun shone onto the statues of the gods, along with one of Ramses himself. Among the valuable wall decorations discovered are a series of reliefs showing the war between the Egyptians and the Hittite people at Kadesh and inscriptions apparently written by Greek mercenary soldiers c.550 BC. The smaller temple

The Egyptian Army

Foreign military campaigns demanded a highly organized, full-time army. This was garrisoned both in known trouble spots, such as Nubia and Asia, and near royal capitals along the Nile. Infantry was split into platoons of ten; 20 platoons formed a company and 25 companies made up a Division (or an "Army", as Egyptian Generals would confusingly call it). Each company fell under the command of a standard-bearing captain.

The most effective units were archers, grouped in specialized battalions and often assigned to support infantry charges. The Egyptians were good at headlong charges, with their fast chariot cavalry (organized in groups of 50), expert javelin-throwers, and fearsome hand-to-hand sword fighters. But they had little idea of how to break a besieged city and were usually reduced to camping outside to await the effects of starvation.

Man-made Lake Nasser—modern needs endangered ancient monuments.

c.1600 BC	c.1300 BC	c.1250 BC	c.1200 BC	c.1100–900 BC	814 BC	c.800 BC	776 BC
Mycenean civilization begins in Greece.	Settlers arrive in Tonga, Fiji, and Samoa.	Abu Simbel temples carved, under order of Ramses II.	Greeks destroy Troy.	Chinese dictionary compiled.	Phoenician colony founded at Carthage.	In India, Aryans spread southward.	First Olympic Games, held in Greece.

CHAPTER THREE

WESTERN ASIA AND THE NEAR EAST

left: *Glazed brick relief of an archer of the Achaemenid period, c375 BC.*

It is a land immortalized in the Bible and the magical folk stories of Arabian Nights. Amid the fog of part-fact, part-fantasy that envelops so much of ancient history in Mesopotamia and the Near East, there lies the origins of the world's first great cities—Babylon, Nineveh, Ur, Persepolis, Ebla, and Jericho. Here archeologists have discovered urban planning and civil engineering of scarcely believable efficiency; societies that could channel drinking water across a 30-mile network of canals and aqueducts at a time when much of the world had just emerged blinking into the light of post-Stone Age technology.

Israelite altar from the 10th century BC.

BLACK SEA

● Ankara

TURKEY

MEDITERRANEAN

Mount Carmel ■

ISRAEL

Jericho ■

Masada ■

EGYPT

● Cairo

RED SEA

The spread of innovation in structural design, farming, and metallurgy had implications in the form of wider trading links and, inevitably, a fierce ambition among rulers to protect their wealth and create new empires. Within the space of a few hundred years, Mesopotamia—the land now shared mainly by Iraq and Syria—formed the battleground on which countless kingdoms and city states tested their military might. Sumerians, Assyrians, Persians, Babylonians, and Chaldeans all claimed it for their own, their respective stars rising and falling as time passed.

This was also a period of emerging faiths, in which Jews and early Christians were persecuted by the pagan Roman empire and responded with acts of martyrdom and even terrorism. One of the most remarkable and tragic shows of defiance was played out on King Herod's former palace fortress, the Rock of Masada, where a thousand men, women, and children withheld the might of the Roman Tenth Legion for two years, before committing mass suicide. Like so many thousands of others in the ensuing years, they believed theirs was a land worth dying for.

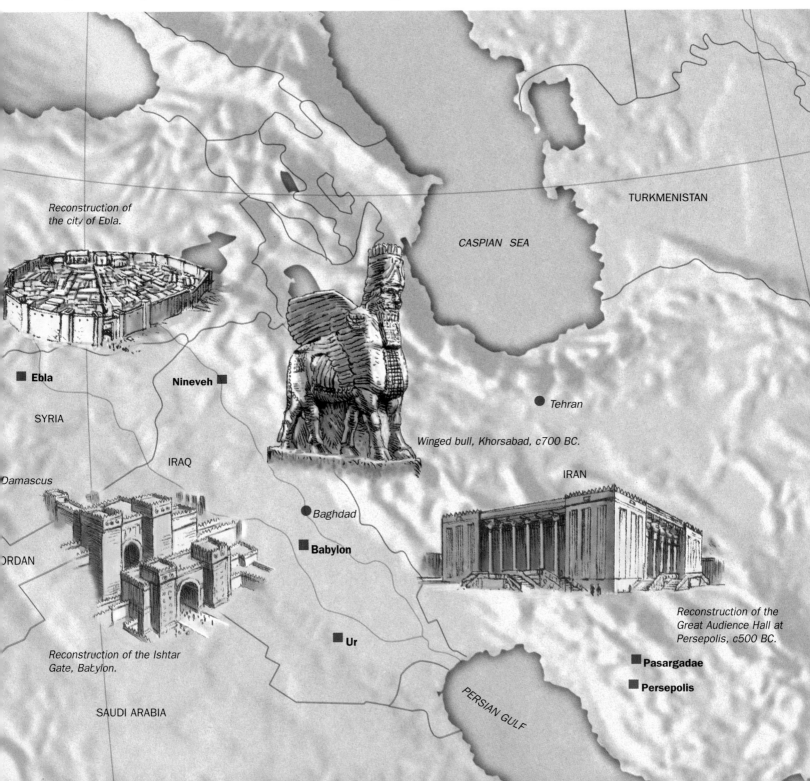

Reconstruction of the city of Ebla.

TURKMENISTAN

CASPIAN SEA

■ Ebla

Nineveh ■

SYRIA

● Tehran

Winged bull, Khorsabad, c700 BC.

IRAQ

IRAN

Damascus

● Baghdad

■ Babylon

RDAN

Reconstruction of the Ishtar Gate, Babylon.

■ Ur

Reconstruction of the Great Audience Hall at Persepolis, c500 BC.

■ Pasargadae

■ Persepolis

SAUDI ARABIA

PERSIAN GULF

MOUNT CARMEL
Battleground of Elijah and the false prophets

One of the most sacred sites mentioned in the Old Testament is Mount Carmel, the mountain on which Elijah did battle with false prophets of the Phoenician god Baal. Elijah's struggle involved a contest of miracles, which he finally won by asserting that for three years there would be no rain. He then assembled the people of Israel on the slopes of Carmel and put the Baalite prophets to death.

Although there is no archeological evidence in support of Elijah's life, Mount Carmel has yielded plenty of evidence about the activities of the

left: *A terracotta sculpture believed to be of Middle Eastern design and dating to pre-Old Testament times.*

Paleolithic people who lived there up to 200,000 years previously—people who are key to our understanding of human evolution. The cave sites of Tabun, el Wad, Skhul, and Kebara first attracted the attention of palæoanthropologists in the 1920s, while advances in dating methods in the 1950s helped to plot out occupation of the site by assessing the style of stone tools that were recovered.

The very first inhabitants were primitive *Homo sapiens*, who looked more like the Neandertals of Europe than the people of today. They used crude tools such as hand axes and scrapers fashioned from flakes of stone. Later, in the Middle Paleolithic period, they adopted the more thoughtful Levallois technique (named from a French site), in which a block of fine-grained flint is struck so that smaller flints of a set size and shape are created. Later still, tools were made on standard flat rocks in a "factory" setting similar to a famous site at Aurignacian, France.

Early hunters' diet

Analysis of animal bones discovered in the caves showed what these early

Who Killed Neanderthal Man?

Solving the mystery of Neanderthal Man's demise is still largely conjecture. However, one of the most imaginative theories has resulted from DNA genetic research revealing that domestic dogs have been man's best friend far longer than previously thought. One study claimed that three-quarters of modern dog species could be traced directly to a single she-wolf who lived more than 100,000 years ago. The theory espoused by Dr David Paxton, an Australian veterinary scientist, is that wolves "adopted" humans after realizing that early settlements meant a ready source of scraps and meal leftovers. Humans found the wolves useful as guards and while hunting. More importantly, they relieved humans of the need for a developed sense of smell, allowing them to instead evolve facial characteristics that encouraged a more sophisticated ability: speech. The Paxton idea is supported by some accepted truths about Neanderthal Man. One is that he didn't associate much with wolves; another is that he retained a skull structure that made speech more difficult.

c.400,000 BC	c.300,000 BC	c.200,000 BC	150,000–38,000 BC	c.128,000 BC	100,000 BC	50–30,000 BC	32,000 BC
Date of spear found in Germany, oldest wooden weapon discovered.	Date of a hut in France, oldest discovered manmade structure.	Paleolithic people live in caves on Mount Carmel.	Middle Paleolithic period, when flint tools were used.	Sea temperatures and levels rise as Ice Age ends.	"Modern human" remains from this period recovered from Mount Carmel.	European and Asian climate grows colder again. Humans arrive in Australia from southeast Asia.	Cave art begins to appear across Europe.

Renowned as the site of Elijah's power-struggle with false prophets, Mount Carmel is gradually revealing its ancient past.

hunters liked to eat—goat, boar, wild horses, deer, and gazelle all figured high on the menu. Intriguingly, they also gave a broad indication of climate change. Excavations through stratified layers of material in the caves showed distinct periods in which venison was far more popular than gazelle meat. Gazelles favor a dry, open, desert-like grazing area, whereas deer prefer the woods and heavier ground cover associated with wetter conditions. By comparing the bone data with known

above left:
Faces with exaggerated features are a common theme among artists of the first true civilizations.

right: *A decorated stone animal carving.*

Ice Age advances in Europe, a useful foundation was laid for an overall interpretation of the Mount Carmel caves.

Hominid skeletons in the Tabun and Skhul caves were a further exciting find. These suggest that Carmel residents had both Neandertal features (like a pronounced brow) and those of modern humans (a high forehead). This combination implied some kind of evolutionary transition between Neanderthal Man and humankind as we know it today. Anthropologists now generally accept that the 100,000-year-old Skhul finds, together with others at Qafzeh, near Nazareth, are early examples of modern humans and date to precisely the same period as more obvious Neandertal skeletons found at Tabun. It seems they lived in the same neighborhood at the same time.

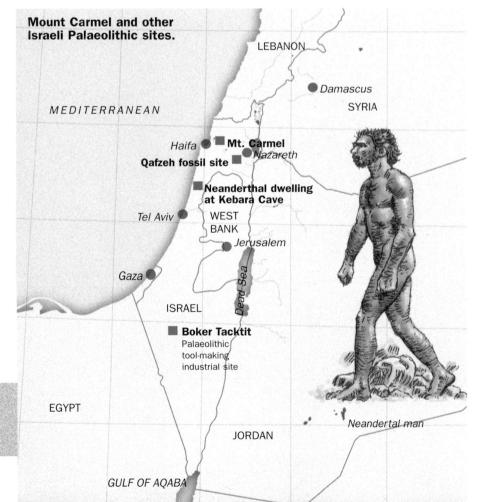

Mount Carmel and other Israeli Palaeolithic sites.

LEBANON

MEDITERRANEAN

Damascus
SYRIA

Haifa • ■ **Mt. Carmel**
■ *Nazareth*
Qafzeh fossil site ■

■ **Neandertal dwelling at Kebara Cave**

Tel Aviv ●
WEST BANK

● *Jerusalem*

Gaza ●

Dead Sea

ISRAEL

■ **Boker Tacktit**
Palaeolithic tool-making industrial site

EGYPT

JORDAN

Neandertal man

GULF OF AQABA

ARTIFACTS OF JUDAISM
The Rock of Masada and the Dead Sea Scrolls

The Rock of Masada is one of the Jewish world's greatest symbols of defiance and bravery. Rising out of the desert on the west coast of the Dead Sea, it was the dramatic natural fortress chosen by King Herod for his summer palace, built between 36 and 30 BC. Herod—portrayed in Christian texts as a puppet king of the Romans—died in 4 BC; 70 years later his stronghold was occupied by Jewish zealots, effectively a terrorist group that masterminded a general uprising against the pagan Roman emperor. They were driven from Jerusalem in AD 70 and made their last stand at Masada. Under the leadership of Eleazar, a group of a thousand held the Tenth Legion at bay for almost two years.

For the Romans, there was no chance of storming the sheer sides. They tried various tactics, like building a 2-mile (3.2km) containment wall around the base of the rock and a massive earthen ramp up the west side, but neither had any effect. The zealots, meanwhile, had cause to thank their old enemy Herod for the massive water cisterns he constructed precisely to withstand a long siege. They had food supplies, arms, and a burning will to avoid surrender.

The sequence of death

Yet, after two years, even the most fanatical zealot accepted that the siege could not go on. According to the Jewish historian Josephus, it was agreed that the garrison should commit mass suicide; men killing their families, ten men chosen by lots to kill the rest of the fighters, and one man chosen by lot to kill the remaining nine and himself. By any historical standards, it was an extraordinary act.

Between 1963 and 1964 Yigael Yadin, an Israeli archeologist,

Key New Testament sites

MEDITERRANEAN

LEBANON

Damascus

SYRIA

Haifa

Qafzeh fossil site

Nazareth

Tel Aviv

WEST BANK

Beit Guvrin
Roman and Byzantine remains

Jerusalem

Qumran Cave
Discovery of the Dead Sea Scrolls

Bethlehem

Dead Sea

Gaza

Herodium
Roman settlement of palaces, baths, etc

Rock of Masada
Herod's fortress palace

ISRAEL

JORDAN

EGYPT

GULF OF AQABA

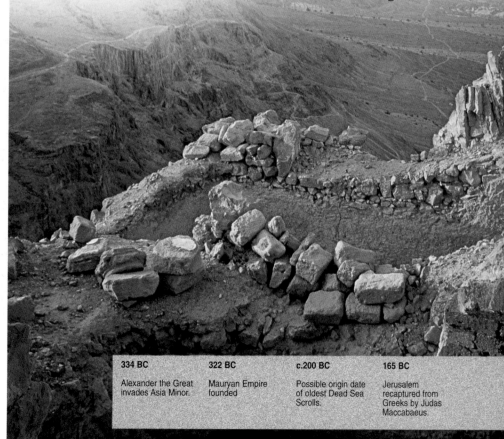

334 BC	322 BC	c.200 BC	165 BC
Alexander the Great invades Asia Minor.	Mauryan Empire founded	Possible origin date of oldest Dead Sea Scrolls.	Jerusalem recaptured from Greeks by Judas Maccabaeus.

King Herod's summer palace became the focus of an extraordinary act of religious defiance.

conducted a massive excavation of Masada, an operation as important for focusing the national identity of the fledgling state as for the historical information it gathered. Yadin concentrated on the palace and its associated bathhouses around the precipitous northern tip of the rock, but also found a small synagogue, ritual baths, and some Old Testament scrolls that had been buried beneath the synagogue floor to prevent them falling into Roman hands. Above all,

he found 11 ostraka—shards of pottery carrying the names of some of the defenders. Was it possible that these were fragments used by the zealots in their lottery to decide the order of death?

above left: *The Qumran Caves; the base of a Jewish brotherhood and the spot where the Dead Sea scrolls were hidden.*

below left: *The Rock of Masada—a symbol of Jewish resistance.*

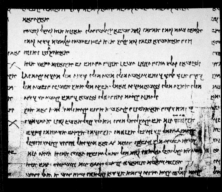

The Dead Sea Scrolls

In 1947 some Bedouin wandering among caves near Khirbet Qumran on the northwest shore of the Dead Sea stumbled upon a hidden cache of Hebrew and Aramaic manuscripts written on leather or papyrus. The precise circumstances of this find have never been fully explained, but there is no doubt of their authenticity. Further investigations by the authorities revealed more scrolls, including two made of copper.

The 600-plus scrolls include rules of discipline (relating to an unspecified Jewish brotherhood), hymn books, biblical texts, and various predictions of apocalypse. There is the oldest known copy of the Book of Isaiah and fragments of every Old Testament book other than Esther. All seem to have been written between 200 BC and AD 68; archeological investigations support the later date. It appears that the community was attacked in AD 68—probably by the Roman general Vespasian—as part of the Empire's response to the zealots' uprising.

The Qumran brotherhood seems to have modeled itself on Moses's Israel and considered that its role was to prepare for Judgment Day. Members were ranked according to their purity, had to serve a two-year probation, and could be promoted or demoted at a general election held each year. Spiritual direction was provided by three priests and seems to have closely followed New Testament teachings. It is noteworthy that John the Baptist came from the Qumran area, a man whose preaching was reflected in the later teachings of Jesus.

c.138 BC	36–30 BC	4 BC	27 AD	43 AD	58 AD	c.68 AD	105 AD
Central Asia explored by Chang Chien.	King Herod's summer palace constructed at Rock of Masada, on west coast of Dead Sea.	Death of King Herod.	Jesus baptized	Romans invade Britain.	Buddhism introduced to China by Emperor Ming Ti.	Jewish zealots commit mass suicide; last Dead Sea Scrolls written.	Paper first used, China.

PERSIA AND HER CITIES
Stories set in stone

At Naksh-i Rustam, near the city of Persepolis in southwest Iran, a cliff face is adorned with a series of spectacular royal tombs carved from the rock. This is the burial ground of the Persian kings, a royal dynasty that rose during the sixth century BC to create an immense empire stretching from Egypt and western Turkey to central Asia. Although they made Babylon their capital, they never shunned their roots, and both Persepolis and its older neighbor, Pasargadae, were designed to accommodate ceremonial needs, such as coronations and state funerals.

The founder of the empire, Cyrus the Great, built a palace retreat at Pasargadae in a period when his forces had underlined their superiority with victories over the Medes, Lydians, and Babylonians. Cyrus was succeeded by Cambyses, who added Egypt to this clutch of dominions, and then Darius, who took the crown under obscure and slightly suspicious circumstances. It was Darius who crushed civil unrest and established a more organized administrative regime in which Persia was divided into satrapies, or provinces. He also commissioned the construction of Persepolis.

The new city was built on a series of platforms and sweeping staircases centered on a huge terrace measuring 1,400 by 1,000 feet (435 by 310m). On this were set the main royal and government buildings, such as the Treasury and Apadama (meeting hall). These were impressive, pillared structures decorated with the statues of winged bulls around doorways, an idea borrowed from the earlier Assyrians.

Elsewhere, intricate stone reliefs paid tribute to the king with illustrations of his court, senior officials, armies, and a submissive troop of vassal regions bearing tributes. This use of monumental masonry to bolster royal pride was a feature of the regime. Darius even used a cliff at Behistun in western Iran to counter criticism by inscribing at length, and in three different languages, his accession and strategy to end civil war.

Massacre of the Persian fleet

It was Darius, and later his son Xerxes, who waged an epic war against the Greeks. A series of battles at Thermopylae, Marathon, and Salamis were portrayed by later Classical historians as a confrontation between the forces of freedom and oppression, with the Greeks fighting a determined rearguard action against overwhelming odds. By 480 BC Xerxes' advance through Greece was unstoppable and he had added Athens to territory controlled by the Persians. With some Greek leaders demanding a retreat to Corinth, the inspirational general Themistocles

left: *This elaborate stone relief bordering a doorway is typical of Persian architectural style.*

6th century BC	539 BC	509 BC
Rise of Persian kings.	Persians conquer Babylon.	Roman Republic founded.

The mighty Persian empire was first halted by a wily Greek general—then destroyed by Alexander the Great.

instead persuaded them to confront the Persian Navy head on.

Themistocles cunningly sent messengers to the enemy claiming that the Greeks' own Athenian-dominated navy was prepared to collaborate and that if Xerxes attacked he could expect a walkover. Xerxes was hoodwinked—when his 350 ships arrived they found the Greek vessels backing into the bay at Salamis. The Persians pressed forward, only to find themselves trapped and forced into hand-to-hand fighting, just as Themistocles had wanted. More than 200 Persian ships were sunk, but only 40 were lost by the Greeks. The battle effectively ended Persian ambitions in the West.

Within 150 years, Persia as a nation state was in ruins. In the Macedonian general Alexander the Great they found themselves up against the most brilliant, ruthless military leader Asia had ever seen. Alexander occupied Persepolis in 330 BC and put the city to the torch—revenge, it was said, for Xerxes' burning of Athens 150 years earlier. Almost overnight, Persia was subsumed into Alexander's fledgling empire.

Persepolis has left a legacy through its many stone inscriptions that have helped historians decipher several important ancient languages of the Near East including Akkadian, a key that unlocked the culture of Mesopotamia. The style of Persian art and architecture also helped establish the ethnic and religious background of the region during a time of great upheaval and instability.

above: *Detail from the Palace of Xerxes* and **above left:** *a gold armlet with finely-wrought griffin motifs found in a hoard of treasure near the River Oxus (today called Amu Darya).*

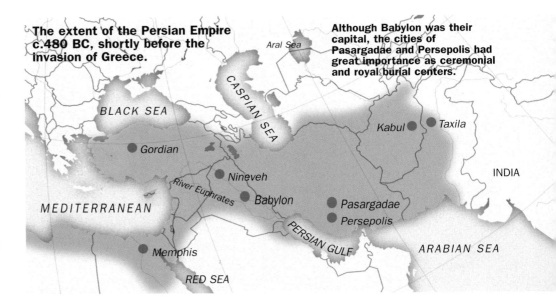

The extent of the Persian Empire c.480 BC, shortly before the invasion of Greece.

Although Babylon was their capital, the cities of Pasargadae and Persepolis had great importance as ceremonial and royal burial centers.

Aral Sea

BLACK SEA

CASPIAN SEA

Kabul

Taxila

Gordian

River Euphrates

Nineveh

Babylon

Pasargadae

Persepolis

MEDITERRANEAN

INDIA

Memphis

PERSIAN GULF

ARABIAN SEA

RED SEA

c.500 BC	c.480 BC	449 BC	447 BC	c.330 BC	290 BC	247 BC	224 BC
Iron first used in Africa.	King Xerxes adds Athens to Persian Empire, after advance through Greece.	First Roman code of laws established.	The Parthenon is built on the Acropolis in Athens.	End of Persian nation state. Alexander the Great occupies and torches Persepolis.	Roman conquest of central Italy.	Kingdom of Parthia founded by Arsaces I.	Colossus of Rhodes, one of the Seven Wonders of the Ancient World, destroyed in earthquake.

ASSYRIAN MAGIC AT NINEVEH
The palace-city

The land of Mesopotamia, between the rivers Tigris and Euphrates in Iraq, is rightly dubbed the "cradle of civilization." It was home to Western Asia's most prolific early urban cultures and, to the chagrin of many a history scholar, endured ever-changing political boundaries as first one then another ruler laid claim to the territory. During the three millennia from 3500 BC onward, Mesopotamia was controlled by the likes of the Sumerian, Babylonian, Assyrian, Chaldean, and Persian peoples, and featured heavily in Old Testament writings.

From their stronghold in northern Mesopotamia, the Assyrians began to flex their military muscle around 1350 BC. They held Babylon in 1225 BC, and for a time around 1100 BC seized control of the eastern Mediterranean lands. The expansion of their empire was thwarted for 200 years as Aramaean and Chaldean tribes fought back, taking Babylonia c.915 BC. This motivated the Assyrians to re-group and re-assert themselves, and by 730 BC their empire was at its height, stretching through the whole of the Middle East to Egypt and back to the Gulf. For the most part they were content to leave conquered kings in command— provided the necessary tributes were forthcoming. More awkward foes were summarily annexed.

During this golden era—from the Assyrian point of view—the city of Nineveh became capital of the empire. It had long been known as a religious center and its statue of the goddess Ishtar was renowned for its healing powers. But it wasn't until Sargon II, who ruled between 722 and 705 BC, that the first steps were taken toward raising its profile. Sargon built a library and his successor, Sennacherib, who ruled until 681 BC, made it the Assyrian capital instead of Calah (now called Nimrud).

Sennacherib's unparalleled home

Sennacherib wasted no time in making his mark. The ancient city was replanned to create wide streets and squares, parks and flower gardens, and a wonderfully named royal residence, The Palace Without A Rival. Drinking water was supplied from 30 miles (50km) away through an ingenious system of canals and aqueducts. And like all Assyrian palace-cities, the defensive fortifications included thick outer walls interspersed with fortlets and elaborate gateways.

left: *Carved ivory animals such as this resting lion were highly prized among wealthy Assyrians.*

c.1700 BC	c.1500 BC	c.1350 BC	c.1323 BC	c.1250 BC	c.1225 BC	c.1100 BC	753 BC
Ukrainian pottery is imported to China.	Widespread use of iron weaponry in Near East.	Birth of Assyrian Empire.	Death of boy king Tutankhamen.	Height of Mycenean civilization.	Assyrians control Babylon.	Assyrians seize eastern Mediterranean lands.	Rome established on River Tiber.

For all their military might and dabblings in alchemy the Assyrian empire had a fatal weakness—territorial greed.

above: *An exquisitely-carved ivory inlay from Calah (now Nimrud) and* **right:** *a bas-relief depicting mounted cavalry, taken from Ashurbanipal's palace at Nineveh.*

The palaces at Nineveh, and other important centers such as Khorsabad and Calah, tended to be designed around large, internal, circular courtyards. There would be blocks of rooms assigned for private royal apartments, state business, and ceremonial occasions, as well as more functional areas for kitchens, maintenance staff, and storage. Main doorways would be guarded by 12-foot (3.6m) high statues of mythological part-human, part-bull winged creatures, while carved panels illustrated the king's great deeds on the battlefield, in hunting parties, and at worship. This was propaganda extolling the king as the sole source of Assyrian influence and prosperity.

Behind the scenes, rulers such as Ashurbanipal, who reigned from 668 to 627 BC, devoted themselves to creating a library of ancient knowledge, including numerous cuneiform clay tablets, written in Akkadian script, devoted to alchemy and magic. Some of these tablets were uncovered by the self-taught British cuneiform expert George Smith in the 1870s and carried historically unique Mesopotamian accounts of the Great Flood. Others produced fascinating evidence of the day-to-day running of the royal household and the operation of the Treasury.

Like many empire-builders before and since, the Assyrians' downfall lay in their territorial greed. They could not hope to maintain control over such a vast area, and in 612 BC combined attacks by the Medes and Chaldeans resulted in the sack of Nineveh. The Medes occupied Mesopotamian hill country while the Chaldeans, under Nebuchadnezzar II, controlled Babylon until the coming of the Persians.

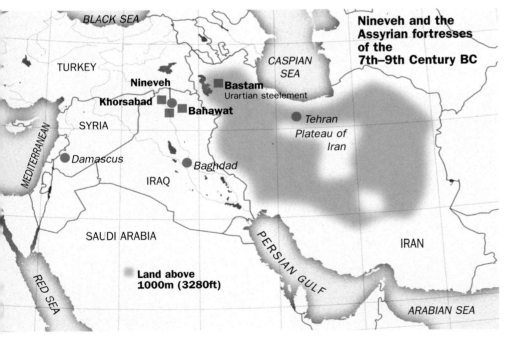

Nineveh and the Assyrian fortresses of the 7th–9th Century BC

BLACK SEA
TURKEY
CASPIAN SEA
Nineveh
Khorsabad
Bastam
Urartian steelement
Bahawat
SYRIA
Tehran
Plateau of Iran
Damascus
Baghdad
IRAQ
MEDITERRANEAN
SAUDI ARABIA
IRAN
PERSIAN GULF
Land above 1000m (3280ft)
RED SEA
ARABIAN SEA

c. 730 BC	722-705 BC	705–681 BC	668–627 BC	650 BC	c.640 BC	612 BC	539 BC
Height of Assyrian Empire.	Reign of Sargon II. Redevelops Nineveh, capital of Assyrian Empire.	Sennacherib reigns. Makes Nineveh capital of Assyria.	King Ashurbanipal creates library in Nineveh.	City of Lepcis Magna, east of Tripoli, established by Phoenicians.	Assyrians attempt genocide on their ancient enemies, the Elamites.	Medes and Chaldeans sack Nineveh.	Persians conquer Babylon.

NEBUCHADNEZZAR AND BABYLON
Wonders of the ancient world

At its peak, Babylon was the largest city in the world. It covered more than 2,500 acres (1,000 ha) and had some of the greatest landmarks of the time, such as the Hanging Gardens, the Ishtar Gate, and a 300-foot (92m) ziggurat linked to biblical stories of the Tower of Babel. The city's importance as a capital dates back to the late third millennium BC, when its position at the hub of overland trade routes between the Gulf and the Mediterranean underpinned its economy.

But it was not until Chaldean king Nabopolassar wrested control of Babylon from the Assyrians in 625 BC that it flowered into an awe-inspiring metropolis. Nabopolassar, and more significantly his son Nebuchadnezzar II, rebuilt the Etemenanki ziggurat in Babylon and designed new palaces, wide pavements, and awesome fortifications. Nebuchadnezzar also commissioned the Hanging Gardens, an arrangement of stepped and planted terraces that became one of the Seven Wonders of the Ancient World. Further afield, their forces conquered much of Palestine and Syria, creating the wider kingdom of Babylonia.

Our knowledge of Babylon owes much to the work of German archeologist Robert Koldewey, who uncovered many of Nebuchadnezzar's buildings between 1899 and 1917 AD. He proved that the site encompassed two cities. The outer city stretched across 3 square miles (7 sq km) and was protected by a triple wall so thick that a four-horse chariot could turn around on top without unhitching.

Love, war, and gold

The triple wall merged in the northeast with the palace of Tell Babil, while to the west it connected to the inner sector housing the core of Nebuchadnezzar's powerbase. Here lay the sacred and royal chambers, protected by their own defenses and set at the head of a processional route leading to the Ishtar Gate. The gate, named after the goddess of love and war, was decorated with molded and glazed colored bricks. These provided a colorful background for the dragon and bull shapes that adorned the sides of a high arch.

below: *An image of Babylonian religious mythology—Ivriz, the god of weather.*

The Tower of Babel

According to the Old Testament, the tower was built by the descendants of Noah on Babylonia's Plain of Shinar. The aim was to make it reach Heaven, but such arrogance infuriated Jehovah, who caused the builders to speak in hitherto-unknown tongues. He then scattered them across the face of the earth—a neat explanation for the spread of languages. Some scholars believe the story was inspired by the collapse of the Etemenanki ziggurat in Babylon, later restored by Nabopolassar and Nebuchadnezzar II.

776 BC	729 BC	625 BC	551 BC	509 BC	500 BC	490 BC	482 BC
First Olympic Games, held in Greece.	Assyrian King Tiglath-Pileser III quells a Babylonian revolution; becomes King of Babylon.	Chaldean king Nabopolassar gains control of Babylon from Assyrians.	Confucius is born.	Roman Republic is founded.	Sinhalese Aryan people reach Ceylon.	Persians defeated at Athens in Battle of Marathon.	King Xerxes of Persia curbs a rebellion in Babylon by destroying temples.

Babylon's awesome defenses produced an aura of invincibility. Yet Nebuchadnezzar's dynasty was short-lived.

above: *A panoramic view of the Ebla excavation. The tablets unearthed are crucial to our understanding of Bronze Age farming and trade.*

Robert Koldewey also found the museum where Nebuchadnezzar kept his much-prized Mesopotamian antiques, and a complex of underground rooms with vaulted ceilings, wells, and an asphalt layer of waterproofing. Although Koldewey believed these rooms served as the foundations of the Hanging Gardens, the evidence is sketchy. More certain is the site of the Temple of Marduk, some half a mile (1km) south, along the processional avenue. According to Greek historians, who were occasionally known to exaggerate, the god's statue and associated cult equipment involved the melting of 20 tons of gold. They claimed that two tons of frankincense were used every year.

The glories of Babylon did not last. Within 23 years of Nebuchadnezzar's

The Ebla Tablets

The Ebla tablets comprise some 20,000 clay blocks inscribed with forms of the old Persian language and Akkadian script. They were found by Italian archeologists investigating a Bronze Age city at Tell Mardikh, Syria, the modern name for Ebla. They were quickly shown to be a unique archive of state records, including details of livestock and grain reserves, textile and metal production, temple offerings and overseas trade. They proved that the long-held view of Near East communities as mere satellites of Mesopotamia was fatally flawed.

son, Amel-Marduk, succeeding the throne, Cyrus the Great's Persian army had captured the city. Later still, in 330 BC, it fell to Alexander the Great, who dreamed of making it the central capital of his empire. But

Alexander died before his plan could be realized, and for the next thousand years Babylon's importance steadily declined until, by the rise of Islam in the seventh century AD, it was almost an afterthought on ancient maps.

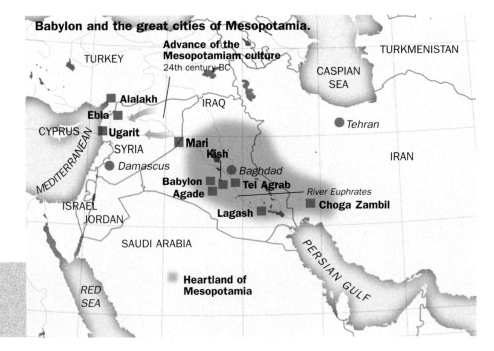

Babylon and the great cities of Mesopotamia.

4th century BC	c.330 BC	323 BC
Iron-smelting furnace in use in Taruga, Nigeria.	Babylon falls under Alexander the Great's control.	Death of Alexander the Great.

HUMAN SACRIFICE AT UR AND THE GREAT FLOOD

Lands of Abraham

Picture the scene during the momentous climax of a royal funeral in the Sumerian city of Ur. The body of the king lies in a pit leading to his underground tomb. Around him stand members of his household who have volunteered to travel into the afterlife with him. There are the ranks of his ladies-in-waiting, armed soldiers clutching javelins, senior male courtiers—even oxen, ready-hitched to their carts. As the last rituals are performed by religious officiants, so the killing begins.

Today we can barely imagine the mixed feelings of the doomed royal entourage. All that is clear is that the slaughter was sometimes on a grand scale. One excavated grave contained the remains of 68 women and six men, clad in the finest robes and laid in neat rows. Another grave ensured the king's security and his easy exit to eternity—the bodies of soldiers and their ox-carts were in an outer chamber, while those of nine women were in the burial room.

In total, more than 2,500 graves were unearthed in the "Royal Cemetery" at Ur, many of them attributed to commoners. Contents ranged from simple pots and beaded jewelry to outstanding works of Sumerian art such as the Royal Standard of Ur, a picture-panel inlaid with mother-of-pearl and semi-precious gems. Other similarly inlaid objects included gaming boards, animal figures, and lyres, one of which bore what appears to be an artist's joke—a depiction of wild animals playing musical instruments.

Perhaps the most stunning example of metalwork produced by the royal smithy was the helmet of King Meskalamdug. This piece was made in electrum, an alloy of gold and silver popular with ancient craftsmen—evidence of the healthy state of the Sumerian treasury. Many such items were recovered by Sir Leonard Woolley in his exhaustive investigations of Ur for the British Museum and the University of Pennsylvania between 1922 and 1934.

above: *Items of jewelry worn by servants of Queen Pu-Abi; later recovered from royal burial pits by Sir Leonard Woolley.*
left: *This carved bull's head adorning a stringed instrument was recovered from a royal tomb at Ur.*

Ur and the Great Flood

Woolley's work covered the site of the city from prehistoric times to its rapid abandonment during the early years after Jesus's birth. The archeological record he produced showed that Ur was probably founded around 5500 BC by an early farming community that produced a distinctive style of painted pot. By 3500 BC they had constructed sophisticated temples filled with ornaments. This period also shows the development of a crude writing— probably to help priests keep track of trading deals—and by 2700 BC this had developed into a definitive script in which rulers could extol their

c.5500 BC	c.5000 BC	c.4000 BC	c.3500 BC	c.3000 BC	c.2700 BC	c.2100 BC	c.1900 BC
Ur founded by early farming community.	Cave paintings and engravings from this time found in Sahara and Zimbabwe.	Plow is invented.	Sophisticated ornamental temples at Ur.	Copper knives and axes made in Palestine.	Script used to record Ur's rulers' achievements and priests' myths.	Ur's great ziggurat constructed under King Ur-Nammu's rule.	According to Bible, Abraham's family leave Ur for Palestine.

The Book of Genesis tells how Noah discovered the secret of winemaking soon after the flood. Did his descendants tend the vineyards of Mount Judi?

achievements and priests record their cult-based myths. In about 2100 BC the city's great ziggurat was constructed by King Ur-Nammu, tangible evidence of the power and influence he held over Mesopotamia and the important trade routes along the Euphrates to the sea and across land to the Mediterranean.

It is soon after this that biblical stories become woven into the city's history. We are told in Genesis chapter 11 that Ur was the starting point for the departure of Abraham's family to Palestine in about 1900 BC. Intriguingly, Woolley's deepest explorations discovered the ruins of primitive huts dating to the very earliest occupation of the site. These huts were covered in an 11-foot (3.35m) layer of mud and river silt that seemed to correlate with

accounts of the Great Flood.

The debate over the flood and the existence of Noah's Ark seems unlikely to go away. While some archeologists insist that Ur only offers evidence of a localized flood, others believe there is a powerful case for treating this and certain other Old Testament accounts as historically sound. Since about AD 1000, the Ark's

below: *A clay tablet recovered from the site of Ur. These were used by priests to develop the first, crude forms of writing.*

above: *Reconstruction of the Ziggurat at Ur.*

supposed landing place, Mount Ararat, was linked to Mount Aregats, far away in northeast Turkey. Yet much earlier Christian and Jewish traditions, along with the Koran, place it on Mount Judi (or Judi Gargh), just 100 miles from the Tigris Valley. It was from here that Assyrian ruler Sennacherib returned in the seventh century AD, with a plank he claimed originated from the Ark.

Another curious detail supports the biblical account. According to Genesis, when Noah returned to dry land he soon discovered the secret of wine-making. Is it coincidence that the first evidence of viniculture has been found in Mesopotamia—in the shadow of Mount Judi?

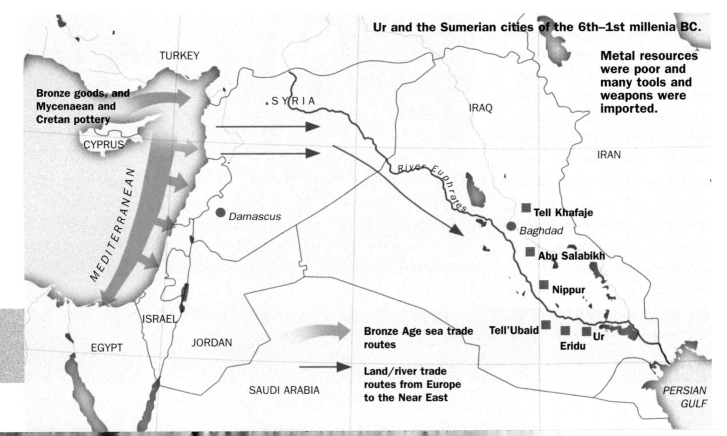

Ur and the Sumerian cities of the 6th–1st millenia BC.

Metal resources were poor and many tools and weapons were imported.

TURKEY

Bronze goods, and Mycenaean and Cretan pottery

CYPRUS

MEDITERRANEAN

. SYRIA

IRAQ

IRAN

River Euphrates

• Damascus

Tell Khafaje

• Baghdad

Abu Salabikh

Nippur

ISRAEL

EGYPT   JORDAN

Bronze Age sea trade routes

Tell'Ubaid

Ur

Eridu

Land/river trade routes from Europe to the Near East

SAUDI ARABIA

PERSIAN GULF

CHAPTER FOUR

ANCIENT GREECE AND THE AEGEAN

GREECE

Vergina (Aigai) ■

The priestess of the Oracle at Delphi.

Delphi ■

Mycenae ■

■ Pylos

The role of Ancient Greece in shaping the culture of western society can hardly be overstated. This divided yet immensely powerful civilization boasted a mythical world of gods and heroes, a history of fantastic triumph and glorious failure, and a democracy that could rival many in the world today. Here was a people who valued art for art's sake, who prized beauty as highly as wealth, and who showed a level of religious tolerance sadly lacking in later eras.

Yet it would be wrong to portray the movers and shakers of the Greek world as arty wastrels preoccupied with spiritual affairs. They made major advances in philosophy, medicine, and natural science, were thorough historians and geographers, good architects, innovative administrators and economists, courageous explorers, and superb battlefield tacticians. It is no coincidence that in military academies around the world, the conquests of the Macedonian general Alexander the Great remain relevant to the theory of warfare.

This chapter looks at some of the greatest legacies of the Greek-speaking people, from the opulent early palaces of the Bronze Age Mycenaeans to the birth of literacy on Crete, expansion of the empire, and awe-inspiring landmarks of Athens. It also explores the truth behind Troy—once considered a mere poetic fantasy, now regarded among the greatest and most fascinating of Greek cities.

A lonely set of pillars testifies to the ancient splendor of the island of Delos.

IONIAN SEA

Philip of Macedon, father of Alexander, from a small ivory carving found in the royal tomb at Vergina.

Alexander the Great, from a Roman statuette. His conquest of Western Asia started in Troy.

■ Troy

AEGEAN SEA

TURKEY

Athens

■ Delos

Reconstruction of the fortress at Mycenae.

■ Akrotiri

SEA OF CRETE

CRETE   ■ Knossos

The sport of bull-vaulting, as depicted on a mural at Knossos.

ATHENS: THE ACROPOLIS AND AGORA
Cradle of democracy

Just as the pyramids provide instant worldwide recognition of Egypt, so the Acropolis of Athens is the abiding symbol of Ancient Greece. Towering 500 feet (150m) above the city, like some watchful sentinel of the Classical World, this natural hill fortress was at

above: *Ruins of the entrance to the Acropolis of Athens, and what the imposing complex of temples looked like in its heyday in the 5th century BC (right). The gilded statue of Athena and the Parthenon, on the right, dominate the skyline.*

the hub of Greek affairs between 600 and 350 BC, when Athens had secured domination over all rival cities. At this time, Greece was a loose collection of alliances between *Poleis*—communities of essentially equal citizens—and more urbanized city-states.

The term acropolis stems from the Greek word "akros," meaning highest, and "polis," meaning city. Early Greeks tended to build their settlements on flat land, near high outcrops that could act as defendable sanctuaries in times of war. As a result, most cities boasted an acropolis and the word came to mean both the high ground and whatever was constructed upon it. Often an acropolis would encompass several roles, such as a public meeting place, the citadel of a ruler, and the focus of religious activity.

The Acropolis in Athens seems to have been occupied from Neolithic times (c.5000 BC). During the height of the Mycenaean civilization (c.1450–1200 BC) it was a formidable garrison city, but there is no clear idea of its role for the years after this period. In 490 BC the Athenians began a major temple-building program there, in gratitude to the gods for delivering victory over the Persians in the Battle of Marathon.

Ten years later, with the foundations in place and marble columns taking shape, the Persians hit back by routing the Greek army at Thermopylae, sacking Athens and laying waste to the Acropolis. It was 30 years before Athenians began rebuilding—an agreed period of reflection on the hated Persians' sacrilegious treatment of the gods.

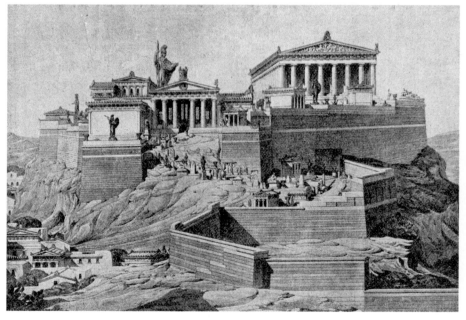

c.5000 BC	4236 BC	c.4000 BC	c.4000 BC	c.3100BC	c.1750 BC	c.1450 BC	c.600–350 BC
Site of Athens first settled.	First date in Egyptian calendar.	First farmers in Britain.	Cities emerge in Euphrates valley, Mesopotamia.	Pictographic writing invented in Sumer.	Hammurabi founds Babylonian Empire.	Mycenaean civilization flourishes.	Acropolis is hub of Athens.

Just as Athens dominated the Greek states, so the Acropolis towered over the city it protected.

The Temple of Apollo

The town of Delphi, some six miles (9.5km) inland from the Gulf of Corinth, was thought by ancient Greeks to be the center of the earth and the spot where the god Apollo overcame the serpent monster Python. The ruined temple itself is set on a dramatic site beside Mount Parnassus and once supported a lucrative cult centered on a chief priestess named Pythia, said to be the living incarnation of Apollo. Wealthy individuals and public officials regularly consulted her and the Sacred Way path to the temple was piled with valuable tributes from the main Greek city-states.

A showpiece for Athens

When work did restart, under the direction of the leading politician Pericles, the intention was to "grandstand" Athens as the dominant Greek city-state. The rich natural resources of its main province, Attica, were made available, together with support from the temples, tributes from neighboring states, and a sizable chunk of the spoils of war (following a long-awaited final victory over the Persians).

By far the largest new structure on the Acropolis was the Parthenon, built wholly from marble obtained in the great quarry at Mount Pentelikon, and measuring 228 by around 100 feet (70 by 31m). This temple to the goddess Athena, protector of the city, had eight giant columns at the front and 17 at the rear. It contained two main sections, a chamber that housed the massive gold-and-ivory statue of the goddess, and a smaller one that was the temple treasury. An internal frieze running for 525 feet (160m) is thought to have depicted one of Athens' most important rituals—the Panatheniac Procession. This ceremony involved people filing up to the Acropolis to present a wooden statue of Athena with a fine new dress.

The other outstanding archeological remnant of old Athens is the agora, a market place and religious ceremonial center that stands in a hollow between the Acropolis to the south and the Areopagus, or Hill of Ares, to the north. By the sixth century BC, the agora had become a famed debating arena for politicians anxious to shrug off aristocratic rule in favor of democracy. It was closely identified with good citizenship, and criminals were not permitted to enter. To ward off felons, marker stones were clearly inscribed with the words, "I am the boundary of the agora."

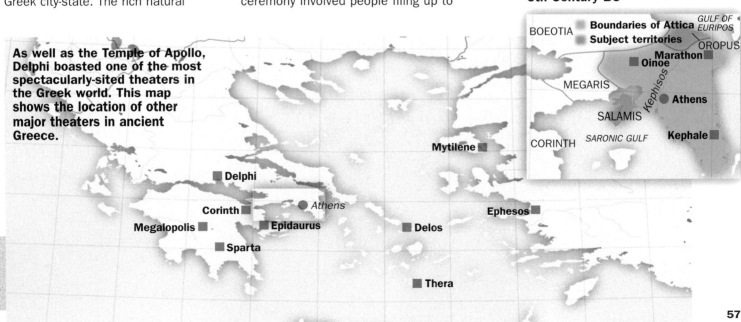

As well as the Temple of Apollo, Delphi boasted one of the most spectacularly-sited theaters in the Greek world. This map shows the location of other major theaters in ancient Greece.

Athens and the growth of the Attica province during the 6th Century BC

Boundaries of Attica
Subject territories

BOEOTIA
GULF OF EURIPOS
OROPUS
Marathon
Oinoe
MEGARIS
Kephisos
Athens
SALAMIS
CORINTH
SARONIC GULF
Kephale

Mytilene

Delphi

Corinth
Athens
Megalopolis
Epidaurus
Delos
Ephesos

Sparta

Thera

Knossos

AIGAI CITY AND THE MACEDONIANS
Burgeoning empire of an astute leader

Within the span of 20 years, the Macedonian Empire grew from a squabbling bunch of rival noblemen into the most feared and efficient military power of its day. Much of the credit goes to Philip II, father of Alexander the Great, who unified the kingdom and embarked on war with his neighbors—astutely seizing a gold mine in the Athenian colony of Amphipolis to pay the bills. Between maneuvering himself onto the Macedonian throne in 359 BC, and finally conquering the Athenians at the Battle of Chaeronea in 338 BC, Philip was acknowledged as undisputed leader of the Greek-speaking people. He was assassinated in 336 BC as he

prepared to conquer the Persians—a plan subsequently taken over and brilliantly executed by Alexander.

Philip's ancient capital was Aigai, a city in northern Greece that now lies beneath the modern town of Vergina. It was the area in which the Macedonians buried their kings; excavations by the Greek archeologist Manolis Andronikos in 1977 concentrated on the Great Tumulus, an earthen mound 46 feet (14m) high and 360 feet (110m) in diameter.

The first tomb Andronikos found had clearly been looted by robbers, although some interesting wall paintings were intact. But the second looked far more promising. It had a

above: *The cuirass of Philip II of Macedonia, located within the second burial chamber.*

vaulted ceiling and was decorated at the entrance with a 18 foot (5.5m) long painted hunting scene; a labor of love that indicated the deceased must have been of high birth. More importantly, the two massive slabs sealing the burial chamber stood intact, indicating that it had not been plundered. The archeological team gained access by using a time-honored technique beloved by ancient tomb raiders—removing the keystone. This wedge-shaped stone at the top of the entrance arch locked the monumental structure's entrance together.

Vergina—Ancient capital of Macedonia

BLACK SEA

Vergina (Aigai)

AEGEAN SEA

Macedonian empire 359BC

Expansion of territory by 336BC under the rule of Philip II, father of Alexander the Great

359 BC	c.359–340 BC	357 BC	356 BC	338 BC	336 BC	335 BC	334-333 BC
Philip II becomes king of Macedonia.	Philip turns Macedonia into nation geared for war.	Marriage of Philip to Olympias, mother of Alexander the Great.	Alexander the Great born.	Philip conquers Athenians at Battle of Chaeronea.	Assassination of Philip. Alexander becomes king.	Alexander's army destroys Thebes.	Invasion of Turkey.

The discovery of the burial tomb of Philip II of Macedonia, the architect of Greek supremacy.

left: *Gold chest bearing the starburst design.*

Reconstructing a Greek king

Inside the second tomb, Andronikos found all the trappings of an undisturbed royal grave: silver drinking vessels, bronze armor laid against the walls, a gold-and-silver headband placed inside a helmet, and piles of gold and ivory chips that had inlaid a since-rotted ornamental shield. It was soon established that the chamber had been fitted with wooden furniture, including a couch, but 2,000 years of damp conditions had taken their toll.

Fortunately, the most important find remained in superb condition—a marble coffin containing a 24-pound (11kg) gold chest bearing a starburst design, the insignia of Macedonian royalty. Inside this were some cremated remains that had once been wrapped in purple cloth and topped with a gold oak wreath. Forensic analysis of these suggests the dead man was aged between 35 and 55 and some 5' 8" (1.7m) tall.

A room leading from the main chamber contained similar items: bronze armor, wooden furniture, and a particularly beautiful gilded silver arrow sling depicting a battle in a temple sanctuary. A second gold chest containing more cremated remains, this time of a woman in her 20s or early 30s, again wrapped in what must have been a fine-quality gold-and-purple cloth.

The case for confirming the tomb as that of Philip II is overwhelming. Apart from the historical evidence that Aigai was the burial ground of kings, there is the presence of the star emblem (both on the chest and the headband), the age of the deceased (Philip was 46 when he died), and the date of the artifacts and paintings (all mid-fourth century BC).

Most compelling of all is the reconstruction of the cremated skull by a medical forensic team, who produced a clay model of the man's facial features. There were traces of damage and scarring to one eye—an injury known to have been suffered by Philip—and the modeled face bore striking similarities to contemporary portraits of the king.

above: *The excavation team managed to gain access to the tomb by removing the key stone at the top of the doorway.*

left: *The entrance to the royal tomb within the earthen mound of the Great Tumulus, Vergina.*

332 BC	330 BC	329 BC	326 BC	325 BC	324 BC	324 BC	323 BC
Territories of present-day Lebanon, Israel, and Egypt conquered.	Persia (modern-day Iran) invaded.	Afghanistan and part of central Asia taken.	Alexander's army invades western India.	Army marches through deserts of southern Persia.	The force returns to Persepolis, which it destroyed six years earlier.	Alexander the Great marries daughter of conquered Persian king Darius.	Death of Alexander the Great.

THE DISCOVERY OF TROY
Homer's literary legacy

Until the 1870s the prehistoric Greek city of Troy was considered to be a piece of fiction; the product of Homer's fertile imagination in epic poems describing the Trojan Wars. According to legend, it was attacked by the Greek king Agamemnon in an attempt to rescue his brother's wife, Helen, beautiful daughter of the god Zeus. The outcome is well known: Circa 1260 BC, after a ten-year siege, Agamemnon's forces constructed a giant wooden horse, supposedly an offering to Athena but filled with warriors. Agamemnon apparently sailed away and the Trojans hauled the horse inside their defensive walls. That night, Greek impostor Sinon released the hidden warriors, who promptly opened the city gates, allowing the returning Greek army to storm through.

The possibility that there was some truth in the Siege of Troy was recognized by Greek writers a thousand years later. The idea was largely sneered at by 18th and 19th century historians, until German archeologist Heinrich Schliemann turned the received wisdom on its head. Schliemann had been fascinated by Homer since the age of eight, when his father, a pastor, read the *Iliad* and *Odyssey* to him.

Schliemann became convinced that some of Homer's work was

above left: *A 16th-century BC royal death mask recovered from Mycenae. The archeologist Schliemann believed it was "the face of Agamemnon."*

The Nine Ages of Troy
A chronology of the separate cities discovered at Hissarlik

Troy 1: A walled settlement built of stone and clay, dating to around 3000 BC.

Troy 2: A huge prehistoric fortress with thick ramparts, a palace, and houses, now known to have been built in the third millennium BC (Schliemann believed this was Homer's Troy).

Troy 3: The layer in which Priam's Treasure was discovered.

Troys 4 & 5: Bronze Age villages built on the remains of "Troy 2" between 2300 and 2000 BC.

Troy 6: Another massive fortress, bigger than its predecessor, comprising walls, watchtowers, gates, and houses and dating between 1900 and 1300 BC.

Troy 7A: A rebuilding of "Troy 6", probably around 1400 BC, following an earthquake (this is now thought to be the "real" Troy).

Troys 7B & 8: Greek villages of simply constructed stone houses.

Troy 9: The acropolis of the Graeco-Roman city Ilion, built in the first century BC.

c.1300 BC	776 BC	c.750 BC	c.675 BC	c.650 BC	592 BC	c.550 BC	335-323 BC
Mycenae richest city in Greece.	Olympic Games established.	*Iliad* and the *Odyssey* are written.	Greek city states increasingly militarized, with almost universal conscription.	Greeks colonize much of Mediterranean.	Lawmaker Solon lays groundwork for Athenian democracy.	First map of then known world produced, by geometrician Anaximander.	Alexander the Great conquers most of known world for Macedonia.

The German archeologist Heinrich Schliemann became convinced that some of Homer's work was historically accurate.

historically accurate, and at the age of 46, after amassing considerable wealth as a merchant in Russia, he visited Greece and Turkey for the first time. The theoretical location of Troy was disputed by academics, but the results of a preliminary dig in 1870 encouraged Schliemann to focus on a manmade mound called Hissarlik ("Place Of The Fortress"), and within three years his team of 150 laborers had driven a series of huge trenches through the site, exposing the layers of several cities.

A fruitful dig

In May 1973, Schliemann spotted gold in one trench. He ordered an early break for lunch and, assisted by his Greek wife Sophie, personally dug up an astonishing hoard of gold, silver, and bronze jewelry, together with many priceless ornaments. He smuggled them out of Turkey, an act that sparked

right: Some of the gold jewelry discovered by Schliemann and his Greek wife Sophie.

fury among Turkish authorities, who understandably felt they had a claim. Priam's Treasure, as it was called, was exhibited in Berlin's Bode Museum and made Schliemann a celebrity. He was adept at media manipulation—a drawing of his wife clad in some of the jewelry was reprinted around the world. His Homer theory had been spectacularly vindicated.

Schliemann initially believed that four separate cities had been built on the site of Troy, but his further analysis in 1889 showed there were seven; most archeologists now accept nine as a more accurate figure. Schliemann thought the second city was consistent with Homer's Troy, although later work by his assistant, Wilhelm Dorpfeld, showed that this layer dated from the third millennium

BC—at least a thousand years before the siege supposedly happened.

Dorpfeld's findings, confirmed in a 1938 dig by Carl Blegen from the University of Cincinnati, revealed the "real" Troy in the seventh layer (nearer the surface), which had been destroyed by fire and correlates with the traditional 1260 BC date given for the climax of the Trojan Wars.

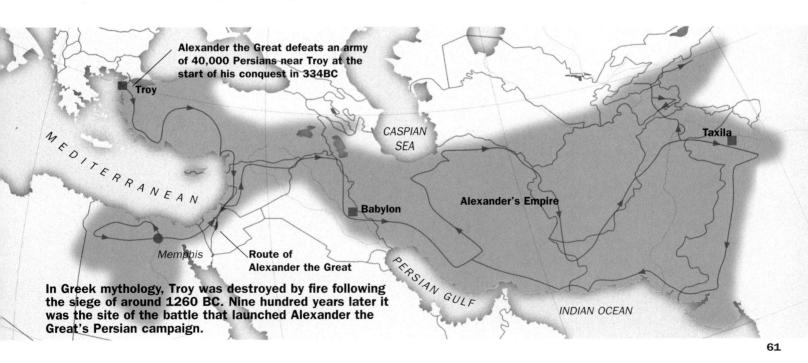

Alexander the Great defeats an army of 40,000 Persians near Troy at the start of his conquest in 334BC

Troy

CASPIAN SEA

Taxila

MEDITERRANEAN

Babylon

Alexander's Empire

Memphis

Route of Alexander the Great

PERSIAN GULF

INDIAN OCEAN

In Greek mythology, Troy was destroyed by fire following the siege of around 1260 BC. Nine hundred years later it was the site of the battle that launched Alexander the Great's Persian campaign.

CAPITAL CITIES OF TROY'S CONQUERORS

King Agamemnon and Nestor's Palace

After his stunning success at Troy, it was natural for German archeologist Heinrich Schliemann to investigate the history of the two great Greek leaders whose forces sacked the city. They were Agamemnon, whose capital was Mycenae, near the town of Minaiki in northern Greece; and Nestor, whose palace was said to be at Pylos—or Pilos, as it is known today—in western Messenia.

Together with Troy and Tyrins, Mycenae and Pylos were the main cities of the Mycenaean culture that dominated the region during the 13th and 14th centuries BC. These people could trace their roots to the first central European and western Asian tribes, who arrived in Greece around 2000 BC. They spoke in an early Greek dialect and wrote on clay tablets in a script that archeologists now call "Linear B."

Schliemann's excavations at Mycenae were less complicated than at Troy, because the city's location was not in doubt. Second century AD historian and travel writer Pausanias had told how Agamemnon's remains were buried inside its "cyclopian" walls—a term used to describe ramparts made of massive chunks of stone—and faithfully described the nearby "lion gates." Both of these landmarks were well-known structures.

Schliemann focused his efforts on an area just inside the gates, and in 1876 uncovered 30 deep shaft graves, arranged in two circles, into which the remains of Mycenaean royalty had been interred. He made some spectacular finds, including Bronze Age weapons, plates, and jewelry. When he unearthed a gold death mask, Schliemann wasted no time in declaring to the world that he had gazed upon the face of

above: *The Lion's Gate in the ruined walls of the hill fortress of Mycenae.*

Agamemnon. This subsequently proved untrue—the mask was dated to the 16th century BC, 300 years before Agamemnon's time.

The elusive city of Pylos

Though Mycenae was another triumph for Heinrich Schliemann, his search for Pylos proved futile. Even the ancient Greek historians were confused as to its whereabouts; their comments spawned the proverb, "…there is a

left: *Ruins of the royal palace at Mycenae. Heinrich Schliemann made some spectacular Bronze Age finds here.*

c.2000 BC	c.2000 BC	c.1900 BC	1840 BC	c.1400–1100 BC	c.1240 BC	c.1200 BC	c.1120 BC
Forebears of Ancient Greeks populate Greece.	Use of sail on seagoing vessels in Aegean.	Irrigation technology improves in Mesopotamia to nurture expanding population.	Lower Nubia annexed by Egypt.	Mycenean civilization at its height.	Moses gives out the Ten Commandments.	Greeks destroy city of Troy.	Mycenean civilization comes to an end.

American archeologist Carl Blegen found a library of clay tablets which, he believed, pinpointed the site of Pylos.

Pylos in front of Pylos and there is still another Pylos." With this kind of advice, and no obvious clues from his fieldwork, Schliemann abandoned his efforts.

By the turn of the century, the hunt had resumed. The discovery of two Mycenaean "tholos" tombs, with their high, stone-vaulted roofs resembling sharpened beehives, had revived interest in Messenia, and in 1939 American archeologist Carl Blegen identified some remains on a hill at Epano Englianos as worthy of investigation. Blegen, a veteran of Troy digs, found painted pottery, old walls, and Linear B clay tablets in his first morning. Regrettably, his discovery was interrupted by the Second World War, and he had to wait until 1952 before resuming.

Over the next 14 years, Blegen painstakingly uncovered a palace closely resembling the royal strongholds at Mycenae and Tiryns.

The Island of Delos

Trade capital of the Aegean

Delos was an important religious site during Mycenaean times; by the seventh century BC it was a focus of worship to the god Apollo. There were regular games, festival processions, and sacrificial rituals, and hundreds of pilgrims presented votive offerings to the islands' statues. However, Delos's strategic importance as a trading center did not emerge until the second century AD, when it became the largest port of the eastern Mediterranean and the key slave market serving both Rome and Athens. During this period the island went through an extensive building program, an entire town mushrooming within the space of a few decades.

There was a distinctive circular central hearth, a bathroom complete with terra-cotta baths, storerooms containing vessels for olive oil and wine, thousands of cups and plates for banqueting, and a record office containing a library of clay tablets which were baked hard (and so preserved) by a fire that engulfed the palace around 1200 BC.

The tablets gave an unprecedented glimpse of Mycenaean palace society—the food rations eaten by textile workers, the bronze raw materials supplied to smiths; even tributes to the gods. They confirmed Blegen's belief that he had found Pylos, although sadly they made no mention of King Nestor. Perhaps Nestor was just a figment of Homer's imagination after all.

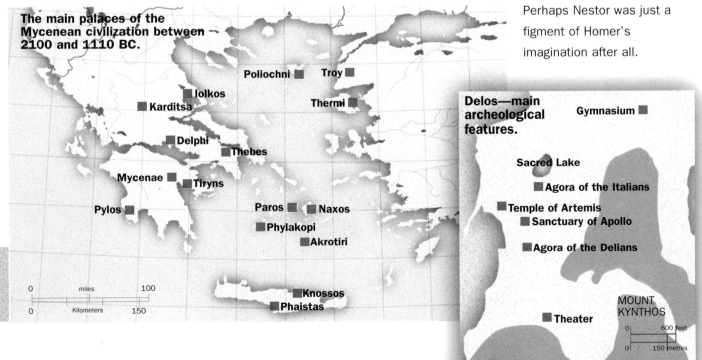

The main palaces of the Mycenean civilization between 2100 and 1110 BC.

Poliochni
Troy
Iolkos
Karditsa
Thermi
Delphi
Thebes
Mycenae
Tiryns
Pylos
Paros
Naxos
Phylakopi
Akrotiri
Knossos
Phaistas

0 — miles — 100
0 — Kilometers — 150

Delos—main archeological features.

Gymnasium
Sacred Lake
Agora of the Italians
Temple of Artemis
Sanctuary of Apollo
Agora of the Delians
MOUNT KYNTHOS
Theater

0 — 600 feet
0 — 150 metres

THE KNOSSOS LEGACY
The palace of King Minos

According to Greek mythology, Knossos, on Crete, was the palace of King Minos, a powerful naval commander who commissioned the architect Daedalus to build a labyrinth to house the Minotaur. As successive excavations have since discovered, bulls and snakes were particularly important religious figures to the Bronze Age culture that occupied Knossos c.2000–1100 BC. These animals, together with dolphins and even the mythological griffin, feature in many of the magnificent frescoes that decorate interior walls.

The existence of a culturally advanced race on Crete was suspected by the German archeologist Heinrich Schliemann (*see* Troy and Agamemnon's Mycenae, *pages 60–63*), but his efforts to buy the Knossos site in 1887 failed when he would not pay the Turkish landowner's asking price. It was left to the British antiquary and journalist Arthur Evans to conclude a deal, and in 1900 he began work.

Evans was convinced that prehistoric Greeks were a literate people, and within a week he had uncovered an artifact he described as "a kind of clay bar, rather like a stone chisel in shape, though broken at one end, with script on it and what appear to be numerals." Pottery finds from a nearby location indicated that this bar was pre-Mycenaean, proving Evans' theory. The discovery of a throne made of gypsum confirmed that Knossos was a royal residence and, mindful of the Greek legend, Evans named it the Palace of Minos and its occupants "Minoan".

above: *A sculpture of a Minoan snake goddess. By about 1100 BC the Palace of Knossos was reserved purely for religious ceremony.*

As the excavation continued, it became obvious that Knossos was the location of several palaces, modified and rebuilt over the centuries in the manner of Troy. The first phase began around 2000 BC and there were regular redesigns until c.1400 BC, when the entire structure was gutted by fire.

left: *Dolphins of the Aegean waters decorate a wall in the Palace of Minos.*

Fisherman with his catch, from a wall painting.

Mountains above 6,000 feet

Key sites of Minoan culture on Crete

MEDITERRANEAN

■ Knossos   ■ Gournia
■ Arkhanes   ● Iraklion

■ Idaean
legendary birthplace of Zeus

Palaikastro ■

CRETE

| 0 | miles | 50 |
| 0 | kilometres | 70 |

c.2300 BC	c.2000 BC	c.2000 BC	c.2000–1400 BC	c.1800 BC	c.1750 BC	c.1500 BC	c.1100 BC
First empire in world civilization (Sumeria)	Minoans produce painted pottery	Bronze Age culture inhabits Knossos	Periodic rebuilding of palaces and other architecture at Knossos	Shamshi-Adad founds Assyrian state	Hammurabi founds Babylonian Empire	Egyptians import wood from Lebanon, fuelling Mediterranean trade	Knossos abandoned as a palace; used only as a religious site

Navigating the Minotaur's labyrinth

It is easy to imagine how the layout of the palace would have seemed like a labyrinth to visitors. The bewildering array of chambers winding around a central court must have been a navigational nightmare. However, close analysis showed that the palace had simply been designed "inside-out;" the court took priority over rooms placed around it. Elsewhere, first-floor chambers seemed to determine the position of those below. The complex included luxury suites decorated with frescos and gypsum floors, state apartments, cavernous storerooms, craft workshops, and an administrative center heavily reliant on the ubiquitous clay tablets.

It is the recovery of these tablets, rather than the Minoans' superb art and craft work, which became Evans' outstanding contribution to Aegean archeology. He recognized three separate scripts and realized they were used successively over hundreds of years. The first, which has some loose links to Egyptian hieroglyphics, is not yet fully understood. Neither is the second, the so-called "Linear A" script, which has been found at other locations in Crete and neighboring islands.

The third, however—"Linear B"—was deciphered by an English architect called Michael Ventris in 1952. It took him 16 years to achieve this feat and at first many experts were highly skeptical. It wasn't until the American university lecturer Carl Blegen (*see* King Agamemnon, *pages 62–63*) applied Ventris's theory during excavations at Pylos that the Englishman was proved correct. Blegen found that not only could he decipher the writings of a clay block, but that several of the words could be linked to adjacent picture-symbols. Though the translation of Linear B was a slow process, it opened up vast areas of Aegean history that had previously been matters of educated guesswork.

Toward the end of the Bronze Age, Knossos was abandoned as a residence and new settlements were established to the north and west. This was perhaps because of the palace's reputation as a sacred site, a belief surely fostered by the myth of the Minotaur lurking in some half-forgotten labyrinth. By c.1100 BC, Knossos was used only by priests, as a venue for religious ritual.

Translation of the 'Linear B' script opened up vast areas of Aegean history.

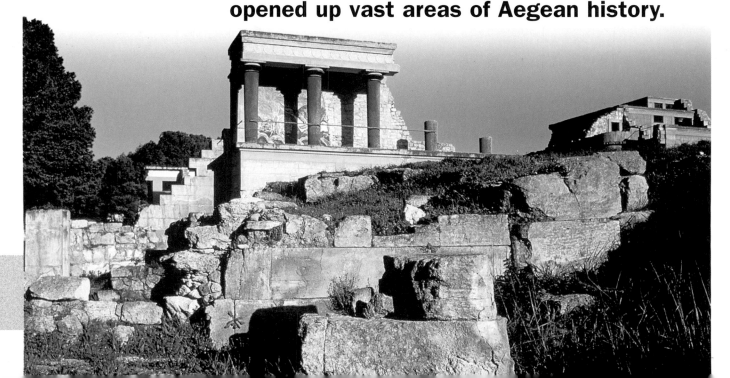

THE BURIED CITY OF AKROTIRI
Preserved under volcanic deposits

The rapid collapse of Minoan culture remains one of the great mysteries of the Ancient World. All we can confidently say is that around 1500 BC, a cataclysmic event occurred on Crete in which palaces, villas—even entire villages—were consumed by fire. The Knossos palace seems to have somehow emerged unscathed, although within a century it too stood deserted.

The phenomenon of an abruptly vanishing civilization is not particularly unusual in archeology, although satisfactory explanations are rare indeed. In the case of the Minoans, the Greek archeologist Spyridon Marinatos thought he had found the answer when he suggested that the eruption of the Thera volcano may have been to blame. There is empirical evidence to show that Thera exploded with great violence around 1500 BC, and given that the volcanic island stands just 62 miles (100 km) north of Crete, it is perfectly feasible that hot ash and molten rock could have rained down on the Minoans.

Marinatos was also curious about the inexplicable movement of giant blocks of stone which, he discovered, had been ripped out of position in the Minoan harbor of Amnisos. The coast here faces due north, directly toward Thera. Could a huge tidal wave have hit Crete at the same time as fire-stones crashed from the heavens?

To say it was a controversial theory is an understatement, and many archeologists and geologists remained unconvinced. The debate continued for 28 years, until in 1967 Marinatos decided to conduct a detailed excavation on Thera to establish more facts about the eruption. This was

below: *The remains of Akrotiri have now been shielded from the elements.*

c.1800 BC	1674 BC	c.1600 BC	c.1550 BC	c.1500 BC	c.1500 BC	c.1500 BC	c.1460 BC
Advanced mathematics is used for accounting in Egypt.	Memphis, the Egyptian capital, falls to the Hyksos.	Shang dynasty in China creates the first urban civilization in that region.	Pharaohs begin to be interred in the Valley of the Kings.	Metallurgy is developed in North America.	Demise of the Minoan civilization.	India is invaded by the Aryans, from Europe.	Thutmose III extends Egypt's empire to Mesopotamia.

right: *Color and detail are well preserved in the city's wall frescoes—even after 3,500 years beneath a bed of volcanic ash.*

easier said than done. The island had been coated in a thick volcanic ash, obliterating the original topsoil strata, and conventional fieldwork techniques were largely irrelevant.

Nonetheless, some prehistoric artifacts had been found in the south of the island, near the village of Akrotiri. When Spyridon Marinatos was told that farmers could not plow certain fields here because they were pitted with stony hollows, he rightly concluded that buildings lay beneath. In the

The ancient island of Thera (now Santorini)

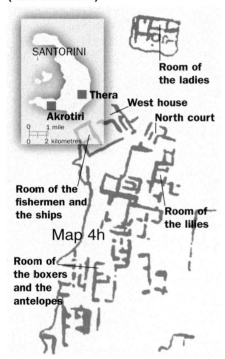

Plan of the excavated buildings of Akrotiri, buried by a volcanic explosion. The best-known frescoes are marked.

ensuing months, Marinatos uncovered the Greek equivalent of Pompeii; a ghost village that had been buried by volcanic ash soon after the eruption.

Inside the abandoned village

The houses were surprisingly intact, some walls extending two or three stories high and bearing brightly colored frescos of social, religious, and military events. Among the finest is the fishermen fresco, which shows naked men carrying stringed fish— perhaps in tribute to some ruler or a god of the sea. Then there is the Antelope Room, in which were found animal drawings of a style and quality equal to anything discovered in the finest of Cretan palaces. Other superb examples include the Room of the Ladies and the Room of the Lilies.

Depressions in the ash that covered every floor were filled with plaster of Paris to reveal the forms of tables and

beds. Basements still contained food storage jars. Yet there was no sign of the people themselves. Akrotirians had obviously been aware that an eruption was imminent and evacuated the village while there was still time. No one will ever know whether they sailed away to safety, but if they didn't they must have died terrible deaths. The volcano's ferocity would have ensured that few living things on the island survived.

For Spyridon Marinatos, the irony of the discovery was that it shot to pieces his apocalyptic theory about Minoan culture. The pottery recovered from Akrotiri is demonstrably different from vessels found in layers of earth on Crete that correspond to the time of the great inferno. All the evidence suggests that Akrotiri was deserted some 20–30 years before the Minoans' speedy demise.

Akrotirians had known that a volcanic eruption was imminent.

c.1450 BC	c.1400 BC	c.1400 BC	c.1350 BC	c.1300 BC	c.1285 BC	c.1140 BC	c.800 BC
Earliest Indian *Vedas* written.	Horses used as transport in central Asia.	Hittites and Egyptians fight to be the dominant empire of Middle East.	New Egyptian religion established, based on solar cult.	Sahara desert advances quickly across North Africa; drives most nomads out of region.	Led by Ramesses II, Egyptians narrowly avoid defeat by the Hittites.	Utica, first Phoenician settlement in Africa, established.	Greece at the height of a Dark Age following collapse of its early Mycenean culture.

CHAPTER FIVE

THE ROMAN EMPIRE

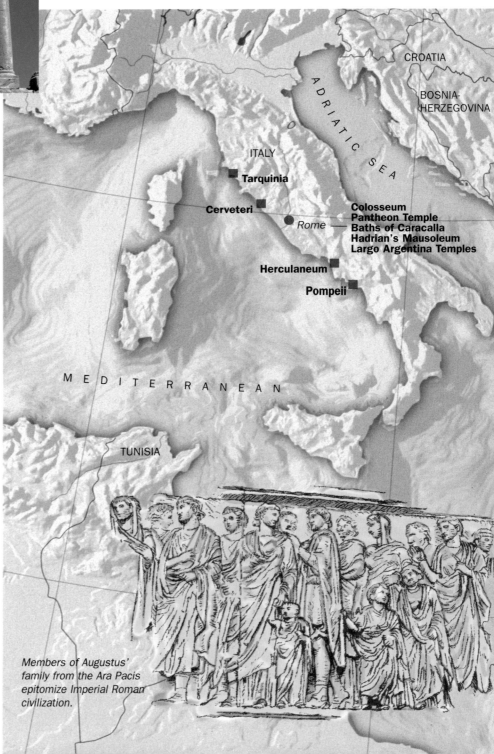

left: *Temple of Jupiter-Baal at Baalbek (Heliopolis), 1st century BC, Syria. Roman architecture brought new grace to the ancient settlement.*

CROATIA

BOSNIA-HERZEGOVINA

ADRIATIC SEA

ITALY

Tarquinia

Cerveteri

Rome —

Colosseum
Pantheon Temple
Baths of Caracalla
Hadrian's Mausoleum
Largo Argentina Temples

Herculaneum

Pompeii

MEDITERRANEAN

TUNISIA

Members of Augustus' family from the Ara Pacis epitomize Imperial Roman civilization.

The golden rule of history is that an empire sustained solely by military might is ultimately doomed. Invasions and brutal repression may work in the short term, but true unification of different cultures and peoples happens by agreement, not aggression.

The Romans, the greatest military power of their age, knew this better than anyone. Their army had triumphed in theaters of war ranging from the freezing northern hills of Britannia to the semi-deserts of North Africa, the mountains of Macedonia, and the huge expanse of Western Asia. Yet although by c.130 BC they controlled a world empire—and were guilty of appalling barbarism in parts of it—they recognized it would only stay Roman if the conquered lands adopted their customs. Therefore, newly founded towns were quickly supplied with all the cherished features of Roman society: temples, shrines, aqueducts, bathhouses, theaters, amphitheaters, libraries, colleges, schools, courthouses, assembly rooms, and countless statues and triumphal arches. No wonder that, even as late as the Middle Ages, many European people still considered themselves Roman.

This chapter looks at some of the great archeological remnants of the Roman Empire, its customs, religion, and technological advances. In addition, two sections are devoted to the Etruscans, a far older civilization that shaped so much Roman thinking and whose language and way of life still remain frustratingly unclear. From their compact heartland in central Italy, these two great cultures laid the foundations of the Western Europe we know today

right: *This fragment of a giant statue of the Emperor Constantine makes an admonishing gesture.*

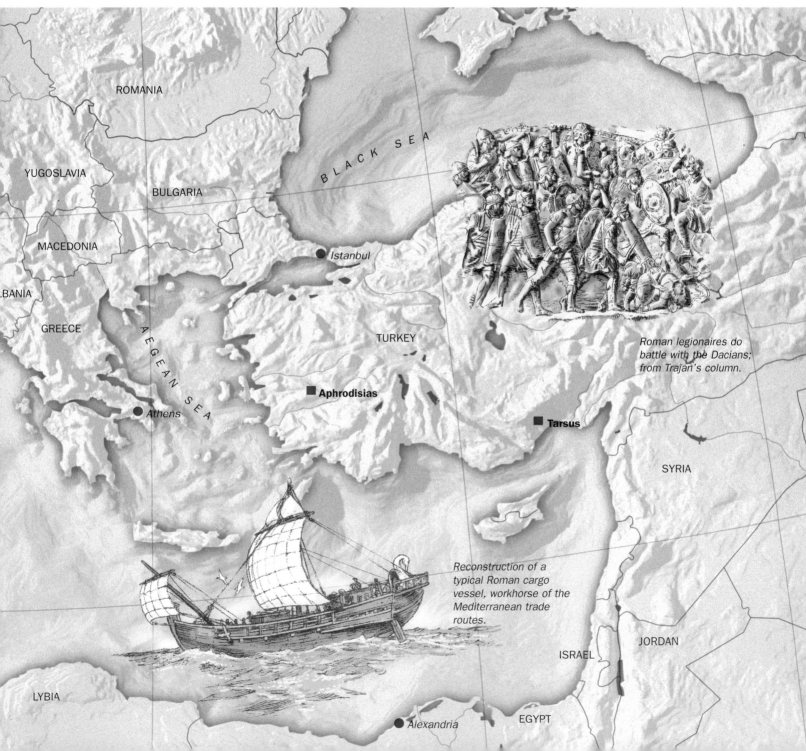

ROMANIA

YUGOSLAVIA

BULGARIA

BLACK SEA

MACEDONIA

ALBANIA

GREECE

AEGEAN SEA

● *Istanbul*

TURKEY

■ **Aphrodisias**

● *Athens*

■ **Tarsus**

SYRIA

Roman legionaires do battle with the Dacians; from Trajan's column.

Reconstruction of a typical Roman cargo vessel, workhorse of the Mediterranean trade routes.

LYBIA

ISRAEL

JORDAN

EGYPT

● *Alexandria*

THE WONDERS OF ROME
Spectacular, extravagant architectural tributes

The Romans lived for their cities, but this is not to say the countryside was unimportant. Wealthy Romans recognized that it was crucial to the provision of quality food and wine, and a useful occasional retreat from urban bustle. But considering their practical genius as civil engineers and their advances in architectural design, the Romans showed limited interest in improving the efficiency of their agriculture or the running of their estates. Toward the end of the empire, the perception that city life was idyllic while country life was hard work had permeated through all social classes, leading to a worrying

Roman settlements established in the early years of expansion 340–200 BC.

Ravenna
Tiber
Volci
Rome
Ostia
Cumae
Paestum
Tarentum
Metapontium
Messina
Segesta
Locri
Lilybaeum
Syracuse

0   100 miles
0   150 kilometers

above: *The Arch of Constantine, set up by the people and senate of Rome. Beyond it is the Palatine Hill and Imperial palaces.*

right: *Trajan's Column; the statue of Trajan on the top was replaced by that of St. Peter in 1587.*

753 BC	510 BC	218 BC	206 BC	149 BC
Rome founded.	Foundation of republic.	Hannibal of Carthage invades Italy.	Rome gains control of Spain.	Rome destroys Carthage.

Roman monuments depended heavily on the goodwill of wealthy citizens.

left: *Detail of the bas-relief on Trajan's Column, depicting his conquest of Dacia. The monument was erected in 113 AD.*

population drift from rural to urban areas. This worsened the housing crisis facing the poor, most of whom lived in overcrowded tenements run by speculative landlords.

The grandeur of Rome was concentrated around The Forum, an open marketplace overlooked by the city's Seven Hills. It contained the Comitium assembly hall and the senate house, together with various commemorative statues and the huge Column of Trajan. Around these was a grid of streets lined by shops, triumphal military arches, monuments, and major public buildings such as the Pantheon Temple, the Colosseum, and the Baths of Caracalla. The cost of these structures was met through public taxation or donations by wealthy citizens and politicians, a form of patronage that tended to encourage a "big is best" school of architectural thought.

Trajan's Column is a good example. It was built c.106–113 AD to mark successful campaigns by the emperor Trajan in Dacia (part of modern Romania) at the beginning of the century. Trajan used the spoils to finance a new-look Forum and the

Roman provinces c.100 BC.

Narbonese Gaul
Cisalpine Gaul
Illyricum
Nearer Spain
Italy
Sardinia
Further Spain
Macedonia
Asia
Sicily
Achaea
Cilicia
Africa

44 BC	c.80 AD	c.106–113 AD	117 AD	118–128 AD	165 AD	400 AD	410 AD
Julius Caesar assassinated.	Colosseum is built; audience capacity: 55,000.	Trajan's column is built.	Roman Empire reaches its greatest extent.	Pantheon built.	Smallpox epidemic in Roman Empire.	The Roman Empire adopts Christianity as its religion.	Roman Empire is invaded and collapses.

CITY PLANNING
The world's first metropolis

above: Legend has it that a she-wolf suckled Romulus (founder of Rome) and his brother Remus.

below: Hadrian's Tomb the way it looked when it was erected.

above: The Castel Sant' Angelo—built as Hadrian's Tomb; later adopted as a fortified citadel by the Church.

right: A detail from the wall of the Forum of Augustus, seen from the Imperial Way, which now bisects the forums of Nerva, Augustus and Trajan and almost covers that of Julius Caesar.

below: The Forum Romanum, looking east from the ramp up to the Capitol. In the center is the Temple of Antoninus and Faustina, and to the right the Colosseum.

Hadrian's Tomb (Castel Sant' Angelo)

Aelian bridge

Bridge of Nero

Odeion of Domitian

Bridge of Agrippa

Bridge of Aurelius

Porta Septimiana

JANICULUM

AQUA AISIETINA

Porta Portuense

Rome at the time of Constantine.

Porta Flaminia

Via Flaminia

PINCIAN

AQUA VIRGO

Porta Pinciana

Porta Nomentana

Temple of Fortuna

SERVIAN WALL

The Ara Pacis has been moved to here

Mausoleum of Augustus

Domitian's Stadium (*Piazza Navona*)

Solar clock of Augustus

Ara Pacis Augustae

Baths of Nero

Pantheon — Temple of Hadrian

Baths of Diocletian

Praetorian Camp

above: *Any map of Rome seems to suggest a city of wide, open spaces between grand public buildings. In fact, everything was filled by innumerable multi-story apartment blocks, with shops underneath like these shown in a model taken from Rome's port of Ostia. It can be seen in the Museo della Civiltà Romana, Rome.*

Enlarged map on page 75

QUIRINAL

Arch of Claudius

Temple of Isis

Saepta Julia

Porticoes of Pompey

Baths of Agrippa

Theater of Pompey

Porticus Minucia Frumentaria

Largo Argentina

Theater of Balbus

Circus Flaminius

Portico of Octavia

Capitol

Pons Fabricius

Theater of Marcellus

Pons Cestius

Bridge of Aemilius

Forum Boarium

Trajan's Column

Forum of Trajan

Trajan's market

VIMINAL

Forum of Julius Caesar

Forum of Augustus

THE SUBURA

Forum of Nerva

Temple of Pax

Temple of Venus and Rome

Colosseum

Arx

CAPITOLINE

Forum Romanum

Palace of Tiberius

PALATINE

Palace of Domitian

Porta Tiburtina

Via Tiburtina

AQUA MARCIA

Portico of Livia

ESQUILINE

Baths of Trajan

Baths of Titus

Ludus Magnus

Arch of Constantine

Palace of Elagabalus

Temple of Claudius

Temple of Claudius

AQUA CLAUDIA

CAELIAN

Castrensian Amphitheater

Porta Asinaria

TRANS TIBERTUM

RIVER TIBER

Bridge of Probius

Circus Maximus

Septizodium

Palace of Septimus Severus

AVENTINE

Porticus Aemilia

Horrea Galbana

AURELIAN WALL

Baths of Caracalla

Porta Metronia

right: *The Appian Gate, seen from outside the city.*

below: *A section of the Aurelian Wall between the Appian and Ardeatina Gates.*

Porta Ostiense

AQUA ANTONNIANA

Porta Latina

Via Latina

Porta Ardeatina

Porta Appia

Via Appia

below: *A section of the outer walls of the Baths of Caracalla, with the cisterns to the left.*

The Roman Empire

Senate decided that the people should match his generosity by building a memorial in his name. The column was sited to the north of the Forum, measured 125 feet (38m) high, comprised 29 massive slabs of white marble from the northern city of Carrara, and once supported a 16-foot (5m) bronze statue of Trajan, clad in military uniform.

Rome's lavish architecture

The column even had an internal spiral staircase, hewn out of the solid stone and illuminated via 40 windows, which allowed spectators to climb to a viewing platform 118 feet (36m) above the city. As if this wasn't enough, the tribute to Trajan included a 656-foot (200m) long carved spiral frieze that told the story of his triumph over Dacia in 155 scenes containing some 2600 figures. This pictorial account of Trajan's own (lost) diary *Dacica* winds around the outer surface and may have been a later addition to commemorate his death, c.117 AD.

The Colosseum was erected 30 years before Trajan's Column by Emperor Vespasian. It was not the first amphitheater in Rome but it was by far

above: *The Colosseum, scene of countless bloody gladiatorial contests. In the center is the complex structure that supported the wooden floor of the amphitheater.*

below: *All that remains of the Circus Maximus (left) are the earthen mounds, with the Imperial palaces on the Palatine (right of center. Far-right is the Arch of Constantine.*

above: *The coffered dome of the Pantheon, and* right *the exterior, showing the cylindrical drum on which the perfect hemispherical dome rests.*

below right: *Bust of Constantine.*

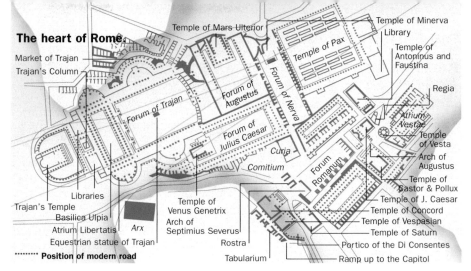

The heart of Rome.

Temple of Mars Ulterior
Temple of Minerva
Library
Market of Trajan
Temple of Pax
Trajan's Column
Temple of Antoninus and Faustina
Forum of Augustus
Forum of Nerva
Regia
Forum of Trajan
Forum of Julius Caesar
Atrium Vestae
Temple of Vesta
Arch of Augustus
Curia
Forum Romanum
Comitium
Temple of Castor & Pollux
Libraries
Temple of Venus Genetrix
Temple of J. Caesar
Trajan's Temple
Arch of Septimius Severus
Temple of Concord
Basilica Ulpia
Temple of Vespasian
Atrium Libertatis
Arx
Temple of Saturn
Equestrian statue of Trajan
Rostra
Portico of the Di Consentes
Tabularium
Ramp up to the Capitol

········ **Position of modern road**

M·AGRIPPA·L·F·COS·TERTIVM·FECIT

the largest. It was used to stage gladiatorial contests, animal fights, and other sporting spectacles. According to later historical records, it was capable of seating 87,000 people—comparable to the largest stadia today—although recent estimates put the capacity closer to 50,000. When Vespasian's son and successor Titus dedicated the Colosseum in 80 AD, its upper sections were built in wood. These were torn down and replaced with stone around 223.

The Pantheon temple, still the best preserved major building of ancient Rome, was constructed between 118 and 128 AD by the emperor Hadrian. It was dedicated to all Roman gods—a factor reflected in its lavish and innovative design—and is considered one of the most important structures in architectural history. It is based on a cylinder beneath a great, semi-spherical vaulted dome of 142 feet (43m) and is illuminated through a single window at the apex.

The Romans' attitude to religion was far removed from present day societies. They saw no need to reinforce social morality with religious teaching—there were plenty of laws and state controls that could perform that job. Their religion was not one of faith; rather of ritual, and gods such as Jupiter, Mars, Minerva, Janus, Lares, and Ceres were worshipped to meet specific goals, such as protection during war or security of the home.

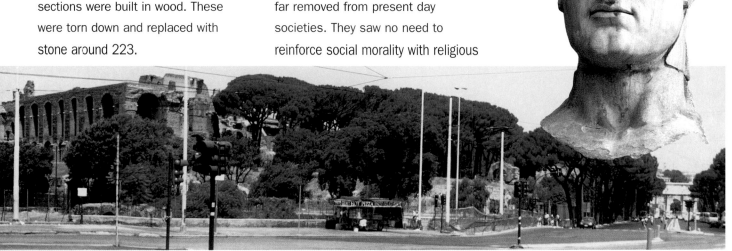

VESUVIUS AND THE DESTRUCTION OF POMPEII

Rescuing a volcano's prey

The volcanic eruption that engulfed the Roman towns of Pompeii and Herculaneum in 79 AD is a story that commands grim fascination. Such was the cataclysmic power of Mount Vesuvius that some residents had no time to escape. In Pompeii's case, 2,000 of them died where they sat or stood, overcome by poisonous fumes, the outlines of their bodies eerily preserved in the black ash and cinders. Many of these images tell their own heart-rending stories; people cowering in hopelessly inadequate places of shelter, or lying head-down on the floor in a vain attempt to survive the choking vapors. Most pitiful of all were the gladiators—kept in chains to stop them escaping or committing suicide.

Pompeii was a Roman colony from 80 BC onwards, and by the birth of Jesus its population was about 20,000, including many wealthy citizens who kept country villas there. It was badly damaged by an earthquake in 62 AD but remained a popular resort at the time of the eruption. Excavations, first started in 1748 and interpreted by the German archeologist Johann Winckelmann,

right: *A well-preserved street in Pompeii. Excavators found advertisements for forthcoming gladiatorial battles.*

have provided a unique insight into the daily life of a provincial Roman town. Apart from its public structures— theaters, baths, shops, and temples— there were some stunning wall paintings, such as those in the Villa of the Mysteries. These are associated with the cult worship of the Greek god Dionysus—which essentially involved heavy drinking and participation in orgies—and seemed to portray a female initiation ceremony.

Other fascinating discoveries at Pompeii include a street off the Strada dell' Abbondanza, which contains houses equipped with first floor balconies 20 feet long by 5 feet deep (6 by 1.5m), superb floor mosaics and frescoes, and even advertisements of

forthcoming gladiatorial battles in the local amphitheater.

Solidifying the dead

A technique was developed for restructuring the bodies of the volcano's victims in plaster. Excavators realized that the original ash bed had been quickly dampened by rain and this had resulted in hardened molds forming around the dead. These molds survived long after the remains had disintegrated, and when liquid plaster was poured inside, an accurate cast could be obtained.

Herculaneum presented a different set of challenges for excavators, because it had been consumed by a 50-foot (15m) wall of mud, rather

80 BC	1 AD	62 AD	64 AD	c. 80 AD	79 AD	1706 AD	1738
Foundation of Pompeii as a Roman colony.	Pompeii's population c.20,000.	Town damaged by an earthquake.	Emperor Nero rebuilds Rome after catastrophic fire.	Roman empire extends north to Scotland.	Vesuvius erupts, burying Pompeii and Herculaneum.	Ruins of Herculaneum discovered.	Excavations begin at Herculaneum.

Gladiators died in their chains as volcanic ash rained down.

than ash. The site was discovered in 1706 AD when it was bought by the Prince of Elbeuf, a man keen to see if the handful of ancient marbles found there were pointers to more valuable treasure. He quickly found the town's theater, but it was not until 1738 that digging began in earnest under the control of the Kingdom of the Two Sicilies.

The technique was to dig tunnels through the mud until a building wall was struck. Once penetrated, this allowed the exploration of the

Herculaneum was burried under volcanic mud; Pompeii under volcanic ash.

Rome
Herculaneum
Pompeii

Ash fallout from Mt. Vesuvius following the eruption which began on 24 August 79 AD. 2,000 people were killed and some streets were buried beneath 50ft of mud and ash.

1748 AD	1750s
Excavations begin at Pompeii.	First tourists visit site of Pompeii.

sheltered rooms inside, and tours of Herculaneum were soon marketed as a fashionable excursion for wealthy European tourists staying in Naples.

The Scottish architect Robert Adam, who visited the town in 1755, was among those who unknowingly witnessed staged "discoveries" of Roman relics. He recalled: "We traversed an amphitheater with the light of torches and pursued the tracks of palaces, their porticoes and different doors, division walls, and mosaic pavements. We saw earthen vases and marble pavements just discovered while we were on the spot

above: *Tombs placed outside the walls of Pompeii in accordance with Roman law. Vesuvius can be seen rising in the background.*

and were shown some feet of tables in marble which were dug out the day before we were there. Upon the whole, this Mediterranean town, once filled with temples, columns, palaces, and other ornaments of good taste, is now exactly like a coal mine worked by galley slaves."

below: *The men's hot room at the Forum baths in Herculaneum. It was buried beneath 50ft (15 metres) of mud.*

left: *A cast of a victim of the eruption—a small boy lies as he died.*

THE BATHS OF CARACALLA
A monument to Rome's hedonism

The baths built by Caracalla are an extraordinary monument to the hedonistic lifestyle of Rome. They were designed to accommodate 1,600 bathers simultaneously, making them the largest indoor public baths ever known—their operating costs must have been a constant drain on the city's purse, at a time when the Roman Empire was starting to crumble.

Caracalla himself was a fleeting and bloodthirsty leader. Born Marcus Aurelius Antoninus (Caracalla was a nickname derived from the Gaulish caracalla cloaks that he made fashionable), he became joint emperor in 211 AD with his brother, Geta. The following year he ordered Geta's murder, along with the massacre of thousands of his sibling's supporters, but then began his sole reign with a major act of reform: the granting of full Roman citizenship to all free-born subjects of the empire. This attempt to build unity among the provinces was not the dawn of a benevolent administration, however. Caracalla's rule was marked by extravagance, double-dealing, and the sadistic persecution of perceived enemies. Perhaps realizing time was short, he must have hoped the baths would restore his standing as ruler. If so, the plan failed. He was assassinated in Mesopotamia by his successor, Marcus Opelius Macrinus, in 217.

The earliest Roman baths are thought to have been built at Pompeii in the second century BC. By Caracalla's time they were a public institution, providing a center for social life, facilities for relaxation and games, and an exercise area. Close by would be shops, meeting halls, gymnasiums, shady gardens, and libraries—indeed, everything necessary for passing a few idle hours with friends.

Baths' facilities and services

The typical baths layout involved a central courtyard surrounded by an *apodyterium* (dressing room), a *calidarium* (hot bath), *laconicum* (steam bath), *tepidarium* (warm bath), and a *frigidarium* (cold bath). Floors and walls were covered in elaborate mosaics and heated by a system in which hot air was blown through a series of in-built chimneys. Water was brought from many miles away, along an advanced system of aqueducts. In addition to Caracalla's giant complex, there were at least four other public baths in Rome, and the ruins of two of these—the Titus and the Diocletian baths—still stand.

A visit to the baths—whether *balnea* (private) or *thermae* (public)—was loaded with ritual. The wealthy, in

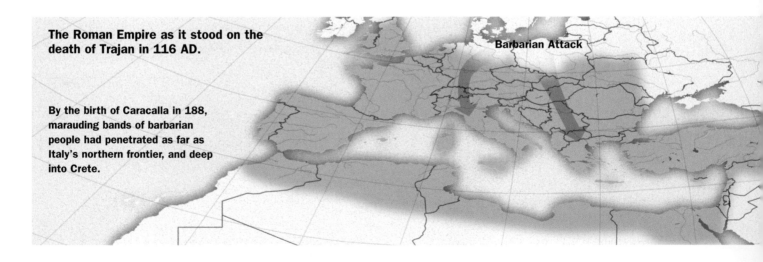

The Roman Empire as it stood on the death of Trajan in 116 AD.

Barbarian Attack

By the birth of Caracalla in 188, marauding bands of barbarian people had penetrated as far as Italy's northern frontier, and deep into Crete.

80 AD	117 AD	c.120 AD	c.200 AD	211 AD	212 AD	c.215	217 AD
Colosseum built in Rome for gladiatorial combat. Audience capacity: 55,000.	Roman Empire reaches its greatest extent.	Emperor Trajan rebuilds road network throughout Italy.	Wealth of empire brings luxury to many Romans; construction of baths increases.	Marcus Aurelius Antoninus (Caracalla) and Geta joint emperors.	Caracalla orders Geta's murder.	Work on baths of Caracalla begins.	Caracalla assassinated.

Slaves were required to remove oil and sweat from their owners' bodies.

above: *Aqueducts carried water into the heart of Rome (reconstruction).*

particular, would come accompanied by teams of slaves responsible for looking after robes, massaging and pampering them, and generally assisting with their needs. Slave roles might include removing oil and sweat from their owner's body using a *strigil*, a kind of metal scraper, washing them with soda bars, or rubbing their master in aromatic oils after exercise. While separate facilities for women were

provided, or at least reserved times for female bathers, there was a gradual trend toward mixed bathing, and in the final years of the Roman Empire. This developed into open sexual promiscuity.

left and above: *Mosaic floor patterns and pictures highlighted the grandeur of the baths, seen in reconstruction (inset).*

410 AD	c.500 AD	c.1400 AD
Roman Empire is invaded and collapses. Dark age in Europe begins.	Teotihuacán, Mexico is largest city in the world (pop. 200,000).	Europe finally regains status as world's most advanced region.

GREAT OUTPOSTS
Alexandria and Aphrodisias

Built on a branch of the Meander River in southern Turkey, Aphrodisias was a classical city of the Eastern Roman, or Byzantine, Empire. It formed part of the province of Asia, a region acquired during an unstoppable period of Roman expansion in the third and second centuries BC. During this period, Rome also conquered Macedonia, which had fragmented into a group of squabbling kingdoms in the power vacuum that followed the death of Alexander the Great.

Excavations on the 1,235-acre (500 ha) site of the city have illuminated much about civic life in the eastern

below: *The theater at Aphrodisias was partly funded by a former slave—Caius Iulius Zoilos.*

empire, including inscribed records of correspondence with various emperors. The Imperial Roman family enjoyed cult status among Aphrodisians, who referred to them as the August Gods—a temple built in their honor contained stonework extolling their great achievements. It mostly focused on the Imperial family between the first emperor, Augustus (who reigned 27 BC–4 AD), and the fifth emperor, Nero (54–68 AD). Augustus is portrayed next to a trophy of the Greek goddess of victory, Nike, while Claudius is shown overcoming an image of Britannia, to celebrate the success of his 43 AD invasion.

Like other Roman cities, Aphrodisias relied heavily on wealthy, generous

citizens to fund the construction of its fine buildings. A freed slave called Caius Iulius Zoilo seems to have paid for at least part of the theater, as well as the Temple of Aphrodite. Broken stone portraits from his mausoleum depict him in both Greek and Roman costume, and there are references to the "manliness" and "honor" that marked out his life.

Some benefactors would leave endowments to the organization of games or musical contests. Athletic events were held in the stadium, and it seems special seats were reserved along one shaded terrace for the gardeners' and gold-workers' associations, both of whom perhaps agreed to underwrite building costs.

Antony and Cleopatra

Alexandria, on the north coast of Egypt, was founded by Alexander the Great in 331 BC. It fell under Roman control in 47 BC, following the arrival of Julius Caesar, who supported Cleopatra against her younger brother. Cleopatra, last of the Ptolemys—the Macedonian royal family who succeeded the pharaohs—was proclaimed Queen of Egypt by Caesar and became his mistress, living with him in Rome after her government was put in order.

On Caesar's assassination in 44 BC, Cleopatra returned to Egypt, famously

331 BC	47 BC	44 BC	40 BC	36 BC	32 BC	31 BC	30 BC
Alexandria founded in Egypt by Alexander the Great of Macedonia.	Alexandria falls under Roman control; Cleopatra becomes Caesar's mistress in Rome.	Caesar assassinated; Cleopatra returns to Egypt —seduces general Mark Antony.	Antony forced to return to Rome and marry Octavia.	Antony and Cleopatra resume relationship.	They begin war against Rome.	Antony and Cleopatra defeated at Antium.	Suicides of Antony and Cleopatra. Alexandria reclaimed by Rome.

Believing a false story that Cleopatra had committed suicide, Antony fell on his sword.

seducing the Roman General Mark Antony when he summoned her to Tarsus in Cilicia (now Turkey) to explain why she had not assisted the civil war against Caesar's assassins. Antony later lived with her in Egypt, but in 40 BC was forced to return to Rome where he married Octavia, sister of the future emperor Augustus (*see above*).

His relationship with Cleopatra resumed in 36 BC, and by 32 BC the couple led Egypt to war against Rome over their claim to the empire's eastern territories. Their fleet was defeated in the 31 BC Battle of Actium and Antony found himself besieged in Alexandria. The following year, believing a false story that Cleopatra had committed suicide, Antony fell on his sword. Soon afterward she too killed herself— supposedly by a snakebite, but more likely by swallowing poison. One of history's greatest love stories ended with Alexandria brought under the direct rule of Rome.

The old city was destroyed in a tidal wave in 335 AD, but many of its archeological treasures—including the entire Royal Quarter—still lie intact on the seabed. In October 1998 some stunning artifacts were recovered by Franck Goddio's diving team, including a statue of the Great Priest of Isis and a sphinx that probably represented Cleopatra's father, Ptolemy XII. A sunken ship, dating from the first century BC, was

also found. Some historians have speculated that it could be the vessel described by Shakespeare and the Greek historian Plutarch, in which Cleopatra first bewitched Antony.

above left: *the remains of Aphrodisias, a city which bestowed cult status on the Imperial Roman family.*
below: *The stadium of Aphrodisias. Special seats were reserved for gardeners and goldsmiths.*

Aphrodisias and other settlements of the eastern Roman Empire.

Istanbul
Ankara
Pergamon   *ANATOLIA PLATEAU*   Eastern empire c.116 AD
Izmir
Athens
Aphrodisias   Tarsus
Antioch

MEDITERRANEAN SEA

The Pharos at Alexandria; the lighthouse was one of the Seven Wonders of the World.

Alexandria

GLIMPSES OF THE ETRUSCANS
Only the dead survive from fragile settlements

History has always been confounded by the Etruscans. Their political influence, culture, and considerable naval might are well documented by Greek and Roman writers, and their fine art and craftwork is beyond question. Yet because their palaces and temples were built of wood-brick combinations, nothing of their architecture has survived. Even their language, a form of Greek, has stubbornly resisted attempts at translation, despite some recent breakthroughs.

There was much debate among ancient scholars on how the Etruscans arrived in the beautiful, fertile valleys that today make up modern Tuscany. According to the Greek historian Herodotus, they came from a land in Western Asia called Lydia. However, his countryman, Dionysius of Halicarnassus, insisted that they were an indigenous race, a view now popular among modern historians. All that can be said with certainty is that they settled among the coastal bogs of Tuscany and built their first towns around Tarquinia at the end of the ninth century BC.

Much of our knowledge has therefore emerged from Etruscan cemeteries and rock tombs— particularly their superb murals (paintings on stone) and frescos (on plaster). Some of the best were discovered in Tarquinia itself; the Tomb of the Leopards (c. fifth century BC) depicts feasting revelers and dancers along its walls, while the Tomb of the Augurs (c. sixth century BC) shows two men wrestling. The Augurs picture may represent an idea that the dead engaged in athletic games. The wrestlers appear to be performing in front of an umpire and there is a pile of metal plates nearby—presumably the winner's prize.

Resting places for the dead
Some tombs reflected Etruscan taste for the good life by attempting to recreate rock "furniture" for the dead. At the Tomb of the Reliefs in Cerveteri (c. third century BC), solid rock "couches" have been carved onto the recliners hewn out of chamber walls.

above: *A fine example of 5th Century BC Etruscan sculpture. This chimera—part of Greek mythology—has the head of a lion, the body of a goat, and the tail of a dragon.*

c.900 BC	814 BC	753 BC	609 BC	581 BC	539 BC	517 BC	509 BC
Area around Tarquinia settled; Etruscan civilization begins.	City of Carthage founded.	Rome founded.	End of Assyrian Empire.	Jerusalem razed by Nebuchadnezzar II.	Greeks defeat Carthage.	Canal from Nile to Red Sea constructed.	Roman Republic founded.

above: *A typically detailed and vibrant Etruscan wall painting.*

right: *This winged horse sculpture, dated to around the fourth century BC, reveals a high level of technical skill.*

The Tomb of the Alcove in Caere is thought to have mirrored domestic Etruscan architecture, with its stone ceiling rafters, fluted pillars, and bed—complete with stone pillow—tucked into a recess. In contrast to these, a much later burial chamber at Volterra, the Inghirami Tomb, is devoid of any painting or stonework, consisting simply of a round room with shelves to support coffins.

Etruscan cemeteries have proved a rich source of pottery and sculpture, deposited for use in the afterlife. In the 18th and 19th centuries, these pieces became highly prized among collectors. Soon treasure-hunters descended on the region and hundreds of artifacts were sold into private and public European collections. The fashion was fueled by travel writers such as the Englishman George Dennis, who in his book *Cities and Cemeteries of Etruria* describes his first sighting of the Norchia necropolis: "We turned a corner of the glen and lo! a grand range of monuments burst upon us. There they were—a line of sepulchres, high in the face of the cliff which forms the right-hand barrier of the glen, some 200 feet above the stream—an amphitheatre of tombs."

One Etruscan method of predicting the future involved laying out the entrails of sacrificed beasts.

509 BC	c.500 BC	490 BC	c.400 BC	c.300 BC	283 BC	First century AD	117 AD
Tarquin the Proud, last of Rome's Etruscan kings, deposed.	Tomb of the Augurs built in Tarquinia.	Athenian shrine at Delphi is first marble building in Greece.	Tomb of the Leopards built in Tarquinia.	Tomb of the Reliefs built in Cerveteri.	Etruscans lose independence to Rome.	Etruscans become full Roman citizens.	Roman Empire reaches its greatest extent.

ETRUSCAN CITIES
The strict design of Pyrgi and Marzabotto

Although Etruscan cities cannot match the richness of Roman tombs and cemeteries in terms of artifacts, they have produced fascinating details about their occupants' ritualistic lives. Two of the most important excavations have been at the port of Pyrgi, near Cerveteri, north of Rome, and Marzabotto, south of Bologna. Marzabotto is particularly compelling, because it seems to have been founded on a system of town planning based on both divine intervention and rigorous mathematical calculation.

According to Roman writers, the ceremony for founding a major Etruscan settlement would begin with an *augur*, or soothsayer, consulting his preferred divination method to ensure that both the time and place were favorable. He would then mark out the main axes of the city, known as the *cardo* and *decumanus*, at right angles, and lay down a grid system for streets in which each square contained an *insula*—a large housing block, similar to today's tenements.

The problem with the Roman accounts was that this method didn't seem to operate in practice. Etruscan town planners inevitably chose good defensive sites which, by the very nature of their high ground or proximity to water, meant strict geometrical design was almost impossible.

The excavations at Marzabotto settled the historical arguments. Here archeologists found a city with streets, houses, and sewers laid out in a precise geometric arrangement, and an acropolis in which five religious temples conformed to the same alignments. The main north-south road, or *cardo*, was intersected by three main east-west routes—the *decumani*. Nor was Marzabotto an isolated example. The city of Pian di Misano, which stands on a plateau close to the valley of the River Po, was built late in the sixth century as Etruscans spread into lowland areas. Again, it was laid out in the cherished grid pattern.

The conclusion must be that Etruscan planners were, above all, pragmatists. In their Tuscan

above: *Entrance to an Etruscan necropolis.*

opposite right: *Husband and wife recline united in death in this sculptured sarcophagus.*

opposite bottom right: *This well-preserved wall painting extols hunters and warriors. Arrows and javelins are aften found in Etruscan tombs.*

Known Etruscan cities/cemeteries of the 1st Millenium BC.

● **The Etrurian heartland**

The quality of Etruscan bronzes, jewelry, and artwork was famed throughout the Ancient World. Despite this, wealthy Etruscans delighted in the purchase of imported treasures— especially for use as grave goods.

c.1300 BC	c.1140 BC	c.1000 BC	c.612 BC	c.539 BC
Egyptians significantly improve wheel and chariot technology.	First colony of Phoenicians in Africa, at Utica.	Phoenician city Tyre becomes important center.	Assyrian capital Nineveh invaded by coalition of forces.	Carthage defeated by Greeks.

The right time—as well as the right site—was crucially important to Etruscan town planners.

heartland, the rugged countryside made it impossible to strictly adhere to the ancient ways of street layout. But where flatter sites became available, they were fully exploited. The Romans showed similar tendencies, in that they loved urban symmetry and deployed it in their new towns wherever possible. Yet their beloved capital grew up around the banks of the Tiber into a maze of winding streets and alleyways that infuriated successive generations of citizens.

Discoveries made during a 1964 excavation at Pyrgi, one of two ports serving the Etruscan city of Cerveteri, proved important for different reasons. Here a team from the University of Rome found the remains of two temples dating to the fourth century BC that contained outstanding examples of sculpture and inscriptions. Among them was a painted terra-cotta wall relief showing the goddess Athena in combat with the Giants—evidence of the great influence the Greek world exerted on Etruscan culture.

In an area between the two temples, excavators recovered three inscribed gold plates bearing dedications to the goddess Uni by someone called Thefarie Velianus. These dedications, repeated in Etruscan and Phoenician, have gone some way to decoding the language of this strangely elusive people.

Merchants of the Mediterranean

With their long history of seafaring, the Etruscans developed a pan-European network of trading. Their first customers were the Phoenicians (who arrived c. eighth century BC), who would barter high-quality jewelry and finished metalware for unworked metals, leather, and wood. The Syrians and Egyptians also brought in fine craftwork, which may have been exchanged for stone carvings and bronzes. The Etruscans loved bronze and were both importers and exporters. Their bronze utensils were particularly popular among the Greeks, while Corinthian vases were highly prized in seventh century BC Etrurian markets.

Bronzes from Asia Minor

● Pisa

Clusium Etruscan cemetery ■

■ Orvieto city and cemetery

Tarquinia ■

■ Veii

Cerveteri ● Rome
or Caere

Faience from Egypt

Ivory from Syria

Phoenician gold and silverware

c.408 BC	c.400 BC	c.390 BC
Acropolis in Athens completed.	Etruscans in decline as Rome expands empire.	Etruscans fight invading Gauls.

CHAPTER SIX

WESTERN EUROPE

There's something about the Celtic western fringe of Europe that imbues ancient places with otherworldliness; a sense that fact and folklore ride a little too closely. Stories about Merlin the wizard assembling Stonehenge, or the patron saint of Carnac, France, turning Roman soldiers into standing stones, are plainly absurd. Similarly, tales of supernatural inhabitants lurking in burial mounds such as Newgrange, Maes Howe, and Sutton Hoo began as fireside yarns or to support pagan mythology.

Yet threads of knowledge, passed on verbally, survive untarnished for centuries. Certainly the Vikings had a forte for this, often preferring to commit their laws and sagas to memory, rather than write them down. The danger of dismissing old tales is that a deep well of knowledge remains untapped. The Celts never bothered with documentation—their entire culture was based on songs and storytelling—and it is presumptuous to assume that verbal history is necessarily less valid than written records. Both can contribute to archeological discoveries.

The point is well illustrated in the final pages of this chapter, recounting the discovery of the "Arthur Stone" at Tintagel Castle, Cornwall, in 1998. For years, historians had confidently dismissed Cornish claims to a sixth century King Arthur figure as romantic fiction. The discovery of the stone indicates, at the very least, that there was a high-status nobleman called Arthnou who built an important structure at Tintagel. It's a long way from proof, but maybe the old stories weren't so far wrong!

The stone rows of Carnac.

PORTUGAL

Skara Brae

Neolithic pendants made at Skara Brae

SCOTLAND

ATLANTIC OCEAN

N. IRELAND

■ **Vindolanda**

Emperor Hadrian, builder of the Roman wall which spanned the breadth of northern England and was named after him.

■ **Newgrange**

IRELAND

NORTH SEA

WALES

ENGLAND

Avebury and Silbury Hill ■

Tintagel Castle ■ **Stonehenge** ■ ■ **Sutton Hoo**

■ **Bush Barrow**

HOLLAND

ENGLISH CHANNEL

BELGIUM

■ **Carnac**

GERMANY

Ritual; monument of the Stone Age: Stonehenge.

Ice age sculputure of a bison

SWITZERLAND

■ **Lascaux**

BAY OF BISCAY

FRANCE

ITALY

Altamira ■ ■**Castilla**

SPAIN

■ **Chauvet cave**

STONEHENGE
Standing stones of many faces

It is a memorial built by Merlin, a druids' ceremonial center, a rallying point for British resistance against the Romans, an astronomical computer, a Roman/Danish/Egyptian/ Phoenician/Greek temple, a focus of "earth" energies, and an early example of architecture by aliens from Mars. Make your choice. It seems that where Stonehenge is concerned, facts just get in the way of good stories. In fairness, this is not altogether true. It *was* an astronomical observatory and, despite all the academic scoffing of past years, it almost certainly *was* used by a religion which evolved into druidism.

Part of the problem in proving or disproving the myriad theories about

below: *After almost 5,000 years, Stonehenge is still an awesome sight.*

Stonehenge is that it is unique, and therefore beyond comparison. Even today, roughly 5,000 years after the first prehistoric builders started work, the stones loom above Wiltshire's bustling A303 main road with a timeless quality of majesty and mystery. Perhaps all the wacky theorists should be forgiven!

So what can we say with certainty? First, that Stonehenge is part of a complex collection of ritual monuments constructed across Britain during the Neolithic and Bronze Age periods. It is among at least 900 circles known to have existed, the earliest of which date to about 3300 BC and the latest to c.1500 BC. Most were begun around 2500 BC, and the first building phase at Stonehenge has been estimated at c. 2800 BC. This

took the form of a circular earthen bank, ditch, erection of the Heel Stone (probably a sighting aid for sunrise on the summer solstice), and a series of 3-foot-square (1 sq m) pits that were filled in shortly after being dug, apparently as part of a religious rite.

Assembling the stone circle

Circa 2100 BC, some spectacular activity began inside this bank with the transportation of 82 bluestones— actually bluish dolerite rock—from the Preseli hills in southwest Wales. Quite how this was done is unclear, but it seems feasible that the stones were transported by barge across the sea, down the River Avon, then man-hauled to Stonehenge. The wheel may well have been invented by this time—and possibly even pulleys—but the work

c.3300 BC	c.3000 BC	c.3000 BC	c.2800 BC	c.2700 BC	c.2650 BC	c.2500 BC	c.2100 BC
Earliest stone circles erected.	Stone rows in Carnac, France erected.	Egyptians learn how to undertake land surveys.	First phase of work on Stonehenge is begun.	Avebury stone circle constructed.	Beginning of age of pyramid building in Egypt.	Main period of stone erection in Europe.	Stones transported from Wales for use at Stonehenge.

The stones have inspired speculation about resistance fighters and human sacrifice.

must surely have involved hundreds of men over many years.

In this way, it seems Stonehenge gradually developed into four concentric ranges of stones. The outermost consisted of 13-foot (4m) high sandstone blocks linked by lintels to create a 108-foot (33m) circle. Then came a circle of smaller bluestones, which in turn enclosed a horseshoe-shaped arrangement of 21-foot (6.5m) high linteled bluestones. These encompassed a single sandstone slab known as the Altar Stone. Running away from the outer bank was the Avenue, a 2-mile (3km) long processional route.

The overall appearance changed several times. It may have originally been a timber construction; the technically sophisticated use of stone tongue-and-groove and mortise-and-tenon joints offers evidence of this. Successive generations seem to have had different design ideas, because at one point the bluestones were dismantled and partly re-erected. For some reason, the Romans desecrated it between 55 BC and 410 AD, a curious act, given that Roman rulers were traditionally tolerant of native religions. This has given rise to speculation about resistance fighters and human sacrifice, a religious act that Rome opposed. Whatever the truth, by the end of the Bronze Age, Stonehenge had lost its position as a revered tribal center.

Avebury and Silbury Hill

Some 20 miles (32 km) north of Stonehenge stand Avebury Circle and Silbury Hill, the two other great pagan ritual centers of southern Britain. Avebury is a henge-type monument of enormous complexity and was built around 2700 BC. As late as the 17th century AD it was said to be in use as a center for "pagan" ceremonies, although these seem to have been more an excuse for deflowering local virgins than the worshiping of ancient deities. At 130 feet (40m) high, Silbury Hill is the largest artificial mound in Europe and continues to baffle archeologists. The theory that it was primarily a burial site is unproven.

Distribution of stone circles and alignments in the United Kingdom.

Stonehenge, Avebury, and Silbury Hill

c.2000 BC	c.1900 BC	c.1500 BC	c.1500 BC	c.900 BC	43 AD	Early centuries AD	c.1000 AD
Lakeside villages constructed in the Alps.	Egyptians begin building temples at Karnak.	In Mexico, the Olmec civilization builds advanced cities.	The last of Europe's stone monuments are erected.	The Chavin temples in Peru are constructed.	Roman invasion of Britain.	Romans desecrate Stonehenge, for unknown reasons.	Adena mound-builders flourish in North American mid-west

THE CARNAC ENIGMA
The stone rows of Europe

The rarest and most odd of all prehistoric European ritual sites are the multiple rows of stone. These occur in varying layouts and sizes in only four places: northern Scotland, Exmoor and Dartmoor in southwest England, and Brittany, in northwest France. None have been found in Cornwall, Wales, or northern England, even though these regions are immensely rich in other types of Neolithic and Bronze Age architecture.

Of all the multiple rows identified so far, the complex at Carnac, Brittany, is by far the largest and most visually impressive, with more than 3,000 stones and dozens of portal dolmens—chambered constructions in which standing stones support a capstone, or roof. The Scottish writer James Miln was among visitors captivated by the Carnac rows and the way they had outlived remnants of Roman occupation. "Independent of the emotions awakened by the view of these battalions of gray stones echeloned along the country," he wrote, "their presence excites the imagination to picture the events which have passed into history since their erection; and one is tempted to ask how it is that the Romans, the masters of the world, came and disappeared, whilst the race of the rude constructors still remains."

Like Stonehenge, Carnac is wreathed in folklore. Some say the megaliths are Roman legionnaires turned to stone by the local patron saint, St. Cornely. Other legends link them to forms of fire or sun worship, an idea supported by charred remains buried at the base of many settings. Often the rows appear to align with notches in distant hills, as though acting as a sighting aid for astronomical observation.

However, the painstakingly accurate surveys by Scottish archeologist Alexander Thom and his son Archie between 1970 and 1974 show that this explanation cannot be generally applied. The Thoms' discoveries disproved claims that Carnac was some precisely calculated piece of prehistoric civil engineering. To the casual eye, many of the rows do seem to run parallel; closer analysis shows they do not.

Accumulated stones from the Bronze Age

The Carnac stones are inconsistently spaced, twist and turn unevenly, and are of varying length and size. This cannot be blamed wholly on 5,000 years of solifluction (the creeping movement of soil). It is far more likely that the rows grew up over many years, added to piece by piece by laborers who were less concerned with geometric niceties than with an overall impression of grandeur and atmosphere.

left: *Sunset over the Carnac rows. Were the stones raised in tribute to the sun's power?*

c.3000 BC	c.2800 BC
Newgrange stone building in Ireland built.	First phase of work on Stonehenge is begun.

Many of the rows seem to run parallel; closer analysis proves they do not.

Carnac—meant different things to different people.

The Thoms concentrated on four main megalithic groups—Ménec, Kermario, Kerlescan, and Petit-Ménec—and surveyed hundreds of other settings using a team of helpers equipped with a formidable array of theodolites, measuring-chains, and ranging-poles. Their work was hampered by the removal or destruction of many stones and in one case—the "fan" arrangement at the shores of St-Pierre-Quiberon—by a rise in sea levels. Even so, their diagrams and charts conclusively proved the haphazard development at Carnac. At Ménec West, the nearest lines to the village itself, 12 rows apparently lead directly to a massive chambered construction a full 300 feet (90m) across. Yet if the five northernmost rows were extended, they would miss the chamber completely! The impression is of stones being added over centuries to an original, simple setting.

The likeliest explanation for Carnac is that it was an important early religious site that, given the large number of nearby burial mounds, was primarily concerned with death and ancestor worship. Later it may have evolved into a more complex center for ritual and sacrifice, perhaps honoring the power of the sun and the flow of the seasons. Its population during the early Bronze Age has been estimated at anywhere between 10,000 and 200,000, based on the size of some of the chambered buildings and the numbers they were designed to serve.

In any event, Carnac is a good example of the danger of compartmentalizing archeological sites, as though they were only ever used for a single purpose. Almost certainly, these strangely haunting stones meant different things to different people.

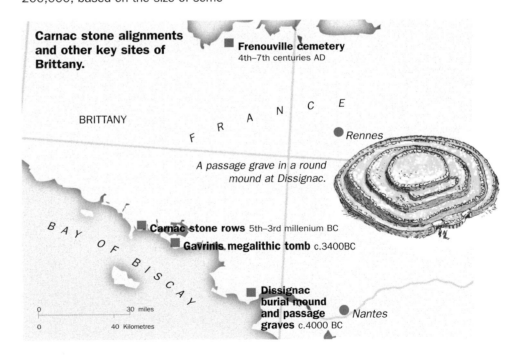

Carnac stone alignments and other key sites of Brittany.

Frenouville cemetery
4th–7th centuries AD

BRITTANY

FRANCE

Rennes

A passage grave in a round mound at Dissignac.

BAY OF BISCAY

Carnac stone rows 5th–3rd millenium BC
Gavrinis megalithic tomb c.3400BC

Dissignac burial mound and passage graves c.4000 BC

Nantes

0 ___ 30 miles
0 ___ 40 Kilometres

c.2000 BC	c.1900 BC	c.1840 BC	c.1750 BC	c.1200 BC	c.1100 BC	c.1120 BC	753 BC
Inuit people living in Arctic.	Irrigation technology improves in Mesopotamia to nurture expanding population .	Lower Nubia is annexed by Egypt.	Hammurabi founds Babylonian Empire.	Greeks destroy city of Troy.	Phoenicians develop alphabetic script.	Mycenean civilization comes to an end.	Rome founded.

ICE AGE ART OF FRANCE AND SPAIN

Vindication of a discredited Spanish architect

In the late 19th century, the notion that Palæolithic artists painted powerful and evocative pictures on the walls of caves was treated with great skepticism by archeologists. Cave drawings had been recognized in France, but because their date was unknown they were assumed to be comparatively recent. The idea that they were produced around 15,000 years ago didn't fit snugly with contemporary interpretations of evolutionary theory.

So when Spanish antiquities collector Don Marcelino Sanz de Sautuola stumbled upon an amazing cluster of bison paintings in a cave at Altamira, near Santander in northern Spain, his claims were controversial. De Sautuola

said he had been digging for prehistoric tools and portable (small rock) art when his young daughter, Maria, saw a bison painting on a roof area. They had been colored with an oily paste and bore comparison to the Palæolithic portable art de Sautuola had seen at the Paris Universal Exhibition in 1878. At the time, portable art was considered to be simply decorative, with no spiritual or cultural significance.

De Sautuola presented his findings to the 1880 International Congress of Anthropology and Prehistoric Archeology in Lisbon, but rather than being feted for a breakthrough, he was treated with derision. The backlash was led by outspoken French palæoanthropologist Emile Cartailhac,

who seemed to believe the entire episode was a plot by Spanish Jesuits to discredit the theory of evolution. The archeological establishment rallied behind Cartailhac and de Sautuola was sent away a frustrated and dispirited man. He died eight years later—just a few years before a clutch of discoveries vindicated his views.

The most clear-cut of these came in 1895 at the La Mouthe cave in the Dordogne. Sediments containing known Palæolithic material had been scraped off a wall to reveal a hidden gallery of figures that had to be extremely ancient. Investigations at the Les Combarelles and Font de Gaume caves in 1901 produced similar results, and by 1902 Cartailhac and his cohorts could no longer hold back the tide. Their embarrassment was not the result of their skepticism— science demands skeptical analysis of any new claim—but the way they had politicized events to crucify de Sautuola's ideas. Cartailhac published a *mea culpa* article in which he acknowledged his mistake—though he pompously tried to justify his reasoning—and new examples of rock art were suddenly pursued.

left: *Animal drawings such as these were cited as evidence for the "hunting magic" theory.*

c.100,000 BC	c.70,000–30,000 BC	c.50,000 BC	c.30,000 BC	c.30,000 BC	c.25,000–10,000 BC	c.12,000 BC	c.10,000 BC
Homo sapiens evolve from earlier human species.	Temperatures drop globally.	First known rock art, in Australia.	Neanderthal people disappear completely after being slowly replaced by *Homo sapiens*.	Most of inhabitable world has been colonised.	Cave art flourishes in Europe.	Pottery is made in most areas of the world.	End of most recent Ice Age; extinction of mammoths and bison in Europe.

It was suggested that the paintings were sexually symbolic.

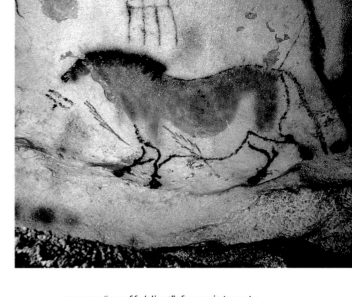

right: *One of the "Chinese Horses" found at Lascaux Cave, Dordogne.*

above: *A so called "Venus" figure with a horn. Ice Age sculpture like this has been found throughout central Europe.*

An enlightened skeptic at work

Emile Cartailhac teamed up with a young priest, Henri Breuil, whose sketchings of cave drawings are still regarded as definitive. Together they worked at several sites, including La Mouthe and Altamira. Between 1906 and 1923 a series of spectacular French discoveries were made, including Pech Merle, with its famous spotted horses, Montespan, which revealed large clay animal statues, and Le Tuc d'Audoubert, which yielded clay bison. Other richly decorated caves were found at Niaux and Les Trois Frères, and in northern Spain caves such as El Castillo,

Covalanas, and Pindal were investigated by prehistoric art expert Hermilio Alcalde del Rio.

France's greatest discovery came in 1940 when four schoolboys discovered a hole in the ground while exploring woods near Montignac, in the Dordogne. Crawling inside, they lit a lamp and noticed unusual colors on the walls. When archeologists investigated, they found an Ice Age picture gallery of awe-inspiring proportions. There were 600 paintings and almost 1,500 engravings, including the Hall of the Bulls—five bull paintings extending up to 16 feet 5 inches (5m)—the largest known works of prehistoric art. In one narrow cave there were even manmade hollows in the ceiling, 17,000-year-old sockets designed to

secure "scaffolding" for painters to access high surfaces.

As the range of cave art unfolded, so the theories multiplied. The idea that it was art for art's sake was first rejected in favor of a "hunting magic" hypothesis, which claimed that prehistoric communities created an animal's image then stabbed it, in the belief that it helped them hunt the real thing. Later, French ethnologist André Leroi-Gourhan suggested that the paintings were sexually symbolic and that many caves were decorated to a standard design. Current thinking is that cave art was a complex discipline rooted in religion or mythology, and that pictures were often re-touched or replaced over thousands of years.

c.9000–8000 BC	c.8000 BC
First civilizations emerge.	The bow and arrow becomes common in Europe.

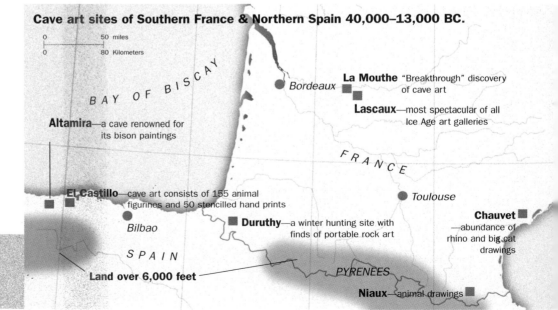

Cave art sites of Southern France & Northern Spain 40,000–13,000 BC.

0   50 miles
0   80 Kilometers

BAY OF BISCAY

Altamira—a cave renowned for its bison paintings

El Castillo—cave art consists of 155 animal figurines and 50 stencilled hand prints

Bilbao

Land over 6,000 feet

SPAIN

● *Bordeaux*   **La Mouthe** "Breakthrough" discovery of cave art

Lascaux—most spectacular of all Ice Age art galleries

FRANCE

● *Toulouse*

Chauvet ■ —abundance of rhino and big cat drawings

■ **Duruthy**—a winter hunting site with finds of portable rock art

PYRENEES

Niaux—animal drawings ■

TOMB BUILDERS OF THE WEST
Neolithic structures in the British Isles

above: *View of the interior of a house at Maes Howe. Some sandstone blocks weigh three tons (over 3,000 kilos).*

On a clear morning, a few minutes after the dawn of the shortest day, the sun's rays travel through a skylight in the roof of the Newgrange passage grave in Ireland's Boyne Valley. This stab of sunlight cuts through the main chamber to illuminate a smaller room at the rear, and for a few minutes the interior of the grave is imbued with a magical atmosphere of light-versus-shadow. To the late Neolithic people (c.3000 BC) who built it, it embraced a relationship between the sun, death, and rebirth; the mid-winter solstice recognized as the beginning of the sun's long climb back to higher skies. At other times of the year, the skylight was manually blocked by a specially imported chunk of quartz.

Newgrange, together with the other great Boyne passage graves at Knowth and Dowth, was probably influenced by tomb builders on the Iberian peninsula. There is clear evidence of trade contacts between the two regions in the form of distinctive Iberian craftwork found at east coast Irish sites, namely decorated stone basins and a particular type of bone pin. Whatever inspired the prehistoric architects responsible, these graves marked a sea change in the sophistication of British Neolithic societies. At Knowth, the remnants of no less than 17 sub-chambers have been found set into the main mound—which is itself 295 feet (90m) in diameter and 36 feet (11m) high. All the Boyne Valley graves show traces of a particular type of stone artwork, such as spirals, geometric shapes, and concentric horseshoes.

Newgrange spawned two isolated imitations in North Wales and northern Scotland, most notably the remarkable 23-foot (7m) high Maes Howe mound on Orkney. This was probably constructed a little later (c.2750 BC) but it incorporates many of the design features of the Irish version—most notably its commemoration of the winter solstice through an alignment that allows the rays of the setting sun to shine down a passageway.

Desecrated by bawdy Vikings

Maes Howe has rightly been described as the finest prehistoric monument north of the Alps. It consists of neatly split sandstone blocks, some weighing three tons, rising through interim stone supports to a superb 14-foot (4.5m) vaulted roof. The blocks were painstakingly leveled and plumbed into position with tiny slivers of stone. Such a labor-intensive project surely involved the cooperation of several tribes, who perhaps shared the finished structure for their burial rituals. Typically, these would involve the careful separation

c.3500 BC	c.3100 BC	c.3000 BC	c.3000 BC	c.3000 BC	c.2800 BC	c.2750 BC	c.2685 BC
First megalithic tombs and circles built.	Construction of Skara Brae begins.	First stone temples erected in Malta.	Stone rows of Carnac begun in France.	Newgrange built.	First phase of work on Stonehenge is begun.	Maes Howe in Orkney erected.	Pyramid building begins in Egypt.

Stone Age mourners removed bones from tombs and scattered them elsewhere.

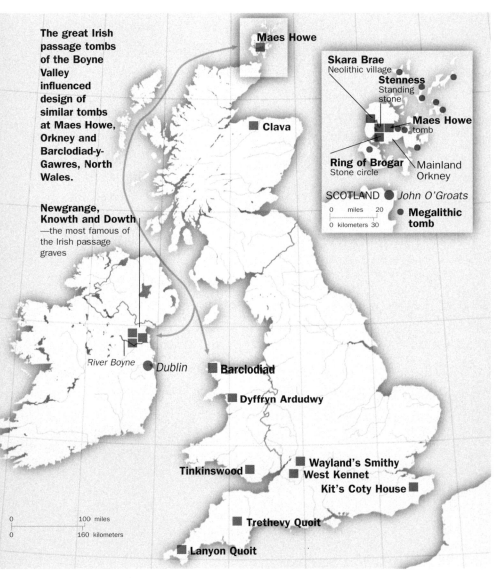

above: *Spiral art now marks the entrance to the burial chamber at Newgrange.*

of skulls and longbones, the smashing of ceramic pots, a presentation of offerings, and the lighting of fires. Recent studies suggest that Stone Age mourners removed bones from tombs and scattered them elsewhere.

Maes Howe was of obsessive interest to the Vikings. They believed burial mounds contained treasure for the taking—if only warriors were brave enough to see off the ghosts and trolls that lurked within. In the 12th century AD, a group of Christian Norsemen broke in and left runic graffiti, boasting of the hoard they had seized, along with lustful comments about a beautiful widow named Ingibiorg. The Vikings may have taken some artifacts (the tomb was bare when 19th-century antiquarians explored it), but it is highly unlikely they found anything of great value. Far richer were the later Bronze Age sites, particularly Bush Barrow in Wessex, where a tribal chief was found alongside gold objects and weapons produced by craftsmen around 1800 BC.

Skara Brae

Skara Brae, on Orkney, is the best-preserved prehistoric settlement in northern Europe. It was built partly underground between 3100 and 2500 BC by the same people who constructed Maes Howe and consists of six houses connected by covered corridors. The interior fittings—all made of stone, because of a dearth of trees on the storm-lashed island—include box-type beds, "dresser" cupboards, alcove store rooms, and some curious rectangular pits that may have been used to soak and store fresh bait for fishing. It was abandoned around 2000 BC, probably because of its exposed position, and wasn't rediscovered until 1850, when shifting sands revealed some of the exterior stonework.

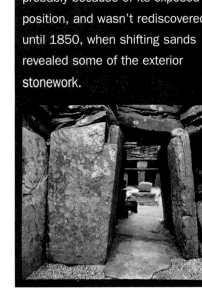

The great Irish passage tombs of the Boyne Valley influenced design of similar tombs at Maes Howe, Orkney and Barclodiad-y-Gawres, North Wales.

Newgrange, Knowth and Dowth —the most famous of the Irish passage graves

Maes Howe

Skara Brae
Neolithic village

Stenness
Standing stone

Maes Howe
tomb

Ring of Brogar
Stone circle

Mainland Orkney

SCOTLAND John O'Groats

Megalithic tomb

Clava

River Boyne ● Dublin

■ Barclodiad

■ Dyffryn Ardudwy

■ Wayland's Smithy
■ West Kennet

Tinkinswood ■

Kit's Coty House ■

■ Trethevy Quoit

■ Lanyon Quoit

HADRIAN'S WALL AND VINDOLANDA
The Romans' barrier and its garrison

The great northern frontier of the Roman Empire was Hadrian's Wall, a 73-mile (117km) boundary built between the Solway Firth and the mouth of the River Tyne in northern Britain. It was designed partly to keep marauding Pictish tribes at bay, but also to show the limit of Roman jurisdiction and to control overland trade across the border. Work began c.122 AD under the orders of the Emperor Hadrian and modifications continued at the time of his death in 138 AD.

In its final form, the stonework was up to 10 feet (3m) thick and around 14 feet high, interspersed with fortlets every Roman mile (1,875 yards; 1,714m). There were a further two observation turrets between each fortlet, a ditch along much of the north-facing side (except where crags offered natural protection), and to the south, large forts capable of housing

above: *A view of Hadrian's Wall looking from Cuddy's Crag, Northumberland.*

thousands of soldiers. A military road—later named the Stanegate—allowed Roman commanders to deploy "rapid reaction" reinforcements in the event of attacks on lightly patrolled sections of the wall.

Although Hadrian's Wall reveals much about Roman defensive structures, it is the garrison at Vindolanda (now Chesterholm) that has allowed a look at the lifestyle of the defenders themselves. Here a large, temporary civilian settlement appears to have been tacked onto an earlier fort—possibly to provide a provincial palace for Hadrian.

Personal effects from Roman Britain

Excavations by the archeologist Robin Birley have produced some intriguing records of everyday activities at this outpost. More than 1500 etched

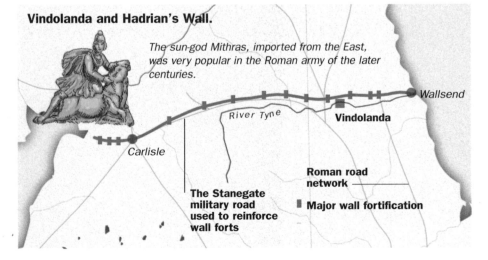

Vindolanda and Hadrian's Wall.

The sun-god Mithras, imported from the East, was very popular in the Roman army of the later centuries.

Wallsend

River Tyne

Vindolanda

Carlisle

The Stanegate military road used to reinforce wall forts

Roman road network ——

■ **Major wall fortification**

43 AD	51 AD	c.117 AD	c.122 AD	c.138 AD	c.140 AD	185 AD	211 AD
Roman invasion of Britain.	Caractacus, leader of British resistance, captured.	Roman Empire reaches its greatest extent.	Work begins on Hadrian's Wall.	Emperor Hadrian dies.	Construction of more northerly Antonine Wall begun.	Antonine Wall abandoned.	Emperor Septimius Severus dies while fighting Caledonians.

One Roman soldier was thankful for a gift of woolly underpants.

top: *Vindolanda looking towards Hadrian's Wall*

wooden tablets and crude paper-and-ink documents give details of duty rosters, stores, supply chains, private relationships, and even the incidence of troops reporting sick. One shows that the First Cohort of Tungrians comprised 752 men, including six centurions. Of these, 456 had been seconded to serve at Corbridge—an important early base for the army of Agricola—and of the soldiers remaining at Vindolanda several complained of "inflammation of the eyes."

Other records suggest that the wives and children of senior military officers were housed at the site. A birthday party invitation from Claudia Severa, wife of the commander Aelius Brocchus, was sent to Sulpicia Lepidna, whose husband Flavius Cerialis had overall responsibility for the Ninth Cohort of Batavians at Vindolanda. In the invitation, Claudia wrote: "On 11 September… for the day of the celebration of my birthday I give you a warm invitation to make sure that you come to us, to make the day more enjoyable for me by your arrival, if you are present."

Other correspondence hints at the frustration many Romans felt at having to endure the privations of life in pagan Britain. A man called Octavius,

below: *The bath house at Vindolanda.*

who had been due to pick up grain and cattle from his brother Candidus, wrote an apologetic letter stating, "I would have already been to collect them, except that I did not care to injure the animals while the roads were bad." Another, separate note fragment was written in reply to a concerned relative or friend, acknowledging receipt of some woolly socks, sandals, and two pairs of briefs.

War on the Wall

By c.140 AD, the activities of Picts to the north of Hadrian's Wall were causing increasing concern to Rome. Emperor Antoninus Pius ordered construction of a second line of defense, some way north of the wall between the Firth of Forth and the Firth of Clyde, in an attempt to squeeze the operations of hostile Caledonian tribes. The Antonine Wall had nothing of the sophisticated fortifications further south and relied on a straightforward turf barricade stretching about 37 miles (58km) and set with 19 forts. It was abandoned almost as soon as it was finished, and in 185 AD the Romans fell back to reinforce Hadrian's Wall. History text books traditionally insist that there were two great tribal assaults on the wall—in 197 and 296 AD—but the archeological evidence for such precise dates is questionable.

SUTTON HOO
The Ghost Boat

Sutton Hoo is a wild, windswept place. An ancient Anglo-Saxon cemetery that has maintained an aura of myth and mystery for centuries, it stands on the edge of an escarpment overlooking the River Deben in Suffolk. Elizabeth I's magician, John Dee, opened a burial mound there, Henry VIII's servants organized treasure hunts, and in 1690 a gold crown weighing about 60 ounces (1.5 kg) was said to have been dug up nearby.

It was at Sutton Hoo in the summer of 1939, as the shadow of war spread across Europe, that Britain's greatest archeological discovery was made. Excavators found the remains of an elegant, 90-foot (27m) buried ship containing early Anglo-Saxon artifacts of such breathtaking quality that they were surely the "grave goods" of a Dark Ages king.

The finds included a ceremonial helmet, a sword engraved with gold and garnet, a "scepter," a battle axe, a shield with dragon and bird motif, silver and bronze bowls, a lyre, a 5-foot 6-inch (1.6m) iron stand (possibly a royal standard), various coins, and 19 items of jewelry unsurpassed by any similarly dated find in the United Kingdom. Among these pieces were a sold gold belt buckle weighing nearly a pound (0.45kg) and decorated with

interwoven patterns featuring animals and birds, and a purse lid exquisitely fashioned in gold, garnet, and millefiori enamel. The prevailing historical view that early Anglo-Saxons were merely primitive tribal warriors—"a convenient stream of flotsam," as one scholar put it—had been decisively challenged. Here at last was evidence that the Saxons had both the notion of nobility and some impressive trade contacts. Several objects came from as far afield as Scandinavia, Egypt, and Western Asia.

Evidence, however, is not proof, and from the moment the dig finished on

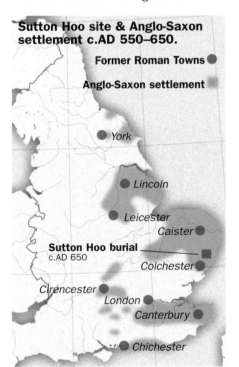

Sutton Hoo site & Anglo-Saxon settlement c.AD 550–650.

Former Roman Towns ●
Anglo-Saxon settlement ■

● York

● Lincoln

● Leicester
Caister ●

Sutton Hoo burial _____
c.AD 650
Colchester ●

Cirencester ●
London ●
Canterbury ●

● *Chichester*

above: *The Sutton Hoo helmet—probably Britain's greatest archeological find.*

August 23, 1939, the Sutton Hoo ship became a monumental controversy. For one thing, there was no ship; only the ghostly impression of it in the sandy soil, the remains of rows of nails, and the metal grave goods. The high acid content of the soil had eaten away everything else, and experts agreed that it could easily have dissolved a body. However, it was also feasible that the boat was a cenotaph or empty tomb, perhaps in honor of some great ruler lost at sea.

King Raedwald or Edmund?

In 1975, after years of intense laboratory work, the British Museum concluded that there had been a body lying at the center of the boat near

410 AD	418 AD	439 AD	451 AD	c.500 AD	c.550 AD	c.600 AD	c.625 AD
The Romans leave Britain, which reverts to tribalism.	A barbarian Visigoth state is set up within the decimated Roman Empire.	Vandals capture the Roman city of Carthage.	An alliance of Romans and barbarians defeats the Huns.	Persia and India are attacked by the Huns.	Invasion of Celtic England by Angles, Jutes, Saxons, Picts, and Scots.	St Augustine converts Southeast England to Christianity, leading way to conversion of entire British Isles.	Burial of Saxon nobleman at Sutton Hoo.

Historians have speculated that the grave is that of martyred King Edmund.

where the sword and jewelry were found. But then a review by forensic experts at Guy's Hospital deduced the exact opposite, insisting that there was no indication of human remains, cremated or otherwise. This idea was initially supported by archeological evidence, in that the position of artifacts within the grave did not square with the presence of a body. Further, there were no personal items, such as finger rings, pendants, pins, clothing fragments, shoe buckles, or gold thread, some of which would surely have accompanied their owner into the afterlife.

However, a complete re-examination of the excavators' original notes in 1979 produced a stunning breakthrough. The 1939 team had noted recovery of a complete set of iron coffin fittings, a glaring fact that had subsequently been overlooked. The position of this metal formed the outline of a since-disintegrated wooden coffin that would have contained all the grave goods found in the central "body area" of the tomb. A coffin is no guarantee of a body, but on balance it seems probable that there was indeed the interment of a Saxon nobleman in a ship which, judging by the dated coins, occurred sometime between 620 and 650 AD.

His name still eludes us. The most likely scenario is that this nobleman led an East Anglian royal dynasty whose heartland lay in the valleys of the Deben and the Alde. British Museum experts have suggested Sutton Hoo is the grave of King Raedwald, of the Wuffinga line, an opportunist ruler who embraced both the new Christian teachings and old pagan ways. More imaginatively, some historians have speculated that it marks the temporary burial of the martyred King Edmund, last of the Wuffingas, who was killed during the Viking Wars.

left: *Very little was left of the actual boat, what is visible in this reconstruction is the discoloration of the sand from the planking.*

c.650 AD	c.675 AD	c.750 AD	c.760 AD	778 AD	c.840 AD	c.800 AD	878 AD
Christianity established throughout most of western Europe and Britain.	Islam is expanding rapidly in Middle East and southern Europe.	Monasteries become widely established in western Europe.	England consists of three kingdoms; Mercia, Wessex, and Northumbria.	Anglo-Saxons establish the penny as the currency in England.	Vikings ravage Britain.	Charlemagne becomes Holy Roman Emperor in mainland western Europe.	Danes are defeated and expelled from Wessex.

TINTAGEL CASTLE AND THE ARTHUR STONE

An inscription questions a myth

Anyone who has stood in the ruins of Tintagel Castle and watched an angry Atlantic Ocean thunder into Merlin's Cave below will understand why thousands of people worldwide are obsessed with the place. It stands on the rugged cliffs of northern Cornwall, a western Celtic outpost with a layout unparalleled anywhere in the world. At various times it has been an Iberian trading post, Ancient British stronghold, monastery, and Norman castle (the remains we see today). But by far Tintagel's most trumpeted and controversial claim is that it is the birthplace of King Arthur.

The very mention of Arthur tends to disturb historians. His birthplace, kingdom, and grave are variously held to be in Cornwall, Wales, Scotland, Cumberland, Wiltshire, Berkshire, and even Brittany, to name but a few possible sites, and all manner of pseudo-historic research has been done to justify dubious claims about the "real" Arthur.

Geoffrey of Monmouth started the

above: *The cliff path to Tintagel Castle, Cornwall.*

trend with his medieval account, *The History of the Kings of England* (which contained numerous errors of translation), and there followed questionable—though effective—attempts by the Church to re-package Arthur as a Christian. Romantic Victorian antiquaries, poets, and sensation-seeking authors have since added their interpretations of Arthurian legend and there is now almost nothing you can say about the poor king that is *not* disputed. The most reliable line has come from the government-backed conservation group English Heritage, which conservatively

suggests that Arthur existed as a successful sixth-century soldier who fought battles all over the country.

On July 4, 1998, the debate took on a dramatic new spin with the discovery of the "Arthur Stone" on a previously excavated clifftop site close to Tintagel Castle. Excavators led by Professor Chris Morris of Glasgow University's Department of Archeology came across a piece of slate inscribed in a distinctive sixth-century script with the name Artognov—the Latin spelling of the British name Arthnou, which later became Arthur. The full inscription read "Pater Coliavificit Artognov" and translated as "Arthnou, father of a descendant of Coll, has had this constructed."

Evaluating the Arthur Stone

The slate, measuring 12 by 8 inches (30 by 20cm) was found a few inches into the earth and, though seemingly a plaque of some kind, had been broken for re-use as a drain cover on some unknown building. Studies of the script, and analysis of the earth in which it was found, appeared to rule out a hoax, and Professor Morris declared, "It is priceless because it is an inscription. There are no inscriptions of this kind found on secular sites. At the moment it is unique. It is the most dramatic find."

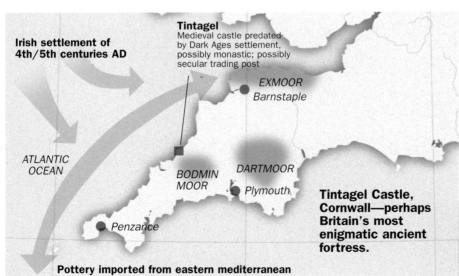

Irish settlement of 4th/5th centuries AD

Tintagel
Medieval castle predated by Dark Ages settlement, possibly monastic; possibly secular trading post

EXMOOR
Barnstaple

ATLANTIC OCEAN

BODMIN MOOR

DARTMOOR
Plymouth

Penzance

Tintagel Castle, Cornwall—perhaps Britain's most enigmatic ancient fortress.

Pottery imported from eastern mediterranean

c.450 AD	c.480 AD
Angles, Saxons, and Jutes begin invasion of England.	Saxons invade the south coast of England and drive the Britons westward.

He is one of the great British heroes. A tough, rough, leader of men.

Academic reaction to the Arthur Stone was positive, though not uncritical. It was pointed out that the name element "Arth" was reasonably common in Britain in the Dark Ages, and the stone could therefore not be seen as proof of King Arthur's links with Tintagel. Nevertheless, alongside evidence offered by rival sites, it was a persuasive find.

Its overall significance lay in the realization that courtiers and officials within a ruler's circle were literate and continuing to read and write Latin long after the departure of the Romans. As Dr Geoffrey Wainwright, chief archeologist at English Heritage, put it: "This is the find of a lifetime. It is remarkable that a stone has been discovered with the name Arthnou inscribed on it at Tintagel, a place with which the mythological King Arthur has long been associated."

He went on: "Despite the obvious temptation to link the Arthnou Stone to either the historical or the legendary figure of Arthur, it must be stressed there is no evidence to make this connection. Nevertheless, it proves for the first time that the name existed at that time and that the stone belonged to a person of status. I hope it will put some meat on the historic figure. He is one of the great British heroes, a tough, rough, leader of men."

above: *The coastline around Merlin's Cave. At one time the castle site was an important international trading post.*

below: *Tintagel's surviving fortifications are mainly Norman. But the Arthur Stone hints at a far older structure.*

c.500 AD	c.500 AD	507 AD	c.550 AD	c.597 AD	c.625 AD	632 AD	c.650 AD
The Sassanic Empire in Persia is partially conquered by the Hephtalites.	Teotihuacán in Central America is the largest city in the world (Pop. 250,000).	King Clovis founds the Frankish kingdom.	The Saxons (now Anglo-Saxons) drive the indigenous Britons further westward.	St. Augustine arrives in Britain to convert the population to Christianity.	Burial of Saxon chieftan at Sutton Hoo in East Anglia, England.	Death of Mohammed, founder of Islam.	The Tang Empire is most successful Chinese dynasty to date.

CHAPTER SEVEN

CENTRAL AND NORTHERN EUROPE

Western societies are not good at dealing with death. The idea of growing old and frail is anathema to a culture that worships youth, beauty, ambition, and material success. There is an obsession with prolonging life that permeates almost all our waking hours; from what we eat and drink to the level of stress we endure at work. Given the option, how many people would today seek immortality?

Such preoccupation was not generally widespread among ancient peoples—mainly because death hovered considerably closer. With adult life expectancy little more than 40 years, the daily dangers of hunting and tribal battles, the debilitating effects of cold and hunger, and the ever-present risk of disease, there was a daily uncertainty that must have concentrated minds on prospects for an afterlife. In societies not yet enlightened by scientific knowledge it was easier to believe in deities. Death was a natural consequence of life. Symbols of rebirth were everywhere in nature. Just as the sun gradually climbed from its winter solstice, so the dead climbed from their tombs to enter the spirit world.

Such thinking is evident in nearly all early civilizations, but ancient Europe particularly illustrates the sheer variety of funerary traditions. In this chapter we look at the incredible Neolithic stone temples and hypogeums of Malta, the strange sacrificial rituals of the Danish boglands, the graves "dripping" with gold at Varna, the mysterious Hochdorf tomb in Germany, and the Viking ship-burials of Scandinavia. On separate themes there is the fascinating story of Ötzi—the world's earliest fully-preserved prehistoric man—and the discovery of the Alpine Lake settlements; an illustration of how archeologists create myths as well as destroy them.

left: *Norse culture contained a variety of terrifying images, to both worship and intimidate. This fierce human mask was carved on the side of the Osberg cart in Norway, c. 850 AD.*

NORWAY

Gokstad and Oseberg Ships

Figurehead from the Oseberg ship.

SWEDEN

N O R T H   S E A

DENMARK
Tollund Man

B A L T I C

RUSSIAN
FEDERATION

BELARUS

Silver panel from the Gundestrop Cauldron, Denmark.

POLAND

CZECH REPUBLIC

Hochdorf
GERMANY

FRANCE

SLOVAKIA

AUSTRIA

Lake People

Hallstatt

Iceman of Tyrol

HUNGARY

ROMANIA

Left: *The oldest wheel found in Europe, built by the Lake People c.3200 BC, and discovered in Zurich. Alongside is a reconstruction of a typical cart of the time.*

ITALY

Gold animal ornament from Varna.

Varna

BULGARIA

Temple complex of Tarxien on Malta.

Maltese Stone Temples

THE HOCHDORF PRINCE
Hidden Celtic tomb

The mountain country around the Hohenasperg, near Stuttgart, southern Germany, was by 500 BC the center of a thriving Celtic community. These people had access to gold, bronze, and iron mines, wide trading links, a prosperous Iron Age economy, and a degree of security delivered by apparently stable leadership. But just how did these Celts—part of a ubiquitous, mysterious race that spread across central and western Europe—organize their society? Were they subject to royal rule, or did they adopt a less structured existence, perhaps led by a religious figurehead? During the 19th and 20th centuries a ring of so-called "princely tombs" circling the Hohenasperg might have provided some answers if only archeologists

had entered them before the tomb robbers. As it was, virtually all the burial mounds were attacked and plundered. All except one; a mound so flattened by plowing and erosion that nobody had noticed it.

Nobody, that is, until an amateur archeologist Renate Liebfried quietly

above: *Stone tumuli in central Europe have long been a target for looters. This one at Pitten, Austria, has survived remarkably well.*

began doing some fieldwork. In 1977 he notified the State Antiquities office of Baden-Württemberg that he had found a "lost tomb" some six miles

Celtic Bronze and Iron Age settlements in Europe.

ATLANTIC OCEAN

NORTH SEA

BALTS

FINNO-UGRIANS

ISLAND CELTS

The Hochdorf Prince's tomb is so far unparalleled in the Celtic world.

GERMANS

Biskupia

SLAVS

The central position of the Hallstatt salt mines allowed miners excellent access to the main trans-European Iron Age trade routes. According to Greek and Roman historians, the peoples of Europe were identified as set out here.

Preist

Hochdorf

Libenice

Rhine

CELTS

Manching

Lyons

Rhone

Hallstatt

ITALIOTES

SCYTHIANS

River Douro

Enserune

River Po

Danube

LIGURIANS

AQUITAINES

ILLYRIANS

BLACK SEA

IBERIANS

THRACIANS

HITTITES

Estimated western limit of Celtic exploration

Estimated southern limit of Celtic exploration

GALATIANS

MEDITERRANEAN

GREEKS

LUVITES

The body was lying on a bronze recliner unparalleled in the Celtic world.

(10km) west of the Hohenasperg, and the following year a full-blown excavation was launched to save the site (originally 20' [6m] high) from further damage. From the moment the team penetrated the core of the Hochdorf burial chamber they knew they had hit an archeological mother lode. So dense were the grave goods that whole sections of earth had to be removed in blocks and minutely dissected in laboratories.

The excavation

The excavation took two summers and cost DM440,000 (about $310,000 or £200,000 at Spring 1999 exchange rates). It revealed a central burial shaft of 1296 square feet (121 sq m) and about eight' (2.5m) deep. Inside were two wooden box structures—the outer one made of oak and measuring 80 square feet (7.5 sq m); the inner 50 square feet (4.7 sq m) and three feet (1m) deep. The space between the two was filled with stones, some containing mineral residues from nearby smelting workshops, and a further 50 tons (51,000 kg) was stacked over the roof, causing it to collapse before the body inside had decomposed. Clearly, the designers meant to make life difficult for robbers.

Inside the tomb the degree of preservation was startling. The body was lying on a bronze recliner unparalleled in the Celtic world, its base supported by the upstretched arms of eight bronze female figures. It had images of wagons and dancers embossed on its back and sides, and had been draped in fur and cloth for the comfort of the departed soul. The deceased, a 5' 11" (1.8m) tall man, was stretched out along it. He wore a conical hat made of birch bark, a gold necklet, and had been dressed in clothes bearing ornaments such as cuffs and hammered gold. A bag on his chest contained a wooden comb, an iron razor, a handful of beads, and three fish-hooks. Around him lay the everyday trappings of nobility; a bronze kettle of Greek design, a small gold bowl, nine drinking horns, and a full-size 15' (4.5m) wagon complete with four huge ten-spoke wheels and harness. Wagons were dear to the heart of the Celtic "princes" and were often included in their tombs. But this one, with its unprecedented iron sheathing, was a truly spectacular find.

Despite all this, the tomb is infuriatingly enigmatic. It tells us only that the Celts revered certain individuals and that important tombs were loaded with the finest treasures Celtic smiths could produce. Whether the Hohenasperg was truly the royal cemetery for a defined Celtic kingdom however remains unproven.

The Salt Mines of Hallstatt

During the lifetime of the Hochdorf "prince" another early Iron Age community was flourishing at Hallstatt, high in the Austrian Alps near present-day Salzburg. Hallstatt's economy was based on salt mining and in more recent times remnants of ancient equipment—picks, hammers, shovels, and even leather rucksacks—have been found in old shafts and timber-shored galleries. In 1734 miners discovered the body of an Iron Age laborer, perfectly preserved by the salt, lying where he'd been killed by a roof fall. In the early 18th century science in Europe was still in its infancy, and the body was reburied without analysis.

The wealth of Hallstatt is obvious in the goods recovered from more than 2,000 graves. These include imported items from the Mediterranean and the Baltic, as well as European-made iron and bronze swords, daggers, axes, helmets, bronze bowls, cups, and cauldrons. The rise of this economy helped establish the first true European towns by c.500 BC.

539 BC	510 BC	505 BC	c.500 BC	c.500 BC	c.500 BC	c.500 BC	c.500 BC	c.500 BC
Persian Empire founded under Cyrus the Great.	Founding of Roman republic.	Democracy established in Athens, center of achievement during Greek "Golden Age".	First European towns established.	Caste system established in India Start of rice cultivation in India.	First Chinese codes of law issued.	Nok Culture begins in northern Nigeria First use of iron in Africa.	Paracus culture flourishes in Peru.

LAKE PEOPLE OF THE ALPS
Innovative Neolithic dwellings

Among the most intriguing and romantic images put forward by 19th century archeologists were the European lake towns. These were supposedly settlements of wooden houses built on pile-driven platforms that stretched out from the shores of Alpine lakes across what is now Germany, Switzerland, Austria, Slovenia, France, and Italy. The idea captured public imagination and for a time artists, novelists, and songwriters extolled the quaint beauty of these "floating islands" beneath a dramatic mountain backdrop.

The find that ignited all this excitement was made during the long, dry winter of 1853–54. During these months the water level of many lakes in the Zurich area dropped by up to a foot (30cm) revealing glimpses of bizarre-looking posts emerging from silt below the waterline. At Obermeilen a local schoolteacher named Johannes Aeppli conducted his own small-scale study and found huge quantities of man-made debris scattered among the posts—typically stone, clay, and wood utensils, and tools made of antlers. These all appeared well-preserved in the cold waters and obviously came from the inhabitants of a sizeable village.

Aeppli took his discovery to Ferdinand Keller, president of the Antiquarian Society of Zurich, and Keller launched his own, more exhaustive survey. He concluded that the posts could have been used in two ways; either to act as foundations for houses on the shore, or to hold up interlocking platforms which stretched across the lake and were themselves used to support structures. Keller embraced the second theory, perhaps because he had read about similar villages in Malaya and the East Indies, and also because of an account by the Greek historian Herodotus describing a lake town in Macedonia.

below: This painting by W. Kranz is supposedly of a Stone Age lake dwelling near Zurich. Archeologists now believe the theory of homes on stilts is wrong.

c.2000 BC	c.2000 BC	c.2000 BC	c.2000 BC	c.1900 BC	1840 BC	c.1800 BC	c.1750 BC
Alpine Lake People.	First metalworking in Peru.	Use of sail on seagoing vessels in Aegean. Minoans produce painted pottery.	Inuit people living in Arctic.	Irrigation technology improves in Mesopotamia, nurtures expanding population.	Lower Nubia annexed by Egypt.	Shamshi-Adad founds Assyrian state.	Hammurabi founds Babylonian Empire.

The water level of the lakes dropped to reveal bizarre-looking posts emerging from the silted bed.

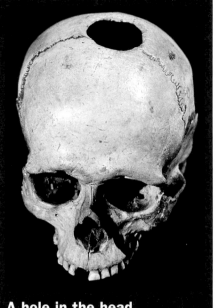

Doubts surface

The problem with Keller's "pile-dwelling" idea was that it didn't seem practical. Why should a stone age culture go to all the trouble of driving logs underwater when it could build far more simply and conveniently by the shore? There was an argument that villages on lakes had better protection than those beside them. Even so, it seemed a heavy commitment for dubious reward and by the 1950s most revisionist studies along the Alpine foreland had concluded that Keller was wrong and that the houses were constructed on the shore. This is not to belittle the overall importance of his work. Studies of the "Swiss Lake Dwellings," as they were popularly called, have produced extremely detailed information about central Europe's early farmers.

The lakeside villages first appeared in the late Neolithic age around 2000 BC and continued in use well into the Bronze Age. They were rectangular in shape and incorporated clay hearths but it is not entirely clear whether they had raised floors or relied on crude wooden planking placed directly onto the muddy ground. Either way, the log piles' principal function must have been to provide a secure footing against subsidence. The inhabitants obviously weren't too fussed about where they hurled their rubbish; excavation of these sites has yielded tens of thousands of broken artifacts, as well as intact stonework and distinctive round-bottomed pots with handles. The handles were important because they allowed food storage vessels to be tied up on the walls or roof—away from the effects of damp or the scavenging of rats.

Other key finds have included well-preserved ax handles (normally only stone axe-heads are found on Neolithic sites) together with various types of cloth and twine. Equally important are the clues to prehistoric man's diet. Traces of wheat, barley, peas, wild fruit and nuts, and seeds have been recovered together with the bones of both hunted wild animals and domestic herds. Excavations on newly discovered lakeside villages look set to continue well into the 21st century and should ultimately provide a comprehensive understanding of late Neolithic man in Europe.

A hole in the head

From as early as 4000 BC, almost all European cultures were using trephaning as a means of "letting out demons" from patients. The operation, carried out with sharpened flints, involved cutting a neat circle in the cranium, Many skulls have been found bearing witness to this early medical cure for madness. The patient was anesthetized by a dose of carefully mixed plants and herbs. Serrated slate was also used for—probably more painful—amputations.

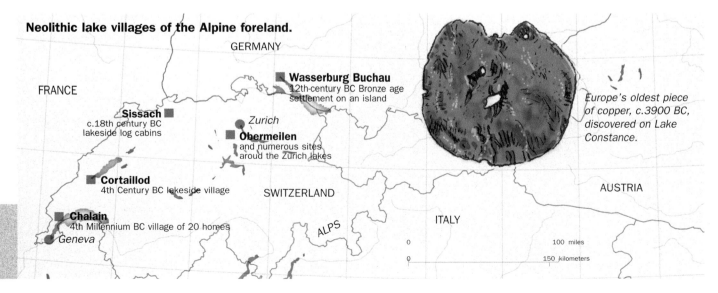

Neolithic lake villages of the Alpine foreland.

GERMANY

FRANCE

Wasserburg Buchau
12th-century BC Bronze age settlement on an island

Sissach ■
c.18th century BC lakeside log cabins

Zurich

Obermeilen
and numerous sites aroud the Zurich lakes

Cortaillod
4th Century BC lakeside village

SWITZERLAND

Chalain
4th Millennium BC village of 20 homes
Geneva

ALPS

ITALY

AUSTRIA

Europe's oldest piece of copper, c.3900 BC, discovered on Lake Constance.

0   100 miles

0   150 kilometers

GOLD OF VARNA
Copper age treasures

Nowhere in the world have archeologists found anything to match the golden graves at Varna. This 6,000-year-old cemetery on Bulgaria's Black Sea coast has produced the largest-ever find of early gold products and illustrates the astonishing wealth of an Eastern European people emerging from the Copper Age. Apart from gold's ability to bestow status and power, the Varna people used it as a key component in their religious ritual. Their dead wore clay masks decorated with it; other bodies had sheets of gold encircling their clothes, and some had gold implements placed next to their genitals. The symbolism is far from clear, except that wealth was

right: This 4th–3rd millenium BC marble piece features gold incrustation. It was found in the Varna cemetery and is thought to represent a female idol.

regarded as equally important in death as in life.

A chance discovery

The cemetery was discovered by chance in 1972 during work on a cable trench along the northern bank of a lake—once part of the Black Sea—near the modern city of Varna. Over the next 14 years 281 late Copper Age graves were excavated across an area of 80,000 square feet (7,500 sq m), an estimated three-quarters of the original burial ground. Interestingly, one-fifth of these were

cenotaphs or "empty tombs" into which great riches had been placed despite the obvious lack of human remains. Only 23 of the graves failed to produce any artifacts. Sixty percent produced between one and ten while the rest proved extremely rich; containing anything up to 1,000 separate items. Curiously, most of the gold was found in the cenotaphs.

In each case the burial ritual was similar. A rectangular trench varying in depth from 8' (2.5m) to 1' (30 cm) was dug and the body (if there was a body) placed inside. Usually the deceased would be stretched out with grave goods arranged beside or on top of him. But sometimes a corpse was buried in the fetal position, with knees drawn up to the chest and head tucked down. Careful study of these

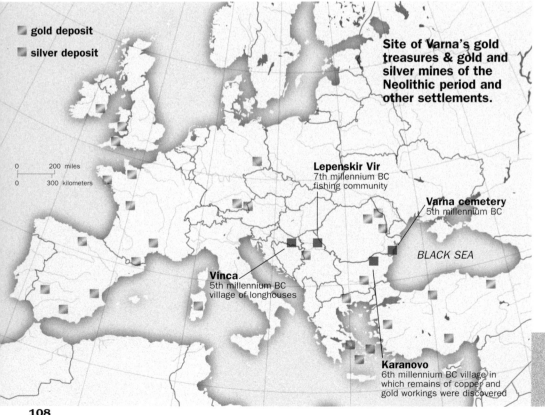

gold deposit
silver deposit

0 — 200 miles
0 — 300 kilometers

Site of Varna's gold treasures & gold and silver mines of the Neolithic period and other settlements.

Lepenskir Vir
7th millennium BC fishing community

Varna cemetery
5th millennium BC

BLACK SEA

Vinca
5th millennium BC village of longhouses

Karanovo
6th millennium BC village in which remains of copper and gold workings were discovered

4236 BC	c.4000 BC
First date in Egyptian calendar.	First farmers in Britain.

Varna treasures were fashioned at a time when prehistoric smiths were experimenting with high-temperature furnaces.

different styles has shown no difference in the type of accompanying artifacts and the reasoning involved can only be imagined.

Of the individual cenotaphs, the ones numbered one, four, and 36 stood out as particularly rich in gold objects. Number one contained 216, which together weighed 38 ounces (1,100g). Number four held 339 pieces together weighing 53 ounces (1,518g), and number 36 produced 857 items, collectively weighing 27.5 ounces (789g). In addition, numbers two, three, and 15 contained clay masks with male characteristics and traces of gold ornamentation. The masks were probably seen as a physical manifestation of the "soul"

they represented.

Among the actual burials, Grave 43 was the most outstanding. It revealed the skeleton of a man aged about 45 and 5'9" (1.75m) tall. Lying beside and on top of him were nearly 1000 gold items, including what may have been a "royal scepter" topped with a stone mace-head and plated with gold along the wooden handle. There were also heavy gold bands around his arms and more mundane items made in clay, stone, copper, and shell. The copper products—hammers, axes, cloak-pins, rings, and ornaments— proved particularly illuminating. Analysis showed these pieces to be among the oldest in Europe, fashioned at a time when prehistoric

above: *Overview of an exquisite shallow tray. The gold discoveries at Varna were found to be 1,500 years older than those of Troy.*

communities were experimenting with the extremely high temperatures demanded in their manufacture.

The Varna people certainly had plenty of precious metal with which to experiment. Large ore deposits are found to the north-west and south-west of their settlement, and in the village of Karanovo, some 150 miles west, remains of copper and gold workings have been dated as early as the sixth millennium BC. However, it is not yet clear whether this economic advantage created a true class structure of Copper Age "noblemen" or whether it was simply a step on the way to a more hierarchical society.

left: *Some graves at Varna held life-size clay masks with gold features, which may have represented a goddess of life and death.*

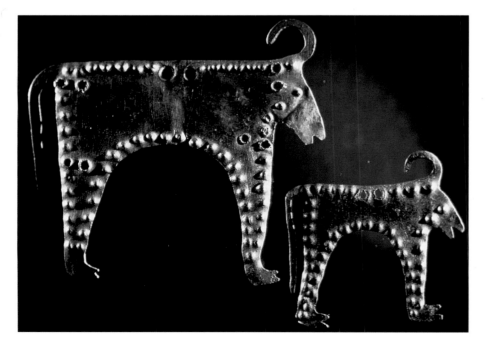

ÖTZI THE ICEMAN
Entombed in ice

The scene: A mountainside high in the Austrian Alps. Staggering beside a glacier, a lone traveler battles through a snowstorm, every step draining his last reserves of energy. Finally he can continue no longer. He collapses into the snow and, within the space of a few hours, has frozen to death. Later, his body is dried by a warm autumn wind before being subsumed into the unforgiving ice of the huge Similaun glacier as it flows down the Ötztaler Alps of South Tyrol.

That should have been the end of a sad, though quite common, story of everyday stone age folk going about their business. Yet in a rather

gruesome twist, the unfortunate man's body was not lost. More than 5,000 years later a sandstorm in the Sahara Desert blew a layer of dust high into the atmosphere, from where it settled on the Similaun glacier. The dust caused heat from the sun to be absorbed, surface layers of ice melted, and on September 19, 1991 a group of German hikers were presented with the ultimate in holiday snapshots—the preserved body of a prehistoric man.

Because of the location at 10,600 feet (3,200m) it was four days before Austrian authorities could recover the corpse and the leather, wood, grass, and flint items which accompanied it. The man—nicknamed Ötzi—was taken to the anatomy department of Innsbruck University and placed in a freezer at 10° Fahrenheit (–6°C) with

98 percent humidity. Over the next few months, forensic examination helped archeologists build up a unique picture of his health and lifestyle in a way that was previously the stuff of science fiction.

Ötzi's secrets revealed

They discovered that Ötzi was between 25 and 40 years of age when he died, about 5' 2" (1.6m) tall, weighed 120lb (54 kg) when found, and could be directly linked to northern European populations through analysis of his DNA. He had terribly worn teeth, suggesting either that he used them as a tool or that he ate a lot of crudely-ground grain.

below: *The body of Ötzi the iceman is carried to Innsbruck University. Forensic tests have yielded extraordinary detail about his life.*

Location of the Iceman of Tyrol discovery.

Alpine peaks above 13,000 feet

GERMANY

Innsbruck

AUSTRIA

River Inn

ATZTALER ALPS

Wildspitze Mountain

SWITZERLAND

Ötzi's copper ax

The Iceman of Tyrol discovered by German hikers near the Similaun Glacier, 300ft inside the Italian border

c.3500 BC	3500 BC	c.3500 BC	c.3200 BC	c.3100 BC	c.3100BC	c.3000 BC	c.3000 BC
First megalithic tombs and circles.	Earliest Chinese city (Lung-shan culture).	First alcoholic drinks made in Middle East.	Early Cycladic civilization in Aegean.	King Menes unites Egypt.	Pictographic writing invented in Sumer.	Village societies established in Amazon.	First stone temples erected in Malta.

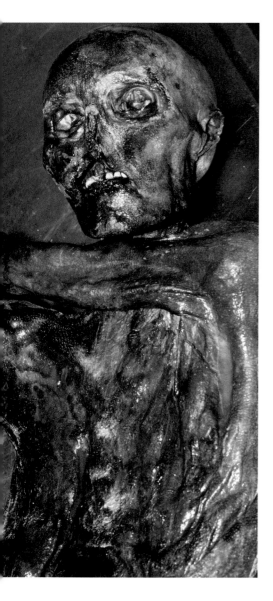

left: *Studies of the 5,000-year-old corpse showed that Ötzi was plagued with health problems before he succumbed to the ice.*

These were found on both sides of his lower back, his left calf, and right ankle, and took the form of a cross near his knee.

It seems likely that these tattoos were therapeutic rather than decorative. Ötzi was a martyr to arthritis in his right hip, lower back, and neck, and analysis of a finger nail showed that he went through lengthy periods of restricted nail growth (corresponding to poor health) over three distinct periods four, three, and two months before his death. He had eight rib fractures, which were either healed or healing, severely blackened lung tissue (too many open fires!), and chronic frostbite in one little toe. Given such a dismal medical record it is a wonder that he was out on the mountain at all, though of course we should not judge hardy stone age hunters by our own standards. Even so, his poor physique and painful limbs were most likely a factor in his demise.

It was later established that Ötzi was found 300 feet (92m) inside the Italian border, and after five years the Austrian authorities transported him back to Italy and a museum at Bolzen.

He was bald and had no beard, but hundreds of curly brownish hairs found near the body, and on his garments, indicated that he had had a haircut shortly before he died. There was a squarish impression in his earlobe—probably from ornamental stone jewelry, and a series of bizarre tattoo marks in the form of half-inch (1cm) blue lines.

The Neolithic clothing, weaponry, and outdoor survival equipment found with Ötzi shows astonishing levels of technical sophistication and handiwork skills. He carried a copper ax, a flint dagger set in ashwood, a sheath of woven grass, a sharpening tool, a hazel and larch backpack, a braided grass mat and grass "carrier bag," a birch-bark "lunchbox" containing a sloe berry (this suggests Ötzi died in the fall), two lumps of tree fungus known to have antibiotic properties (though they may also have been used as tinder), a bone-and-pitch "repair kit," a cloak of woven grass, a leather skirt, a fur cap, and size seven (in modern-day US-size) leather shoes which were heavily repaired. His main hunting weapon was a 6' (180cm) yew bow, probably smeared with animal fat to keep it supple. The deerskin quiver contained 14 30-inch (75cm) arrows, only two of which were sharp enough to fire. Remarkably, these arrows were finished with triple feathering which caused them to spin and fly true. Stone age man, it seems, understood the basics of ballistics.

Tattoo puncture marks on the body may have been an attempt to relieve arthritis.

c.3000 BC	c.2900 BC	c.2750 BC	c.2750 BC	c 2685 BC
Plow first used in China.	First pottery in Americas (Ecuador/Columbia).	Growth of civilizations in Indus valley.	*Epic of Gilgamesh*, an account of a great flood, written in Babylon.	Old Kingdom of Egypt founded; pyramid building begins.

SACRIFICE OR EXECUTION?

Tollund Man

Just as the ice preserved Ötzi, so the acidic peatlands of northern Europe have prevented so-called Bog Bodies from decomposing. Over the years several hundred have been found, usually by laborers cutting peat, and they appear to have been ritually killed; either to present as a sacrifice or as capital punishment. Most of the bodies are dated between the third century BC and the fourth century AD—a time when normal funerary tradition involved cremation—and it may be that the use of peat bogs fulfilled a religious function. Bogs, lakes, and rivers were considered to be dwelling houses of the gods, and weapons and other metal objects were regularly deposited in them as offerings. Outstanding among these is a beautiful silver cauldron of Celtic design found at Gundestrup, Denmark, close to three bog burials. It has 13 separate reliefs, each of which feature a Celtic deity surrounded by actual and mythological animals and various scenes of sacrifice. It is believed to date from around 200 BC and probably came from south-east Europe.

The most famous of all the bog bodies is Tollund Man. He was discovered by two peat cutters at Tollund Fen, Denmark, on May 8, 1950, and when police were called they at first assumed he was the victim of a recent murder. The skin and facial features of the man were perfectly defined, to the point that every wrinkle on his face and the stubble

left: *A cast taken from the head of Tollund Man.*
above: *Illustration showing the position the body was found in.*

c.290 BC	262 BC	224 BC	221 BC	218 BC	206 BC	202 BC	200 BC
Alexandrian library founded.	Ashoka, Mauryan emperor, converts to Buddhism.	Colossus of Rhodes, one of the Seven Wonders, destroyed in an earthquake.	Ch'in dynasty unites China.	Hannibal of Carthage invades Italy.	Rome gains control of Spain.	Han dynasty reunites China.	Etruria falls to the Romans.

A gruesome discovery in the peat bogs of Denmark. Was it ritual sacrifice, or an act of murder?

hair on his chin could be seen. Only the skeletal appearance of the body, and its black coloring, betrayed the time he had lain underground. An archeologist, Peter Glob, soon assured detectives that their only potential witnesses had died two thousand years ago.

Tollund Man was lying naked, except for a leather hood and belt. His eyes were shut and his lips were pursed, almost as though he had been meditating on his fate. The leather noose by which he had been hanged was still in place around his neck and his knees were drawn up to his stomach in the fetal position. We know from a post-mortem examination that his internal organs

were intact and that his last meal was a porridge of barley and wild seeds. The seeds would have been found in late winter or early spring, suggesting that he was killed around that time of year. Other bog people have been found to have similar stomach contents, and some archeologists believe grain porridge was a ritual meal eaten shortly before death.

A cruel death—but why?

Were they criminals, chosen sacrifices—or perhaps both? The jury remains out on this. It is certainly true that some bog victims died agonizing and violent deaths. The Grauballe Man of Denmark (c.310 AD) was found with his throat slit from ear to ear. The Huldremose Woman (c.100 AD), again of Denmark, had been viciously hacked, with her right arm cut off altogether. The Yde Girl of Holland (c.first century AD) had been strangled. The Lindow Man (c.second century AD) found in Cheshire, England, had been struck on his head, garotted, and stabbed in his throat. Gruesome executions were common. An Anglo-Saxon grave (not linked to any bog) at Sewerby in East Yorkshire, England contained the body of a woman who had been buried alive. She was thrown on top of the

coffin of a younger woman, perhaps someone she had allegedly murdered, and weighted down with a rock on her back. Her legs were kicked out, her elbows raised, and her fists tightly clenched indicating her last desperate struggles to escape the inevitable.

Historians such as the Roman Cornelius Tacitus believed bog burial was a punishment in northern Europe for such "crimes" as homosexuality, cowardice, or desertion in battle. It does seem that during the Iron Age, criminals were sometimes executed by being pinned underwater with forked branches and then tossed into a sacred lake or bogland as an offering to appease the gods. Yet although this would account for some of the bog finds, it cannot easily explain all of them. For one thing, there are plenty of female victims— even teenage girls. The Windeby Girl of northern Germany (c.first century AD) was aged barely 14, was blindfolded, and had the left side of her hair shaved off. Other bog bodies were apparently people of status, in that they bore no calluses from manual labor on their hands and had been carefully groomed in preparation for their fate. It is possible that being chosen for ritual killing was an honor, not a punishment.

Tolland Man and associated Iron Age bog sites in Denmark.

0   100 miles

0   160 kilometers

Gundestrop Cauldron found near three bog bodies

JUTLAND

Grauballe Man bog body ■

Tollund Man bog body ■   ●*Arhus*

DENMARK

c.200 BC	c.200 BC	c.200 BC	168 BC	149 BC
Hopewell culture emerges in North American midwest.	Kush (Nubia) develops relations with Pharaonic Egypt.	Teotihuacán emerges from village culture.	Rome defeats Macedonia.	Rome destroys Carthage.

VIKING BURIAL SHIPS
Voyages to Valhalla

The Vikings were obsessed with ships. Their fast, elegant vessels were the key to military power, status, wealth (through pillage-and-plunder coastal raids), adventure, and exploration. Just as crucially, they served as symbols of rebirth following death and a means of traveling into the afterlife. Unlike Christian preachers, who eschewed grave goods and regarded earthly prosperity as meaningless in heaven, Viking poets and saga-tellers had no doubt that a rich man would need all his possessions for the afterlife. Typically, these would include his ship, servants, weapons, wagons, horses, clothing, jewelry, utensils, and even food. The whole approach was one of fatalism. A chieftain in this life would sail off to be a chieftain in the next. A slave could expect more slavery to come. Only a slain warrior could seriously hope to advance his standing by being chosen for eternal feasting in the halls of Valhalla.

The Norse people accepted that the journey into death was spiritual. Burial in an actual ship wasn't strictly necessary because of course not everyone had one. Heathen customs also varied widely. For instance some of the cremated bodies in shallow graves at Lindholm Hoje, in northern Jutland, Denmark, had been burned elsewhere before being taken to the sacred ground and placed in oval stone settings representing ships. Once the symbolic purpose of the stones had been achieved—and the dead person's journey to the god Odin and his Valkyries (handmaidens) adjudged complete—they could be taken up for re-use.

Of the true ship burials so far discovered, two—at Gokstad and Oseberg in Norway—stand out as intriguing time capsules of ninth century Viking life. The Gokstad vessel was found beneath a mound in 1880 and proved to be an 83 foot-long (25m) warship, equipped with both oars and sails. It was built in the time-honored Norse way with overlapping horizontal strakes or planks caulked with animal hair, a slim, shallow profile, and a deep keel. This ensured it was strong enough to handle long sea journeys yet sufficiently maneuverable to enter inland rivers and make landfalls wherever the

above: *A close-up of the intricate carving that has become synonymous with the Oseberg ship. This detail comes from the corner of a sledge.*

master found a convenient beach. Thousands of coastal and riverside communities across Europe learned to their cost how Viking raiders could launch surprise attacks from seemingly unnavigable waters.

The Gokstad ship contained a

The Gokstad and Oseberg sites and other important viking communities.

Kaupang
Viking community c.9th century AD

Bergen

Gokstad
Viking boat burial c.9th century AD

Oseberg
Viking boat burial 9th century AD

Oslo

Valsgarde
Viking chieftain burial site

Birka
Viking trading center

Stockholm

Helgo
Viking village

Gothenberg

775 AD	781 AD	794 AD
Kingdom of Srijaya conquers Malaysia.	Christianity spreads to China.	Capital of Japan is moved to Kyoto.

Only slain warriors could hope to join an eternal feast in the halls of Valhalla.

wooden burial chamber with the skeleton of a man inside. Most of his valuable grave goods had been taken by robbers long ago but there were still the remains of 12 horses, six dogs, and bizarrely, a peacock. There was also a sledge, some small boats, and a massive cauldron. It was a similar story with the Oseberg vessel, found 23 years later, which some scholars believe is the grave of the imperious and manipulative Viking queen Asa (died c.ninth century AD). This burial ship had been robbed of personal items but contained the bodies of two women (one young, one old) together with the skeletons of horses and oxen, a bed, blankets, domestic equipment, and a cart. The saving grace for archeologists was the discovery of wood carvings of immense quality, such as could only have been commissioned by royalty. Thanks to the blue clay and peat soil in which the vessel was buried, this work survived the ravages of time.

Intricate carvings

The best carvings were found on the ship's prow, the cart, and three of the sledges. There are long scrolls of interwoven animal patterns, cartoon-like figures of multi-armed "gripping beasts" (so-named because they are always depicted grabbing themselves, their frames, and surrounding images), elaborate animal heads on the corners of sledges (probably to ward off evil spirits), and pictures of battles between fantastic mythological beasts. One carving, on the front panel of the wagon, shows a man grappling with snakes while a toad-like monster bites him from the side. Quite what all this was supposed to prove in the afterlife is unclear but it seems the lavish intricacy of the Oseberg artwork was in any case only temporarily fashionable.

By the tenth century Viking artists were turning their emphasis towards composition and cleaner, flowing lines.

above: *Hilt of a Viking sword. Fine weapons were both an aid to piracy and a means of legitimate trade.*

below: *The Oseberg ship. Interior carvings were of such fine quality that they could only have been commissioned by royalty.*

800 AD	c.800 AD	c.840 AD	850 AD	863 AD	c.873 AD	878 AD	930 AD
Charlemagne becomes Holy Roman Emperor.	Abbasid culture reaches its height in Mesopotamia.	Arab world invents algebra.	Beginning of Jewish Yiddish community in Germany.	Cyrillic alphabet is created in eastern Europe.	Arabs invent concept of zero in mathematics.	Danes defeated and expelled from Wessex.	Cordoba in Spain is a center of Arab science and trade.

TEMPLES OF MALTA
Stone Age Sophistication

When 18th- and 19th-century travelers began studying the stone temples of Malta, they concluded that the work must have been influenced by the Egyptians, or possibly the great cultures of the Eastern Mediterranean. They were spectacularly wrong. From what we now know, these huge megalithic structures were built long before the rise of the Persians and even before the siting of the first pyramids. If anything, they have more in common with stone age architecture in the British Isles (such as Stonehenge and Maes Howe), and were built at about the same time (c.3000 BC) by an

island "pocket" of Neolithic people able to deploy sophisticated construction techniques.

Just as Stonehenge presented immense transport and logistics problems for its designers, so the Maltese builders had to develop ways of hauling stones weighing 50 tons (51,000 kg) and more using a presumably very limited labor force. They had no metal tools, and certainly no knowledge of writing, yet they appear to have been sufficiently organized to build more than 20 temples while still finding time to farm and fish. One of the most impressive is the great temple at Mnajdra which has a monumental

"trilithon" doorway in which two vertical stones support an overhead crosspiece. Close inspection of the walls here show that they curve inwards as they get higher, suggesting a possible corbelled roof in which projecting stones support those above them.

The Fat Lady of Tarxien
Another outstanding feature of the temples is their statuary, particularly the Fat Lady of Tarxien. She should more correctly be called the "Fat Lady's Legs," as these, together with her skirt, are all that remain. At one time, this statue was about 10 feet (3m) high and probably represented a

below: *An entranceway into one of the Maltese temples. The use of megaliths is evidence of a highly-organized society.*

left: The ruins of a temple complex stand starkly above the Mediterraenean Sea.

below left: A stone altar decorated with spiral patterns. Spiral designs were popular in a number of prehistoric European cultures.

goddess, though it is hard to say which one. Fat lady statues are common in the other temples and may be linked to a female cult of various different deities, the worship of a single idol, or the adaptation of religious mythology from overseas. The Tarxien goddess's appearance is characterized by her outrageously plump thighs and hips; perhaps in recognition of her fertility or simply a way of emphasizing her physical size, and therefore importance. Excavations at this temple have produced a decorated altar and a flint knife thought to have been used for killing sacrifices. A much later cremation cemetery nearby, which dates from around 1400 BC, has yielded pottery and metal daggers.

The Maltese builders kept their dead well away from the temples. Instead of creating nearby burial sites they carved huge tombs, known as hypogeums, out of solid rock and used them for the interment of cremated remains. The hypogeum of Hal Saflieni—discovered by builders working on a new housing estate—is one of the finest examples. It contains a network of some 20 chambers and linked corridors, many of which displayed the rock-carved architectural features of conventional above-ground structures, such as beams and lintels. Some walls were decorated with pictures of cattle. It is possible that these tombs, entered through a roof opening, governed the shape of the later temples. Certainly the Hal Saflieni

complex was in use for many hundreds of years judging by the remains of the 7,000 bodies it housed.

Other Neolithic Sites of Malta

During the late fourth and third millennium BC an innovative Neolithic civilization appears to have prospered both in Malta and some 100 miles north in Sicily. It is likely that there were cultural links between the two islands; the hundreds of rock-cut tombs at Castelluccio, Sicily, bear obvious comparison with early Maltese funerary tradition. Apart from Tarxien, the two most important sites on Malta are Ggantija—a temple apparently dedicated to a nature goddess—and the Brochtorff circle complex in which a tomb with twin chambers contained the remains of some 60 bodies. The Brochtorff central shrine involved worship to various idols, including a carved human head, a rock-carved pig, and a stone storage jar.

2nd–4th millennium temple sites of Malta and Gozo.

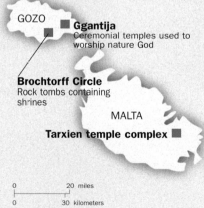

GOZO
Ggantija
Ceremonial temples used to worship nature God

Brochtorff Circle
Rock tombs containing shrines

MALTA

Tarxien temple complex ■

| 0 | 20 miles |
| 0 | 30 kilometers |

Statues of obese women may have been linked to a Maltese female or goddess cult.

CHAPTER EIGHT

RUSSIA AND CENTRAL ASIA

If modern man was born in Africa, Asia was where he grew up. Here, over a million years, the first primitive colonists edged ever northward in search of new hunting grounds; an advance halted only by sporadic shifts from a warm to cold global climate. At some point in Earth's recent past—perhaps only 12,000 years ago—the people who really discovered North America struck out across a narrow strip of land linking Asia and Alaska; land that briefly emerged as sea levels were reduced by the advancing ice. From here, so one popular theory goes, they colonized the whole of the Americas.

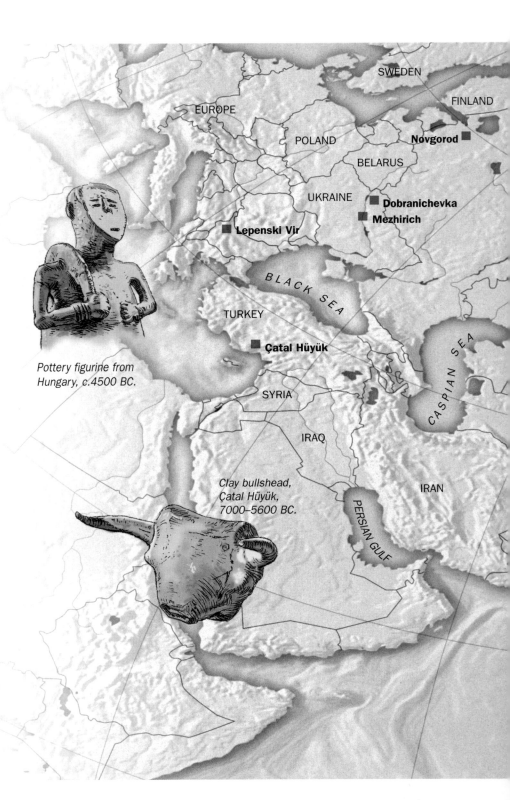

Pottery figurine from Hungary, c.4500 BC.

Clay bullshead, Çatal Hüyük, 7000–5600 BC.

below: *A tripod-shaped altar found in Serbia.*

But central Asia offers much more of an archeological legacy than the mere study of humans in transit. In the mammoth-bone homes of Russia it shows the resourcefulness of early humans battling to survive unimaginably hostile conditions. At the fishing village of Lepenski Vir there is fascinating evidence of an "island culture" in which a traditional way of life was pursued despite major advances in food production nearby. There is the stone age metropolis of Çatal Hüyük, a thriving settlement of 6,000 people that effectively invented urban man. Further east, one of the greatest and most mysterious of the early civilizations—the Indus—emerged to dominate a huge expanse of western India and Pakistan.

Much later, as the Vikings began their assault on western Europe, the first princes of central Russia were carving out their petty kingdoms and city-states, capitals such as the fantastic medieval city of Novgorod with its wooden streets and dwellings. It was here that the awesome hordes of Genghis Khan's successors were finally halted—more out of frustration at the impenetrable bogs and forests than from fear of their enemies.

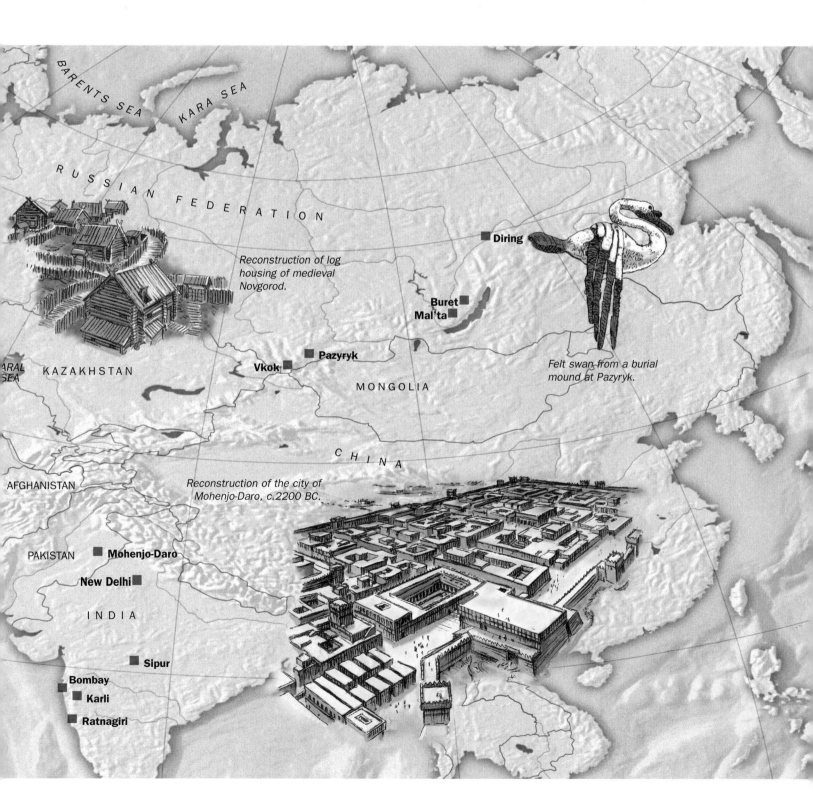

Reconstruction of log housing of medieval Novgorod.

Felt swan from a burial mound at Pazyryk.

Reconstruction of the city of Mohenjo-Daro, c.2200 BC.

HUMAN COLONIZATION OF ASIA
Out of the ice

About two million years ago the first early *homo erectus* humans began to move eastward out of Africa to explore the tropics of central Asia. A million years later the descendents of these colonists were pushing north into a cooler, more temperate climate, and by about 700,000 BC they had settled north of latitude 45° (a line roughly bisecting southern France, the Black Sea, and northern China). These estimates are, it must be said, little

more than estimates. A *homo erectus* jaw and crude stone tools have been found at Dmanisi, in the southern Caucasus mountains of Georgia. These could well date from 1.5 million years ago. Similarly, stone choppers found at Diring, beside the River Lena in Siberia, are thought by some experts to date back a million years—even though the site is 61° latitude and does not match the model theory outlined above. Controversy over these finds seems unlikely to go away.

Neither can we be sure of the various population spreads between *homo erectus*, our own larger-brained *homo sapiens* species, and the European Neanderthal. There are various theories as to why *homo sapiens* emerged as the dominant human form (*see Africa chapter*) but for many thousands of years different types of early human beings coexisted across southern Europe and Asia. One generally accepted view is that the advance north was fueled by an increasing emphasis on meat in the diet, resulting in a need to establish new hunting grounds and temporary settlements. The cooler winters would have forced the colonists to adapt,

left: *Asia has produced some great innovative design such as this 5th–4th millenium BC carpet; the oldest yet discovered.*

Frozen Mummies

Siberia's Altai mountains contain some spectacular frozen tombs dating to much more recent times. Two complexes in particular—at Pazyryk and Ukok—have produced unprecedented detail about the lives of an Iron Age people for whom horses were an integral part of a nomadic life. These tribes would wander far across the mountains, herding sheep and conducting trade as far distant as China and Persia. The consistent low temperatures within the tombs ensured the mummification of bodies inside, some of which were tattooed with imaginative images of wild beasts. Grave goods included leather clothing, felt wall hangings, gold and silver ornaments, jewelry , mirrors, textiles, and wooden trays of jointed horsemeat and mutton. In one grave at Ukok six dead horses had been laid at the entrance to the burial chamber—each killed with a blow to the head.

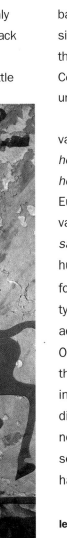

RUSSIAN

Modern political boundaries

Pazyryk

Ukok ■

● Karaganda

KAZAKHSTAN

CHINA

c.4,000,000 BC	c.3,800,000 BC	c.2,000,000 BC	c.700,000 BC	c.250,000 BC
Bipedal (walking on two legs) hominids evolve.	Early hominids live in nuclear family groups.	*Homo erectus* humans begin to move out of Africa to colonize Asia.	*Homo erectus* people live north of 45° latitude.	Some *Homo erectus* populations begin to develop *Homo sapiens* characteristics.

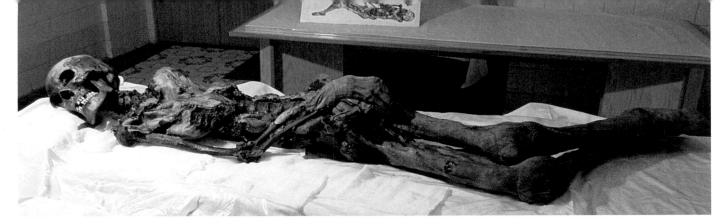

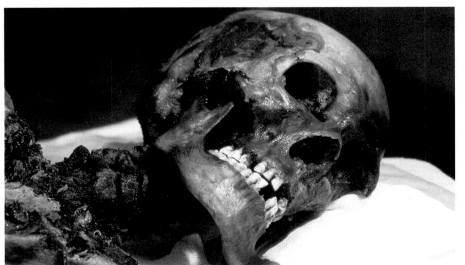

above and left: *The discovery of early human bones and stone tools in Georgia and Siberia is controversial, with some experts attributing dates of 1.5 million years BC. The body and skull of this young woman—well preserved in the ice—is much more recent: c.500 BC.*

seeking out alternative diets, developing warmer clothes, and controlling the use of fire. There is a plausible theory that modern humans were simply better organized than their Neanderthal cousins and this, above all else, helped them become more resourceful and successful.

Whereas central and western Asia had been widely settled by c.500,000 BC, the same was not true of the frozen north! It is likely that the first colonists of the central Russian plains—around Khotylevo on the Desna River for instance or the Altai region of southern Siberia—were relatives of European Neanderthals. Although their fossil remains are extremely rare, the dating of their tools suggests they had no foothold here until c.150,000 BC. During an Ice Age (c.70,000 BC) it is thought these northern outposts were abandoned by the Neanderthal-types, who never returned. Thousands of years later the settlers who replaced them were modern humans.

Onward to the Americas

A crucial clue to the global spread of humanity has now been discovered by Russian archeologists beside a river at Berlekh, in north-eastern Siberia. With its latitude of 71° North, a point inside the Arctic Circle, this 12,000-year-old temporary summer hunting camp is the most northerly Ice Age settlement in the world. The conventional theory is that from areas such as this, prehistoric explorers set out across a land bridge formed by the lowering of sea levels (the result of the advancing ice line). This link allowed them to walk between north-east Asia and Alaska, and strike south and east to discover the New World.

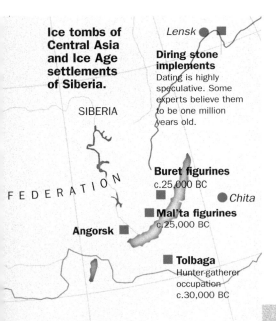

Ice tombs of Central Asia and Ice Age settlements of Siberia.

Lensk ●

Diring stone implements
Dating is highly speculative. Some experts believe them to be one million years old.

SIBERIA

FEDERATION

Chita ●

Buret figurines
c.25,000 BC

Mal'ta figurines
c.25,000 BC

Angorsk ■

Tolbaga
Hunter-gatherer occupation c.30,000 BC

MONGOLIA

0 — 200 miles
0 — 300 kilometers

Prehistoric explorers
set out across a land bridge formed by the lowering of sea levels.

c.100,000 BC	c.50,000 BC	c.30,000 BC	c.30,000 BC	c.25,000 BC
True *Homo sapiens* emerges in Middle East.	Earliest cave art in Australia.	Neanderthal people disappear completely after being slowly replaced by *Homo sapiens*.	Most of inhabitable world has been colonized.	Cave art created in Europe.

NOVGOROD AND MEDIEVAL RUSSIA
Secrets of a city-state

One of the oldest cities in Russia, Novgorod was founded around the 5th century AD on the banks of the Volkhov River near Lake Il'men. In 862 AD it became the royal capital of Rurik, Prince of Novgorod (who effectively created the Russian monarchy), and by 1136 it had won independence from Kiev to form its own mini-kingdom or "city-state." As capital of Great Novgorod during the 13th and 14th centuries it became a key farming and trade center, and later an outpost of the Hanseatic League—a group of trading partners in the Baltic, northern Germany, and central Europe. The city saw off invasions by the Tatars (*see box*) late in the 13th century but in 1478 was overrun by its main rival, Moscow, under Ivan The Great, and its influence gradually declined.

The archeological wonders of Novgorod were not fully appreciated until 1929 when the first digs began under Artemii Artsikhovsky. He confirmed that there were many different periods of construction and found that remnants of timber buildings and wood-surfaced streets had been superbly preserved in the waterlogged clay soil. Since 1950 Novgorod has been regarded as a jewel in Russian history and excavations have continued pretty well non-stop, although the economic crisis of the late 1990s has taken an inevitable toll on funding. This work has given us a fresh understanding of how medieval builders operated and analysis of tree rings in the larger posts has meant dates can be attributed to within 25 years. Equally important has been the discovery of leather and wooden utensils, exquisitely crafted toys, and evidence of the craft skills which powered the city's economy, such as jewelry and shoe making, metalwork, and glassware.

Ordinary homes at Novgorod were built of timber according to traditional models, some of which rose two or even three storeys. They were mostly detached, had their own backyards enclosed by wooden fencing, and occupied residential quarters around the central kremlin or government citadel. The whole city was linked by a network of wooden streets in which three or four long, thin poles were laid lengthways and covered with split logs placed side-by-side to form the street surface. As the logs deteriorated so a new set would be placed on top. At one intersection 28 separate road surfaces have been discovered, dating between 953 AD and 1462 AD.

Medieval manuscripts
The other extraordinary revelation at Novgorod was the surprising level of literacy among the inhabitants. Since 1951 more than 700 birch-bark manuscripts known as *beresty* have been recovered detailing everything from the minutæ of household stores to records of diplomatic and political machinations, and the state of commercial markets. Beresty were

left: *The hub of medieval Novgorod was its kremlin (citadel). Excavators first discovered the birch-bark manuscripts in the Nerevsky district.*

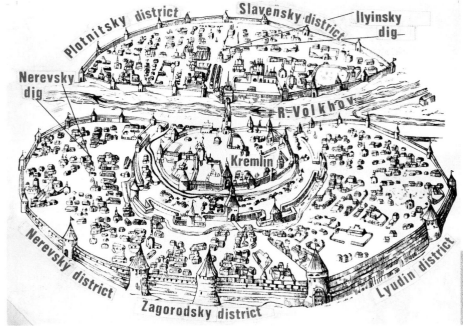

410 AD	c.630 AD	c.1000 AD
Roman Empire is invaded and collapses.	Mohammed founds Islam.	Vikings land in North America.

The army of Genghis Khan's grandson Batu became bogged down in swampland south of Novgorod.

above: *The Cathedral of S. Sofia provides a softer contrast to the power of the Novgorod Kremlin walls,* **left.**

produced by boiling chunks of birch-bark to remove the rough exterior. Once dry, the fine inner layers could be inscribed with a sharpened piece of bone or metal; like using a pen with no ink. The first of these documents, found in the Nerevsky district, were dated to the end of the 14th century but it is thought there may be anything up to 20,000 more lying deeper in the ground. Some of these may well have been written as early as the mid-11th century, holding out the prospect of important breakthroughs in our knowledge of medieval Russia.

Novgorod versus Genghis Khan

In the 13th century the Russian princes faced the first great challenge to their sovereignty from the mighty Mongol armies of Genghis Khan. These forces swept up from the south-east, routing a Russian alliance in the 1223 Battle of Kalka. Despite the vulnerability of his enemy's cities, the Khan recalled the invaders to eastern Asia, and it was not until 1237 that his grandson, Batu Khan, returned intent on conquest. Batu's Tatars (a people originally from Siberia) marched north, seizing and sacking every major town between Kiev and Moscow until they became bogged down in forest and swampland south of Novgorod. This probably saved the city from destruction and Batu turned south-west to ravage Poland and Hungary, and consolidate his "Golden Horde" empire.

above: *A piece of beresty, the birch-bark manuscripts which have provided great insights into medieval urban life. More than 20,000 may still await discovery.*

Novgorod and other Baltic pre-medieval sites.

SWEDEN

GULF OF BOTHNIA

FINLAND

RUSSIAN FEDERATION

Lake Lagoda

Soukajnen
Cairns containing rich hoard of 4th century AD weapons

St. Petersberg

Helsinki

ALAND

Yliskyla
c.AD600 boat grave and cemetery

Toompea Castle
14th century AD medieval castle built by Danes

ESTONIA

Exports
Leather goods, jewelry, metalwork, glass objects

Novgorod medieval city c.9th century AD

BALTIC SEA

LATVIA

| 0 | miles | 100 |
| 0 | kilometers | 150 |

c.1000 AD	1066 AD	c.1250 AD
Polynesians arrive in New Zealand.	Invasion of England by Norman French.	Expansion of Mongol Empire across Asia and Europe.

THE RIVER PEOPLE OF LEPENSKI VIR
Ancient civilization on the Danube

In 1960 members of the Belgrade Archeological Institute were probing likely prehistoric sites along the Danube when they noticed some fragments of pottery protruding from a river bank beside the great whirlpool of Lepenski Vir. Closer inspection showed these were mildly interesting relics from the Starchevo group, the oldest culture of the Danube Basin's neolithic age, but they aroused no great excitement. They would be recorded in a log and filed in some dusty storage room.

Five years later, following the announcement of plans for the joint Yugoslav-Romanian Djerdap hydro-electric dam which would flood many of the Danube's Carpathian Mountain gorges, the University of Belgrade moved in to conduct "rescue" digs at previously identified locations. The operation at Lepenski Vir, run by Dragoslav Srejovic, was considered routine. His archeological team began sinking trial trenches, more in hope than in expectation. A week later they were re-writing history.

Spectacular discoveries

The results from the trenches were nothing short of amazing. Beneath the unremarkable pottery layer Srejovic discovered a completely unknown 7,000-year-old society that

above: *A mask retrieved from the Lepenski Vir site. This possibly represented a god in human form.*

built strange trapezoid buildings arranged so that their wide ends faced the river. The 25 houses were methodically planned (unusual in prehistoric Europe), and they ranged in size from 300 square feet (28 sq m) to 59 square feet (5.5 sq m). As in so many other stone age communities there was a clear recognition that the dead remained a part of the community. The remains of several burials were found within the settlement. Each house was furnished with a central stone-lined hearth sunk into a limestone plaster floor bounded by stone slabs. The roofs were lightly constructed using twigs and saplings, and the interior was decorated with elaborately carved

Lepenski Vir village and later Neolithic sites of western Asia.

c.8000 BC	c.6500 BC
Bow and arrow used in Europe.	Earliest known metallurgy, in Middle East.

They seemed to have adopted an island mentality, cutting themselves off from neighboring people.

boulders up to 2 feet (60cm) high. These limestone rocks—among the earliest examples of three-dimensional stone sculpture—bore humanish faces with fish-like mouths and a decoration thought to resemble scales. Their precise significance remains unclear but, given that fish formed a major part of the Lepenski Vir community's diet, it seems likely they had a religious symbolism, especially as they were often placed next to hearths (fire may have been symbolically linked to the creation of life).

There has been speculation that the sculptures were carved to represent a River God. All we can say for sure is that they fall into three distinct categories: the fish heads; abstract patterns which show no obvious representation; and stones which hint at portraits or undefinable images. All of them are unique in stone age culture—a fact reflected in the 1995 decision by the United Nations Educational, Scientific, and Cultural Organization (UNESCO) to fund the cost of all remaining excavation and protect the site for future generations.

Lepenski Vir's location was heavily influenced by the river whirlpool. This traps algae and lures fish in, ensuring that catches could be made simply and easily through all the seasons. However like other fishing communities in Romania and Serbia, such as Padina, Icoana, Schela Cladovei, and Vlasac, the Lepenski Vir people faced a slow transition from hunting food to farming it. Because of their dependence on the river this transition

left: *A mother-and-child sculpture. This figure may have represented some kind of fertility cult.*

above: *The spectacular "Iron Gates"—the series of gorges that mark the Danube's course through the Carpathian Mountains.*

occurred some two thousand years later than in other parts of central Europe, although by around 5,000 BC they had begun using the sheltered environment provided by hills surrounding the gorge to grow crops and keep domestic animals. Their links with surrounding communities is difficult to assess. In some respects they seem to have adopted an island mentality, cutting themselves off from neighboring people. However there are also persuasive arguments that their artwork influenced ideas at the 4th millennium BC settlement of nearby Vinca, where outstanding examples of a dark burnished pottery have been found.

c.6000 BC	c.6000 BC	c.6000 BC	c.5000 BC	c.5000 BC	c.5000 BC	c.4000 BC	c.4000 BC
Çatal Hüyük flourishes.	First known pottery and woollen textiles (Çatal Hüyük).	Rice cultivation begins in Thailand.	Irrigation techniques developed in Mesopotamia.	First metal tools appear.	Yangshao culture in China produces painted pottery.	First use of plow.	Neolithic settlements flourish in the Balkans.

ÇATAL HÜYÜK
A stone age city

In the years between the eighth and sixth millennium BC the steady advance of Neolithic technology turned into a full-scale revolution. It wasn't just the advances in farming, grain storage, the widening of trade links, and metallurgy experiments with furnaces (important though these were)—neolithic people also began to see the advantages of living together in larger communities. The old nomadic hunting ways were becoming a thing of the past. Of the new cities, Çatal Hüyük, on the Konya plain of south-central Turkey, was like no other. Along with Jericho, it remains the most important Neolithic site in the Near East.

A typical stone age settlement, even by 4000 BC, would be no larger than five to 10 acres (two to four ha), and house a population of perhaps three to four hundred. Jericho was unusually bigger but it paled by comparison to the full-scale metropolis that was Çatal Hüyük. At its peak (c.6250 BC –5400 BC) the city occupied around 50 acres (20 ha) and may have held up to 6,000 people at any one time. This also illustrates how compact it was. There were no streets or grand open squares. Instead, a vast assembly of timber-framed mudbrick houses were packed into one massive tenement, punctuated by the occasional small courtyard. For those joining the community there must have been a hint of culture shock. You entered your house down a ladder from the rooftop door. Your furnishings were simple and practical—fixed clay platforms, benches, hearths, ovens, and waste bins—but you plastered and painted your walls, spread rush matting on your floor, and arranged expensive imported possessions around the place. Oh, and you buried your relatives under the living room floor.

Funerary practices

As seen in previous chapters, stone age man liked to stay close to his ancestors. The funerary arrangements at Çatal Hüyük involved digging a family crypt that was repeatedly re-

below: *The massive Sphinx Gate at Çatal Hüyük was constructed around 1350 BC.*

Flesh was removed from corpses by leaving the dead exposed to vultures outside the city.

above: *An ornamental stag probably made in Çatal Hüyük around 2000 BC.*

opened as necessary. In some cases flesh and tissue was removed from the corpses, perhaps by leaving them exposed to vultures outside the city, and many bodies were wrapped in cloth and placed on their left side. Bones were often sprinkled with red ochre (a form of iron oxide), green malachite, or blue azurite. Analysis of these has shown that many citizens suffered from a persistent anemia, probably caused by a high incidence of malaria. The average life expectancy was 30 for women and 34 for men, and the lower age for women may be partly explained by a high fatality rate among pregnant mothers. There is evidence of a mother-goddess religious cult; some figurines show a plump, seated woman giving birth.

Grave goods included exotic imports; turquoise, sea shells, quality flints, and copper and lead objects which rank among the oldest-known examples of Near East metalworking. These items reflect the success of the city's economy. The nearby area was blessed with a ready supply of obsidian, a natural glass used to make extremely sharp stone tools, and some products found their way as far as southern Palestine and Jericho. Çatal Hüyük's geographical position on key trade routes was a crucial factor in nurturing other craft skills and exports included linen colored with geometric designs which were possibly imprinted with the many carved stone stamps found during excavations. Pottery was still in its infancy and the vessels produced were practical rather than beautiful.

Everything we know about the city suggests its people were followers of sophisticated rituals and attached great importance to symbolic art. Some wall murals have unfathomable meanings—such as a dancing man sporting what appears to be a spotted bow tie around his midriff—while others involved geometric shapes, landscapes, hunting scenes, decapitated bodies beside vultures, animals (especially leopards), people, and human breasts. As in other prehistoric societies, bulls seem to have been sacred. Bulls' horns were often fitted to the ends of platforms, and occasionally several pairs were set in opposite rows down the length of benches.

Çatal Hüyük and associated Neolithic sites.

BLACK SEA

CASPIAN SEA

GEORGIA

• Ankara

TURKEY

Yazilikaya
13th century BC Hittite rock sanctuary

Taurus Mountains

■ **Cayonu**
9th/7th millennium BC agricultural center

IRAN

Çatal Hüyük
6th millennium BC mud house "metropolis"

Hureya
7th/6th millennium BC early farming community

MEDITERRANEAN

IRAQ

SYRIA

0 miles 200
0 kilometres 300

c.7000 BC	c.6500 BC	4236 BC	c.4000 BC	c.4000 BC	c.3500 BC	c.3500 BC	c.3100 BC
Early experiments with copper ores in Anatolia.	First farming in Greece and Aegean.	First date in Egyptian calendar.	First farmers in Britain.	Cities emerge in Euphrates valley, Mesopotamia.	First megalithic tombs and circles.	Earliest Chinese city (Lung-shan culture).	Pictographic writing invented in Sumer.

INDUS VALLEY CIVILIZATION
Priest-Kings of Mohenjo-Daro

Mohenjo-Daro and Harappa are the two defining cities of the Indus Valley civilization which once covered huge tracts of modern Pakistan and north-west India. This Bronze Age culture, comparable to the Minoans of Crete or Egypt before the pharaohs, thrived around 2200 BC and was highly organized, even regimented, in its precise town planning and attitude to fashion. Similar, sometimes identical, artifacts have been found up to 750 miles (1,200 km) apart indicating a uniformity of thought which might not be expected in communities from such diverse locations as the Himalayas and the Indian Ocean coast. There were no obvious signs of palaces or royal leadership but one theory is that this culture was dominated by priest-kings who imposed power through manipulating religious belief rather than using force of arms.

Mohenjo-Daro was laid out in two sections; an inner citadel separated by an open space from a lower residential sector. The

left: *A bronze statue c.2000 BC. The bangles encasing one arm reflected a fashion trend of the time.*

citadel represented the center of government and religious life and contained a number of what are considered to be public buildings built on a huge mudbrick "raft" extending over 20 acres (8 ha), and rising about 20 feet (6m) to protect it from floods. The buildings included a large grain store, an asphalt-lined bath (probably used for religious purification ceremonies), a mini-complex of rooms known, rightly or wrongly, as the priests' quarters, and a large assembly hall in which the roof was supported by stone pillars. The lower district covered about 250 acres (101 ha) and held anything up to 40,000 people at the peak of its occupation. Public hygiene was considered an important part of social order and an efficient sewer, complete with covered drains, connected to private houses—many of which were several storeys high and grouped around a communal courtyard. The streets themselves were up to 30 feet (9m) wide and designed on a methodical grid system of which the Romans and Etruscans would have been proud.

Harappa

Harappa has a very similar layout. It was founded on a series of man-made earth mounds along a dried up section of the River Ravi, in eastern

c.2500 BC	c.2300 BC	c.2300 BC	c.2000 BC	c.2000 BC	c.2000 BC	c.1900 BC	1840 BC
Farming culture flourishes in the Indus region.	Ceramics made in Central America for the first time.	King Sargon unites Sumeria.	Use of sail on seagoing vessels in Aegean.	Inuit people living in Arctic.	Minoans produce painted pottery.	Irrigation technology improves in Mesopotamia to nurture expanding population.	Lower Nubia annexed by Egypt.

Religious leaders controlled food production and distribution to shore up their power-base.

Pakistan. It also has a fortified citadel above workers' living quarters but was designed with a particular emphasis on granaries and grain-pounding "factories." This suggests it controlled food markets and distribution, and its leaders undoubtedly used this to help shore up their religious power-base.

Harappa is less well documented than Mohenjo-Daro, mainly because so many of its structures were demolished for use as ballast during construction of India's western rail network in the 19th century. Among the most curious relics recovered from its ruins are square stamp seals in which soapstone has been inscribed with short passages of Indus script. This lettering, also found on amulets and ornaments, has never been decoded but it may be linked to the Dravidian tongue used today by the Tamil people and others in southern India.

Indus Art

The Indus culture produced a variety of specialized artists, as opposed to a single dominant craft skill. Products included a distinctive type of black-on-red pottery bearing images of fish, animals, and plants, ceramic statues and toys, etched cornelian beaded jewelry, and silver, gold, and bronze ornaments. Bangles carved out of large seashells were fashionable and there were also a number of tool-making factories producing standard flint knives and metal tools. Items with distinctive Indus characteristics have been found all over the Near East and this has forced archeologists to reassess the age of the culture. For a long time it was believed to date only from 1000 BC but artifacts recovered from Mesopotamian sites prove that it must have been far older.

Much of our knowledge about the Indus people stems from the work of Sir John Marshall, director of the Archeological Survey of India, whose team made great strides early in the 1920s. Since then, Pakistani, Indian, and Western scholars have filled gaps in the jigsaw and several linked Bronze Age cultures have been identified at Amri, Sothi, and Gumla. However, the reasons for the sudden demise of the Indus sometime after 2000 BC remains baffling. It is thought some complex ecological and environmental changes caused many settlements to be abandoned en masse.

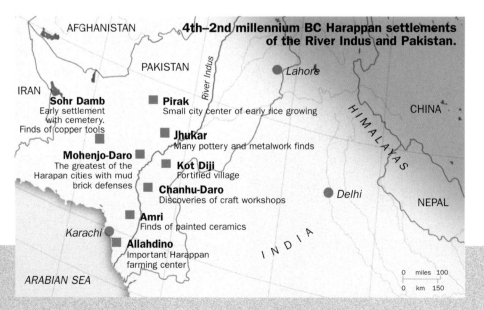

4th–2nd millennium BC Harappan settlements of the River Indus and Pakistan.

AFGHANISTAN

PAKISTAN

River Indus

Lahore

IRAN

Sohr Damb
Early settlement with cemetery. Finds of copper tools

Pirak
Small city center of early rice growing

HIMALAYAS

CHINA

Jhukar
Many pottery and metalwork finds

Mohenjo-Daro
The greatest of the Harapan cities with mud brick defenses

Kot Diji
Fortified village

Chanhu-Daro
Discoveries of craft workshops

Delhi

NEPAL

Amri
Finds of painted ceramics

Karachi

INDIA

Allahdino
Important Harappan farming center

ARABIAN SEA

0 miles 100
0 km 150

c.1800 BC	c.1750 BC	c.1458 BC
Shamshi-Adad founds Assyrian state.	Hammurabi founds Babylonian Empire.	Hatshepsut, the only female pharaoh to rule Egypt, dies.

THE BUDDHA'S LEGACY
The Spread of an Eastern Religion

above: *A Greek contemporary bust of Alexander the Great. His army rested in Taxila before it became a Buddhist stronghold.*

The origins of Buddhism are hazy, but according to legend this great world religion emerged from the teachings of Siddhartha Gautama—the Buddha—who was born in the 6th century BC at Kapilavastu, close to today's border between India and Nepal. The son of a minor king, he became frustrated with his apparently empty and worthless life, and at the age of 29 renounced earthly wealth to devote himself to a search for peace and truth. Through intense periods of meditation the Buddha attained a higher level of consciousness, and achieved "Enlightenment," in c.528 BC. Thereafter he gathered his *sanga* (disciples) and spent the rest of his life as a wandering preacher and founder of monasteries. He is thought to have died about 483 BC.

For more than two centuries Buddhism was merely one of many minor sects based in the ancient north-eastern Indian kingdom of Maghada, a powerful Hindu state.

Following a succession of power struggles the region fell under the control of a skilful military commander named Chandragupta Maurya who established a dynasty and empire extending far into southern India. It was his grandson Ashoka—one of India's bravest and most radical rulers—who ensured that the fledgling religion survived and expanded. Appalled by the savagery involved in his victory over the eastern kingdom of Kalinga in 261 BC, Ashoka converted to Buddhism in 260 BC, adopting a government policy of non-violence and ruling through moral, as opposed to military, means. To spread the word he commissioned inscriptions to be placed on architecture and rock faces extolling morality and compassion, and this was done throughout the Mauryan kingdom, from his capital Pataliputra in the north-east to Taxila and the Gandhara region of the north-west.

A cultural melting-pot

It is at Taxila—a pivotal trading post linking Persian and Greek culture to that of China and south-east Asia—that some of Buddhism's most fascinating archeology can be found.

Until the beginning of the 20th century little was known about Taxila (or Takshasila) in modern-day Afghanistan. It was mentioned in a few Greek and Indian texts and was a resting point for Alexander the Great's army as it marched east. But it was not until the 1912 excavation by Sir John Marshall, the British Director-General of the Indian Archeological Survey, that its importance really emerged. Marshall found the remains of three cities including Bhir Mound (a Persian community dating from the sixth to the first century AD), nearby Sirkap (occupied by Indo-Greeks until

left: *The ruins of Jandial, part of the Taxila excavation. The remnants of three ancient cities were found near this site.*

539 BC	510 BC	505 BC
Persian Empire founded under Cyrus the Great.	Founding of Roman republic.	Democracy established in Athens.

Appalled by the savagery of his army, Ashoka Maurya emerged as one of India's boldest and most radical rulers.

the second century AD), and an outpost of the Parthian empire (centered on modern-day Iran) that had expanded rapidly during the first century AD. This melting-pot of cultures produced an extraordinarily vibrant art style that became known as Greco-Buddhist. It spread across central Asia and evolved into two particularly distinctive, and quite different, decorative techniques— *stucco* (the moulding of plaster or cement), and *schist* (the splitting of rock into thin plates).

Further excavations at Taxila and Sirkap by Sir Mortimer Wheeler in

1945 uncovered many monuments relating to the Buddhist faith, including one describing them as the work of Ashoka's Mauryan dynasty. Communal worship is not a central feature of Buddhism and most of the religion's key ancient buildings tend to be monasteries. However, Wheeler found a number of structures clearly designed for large congregations that were set outside city walls. The most impressive of these was the Dharmarajika, a huge complex comprizing monasteries, temples, and a *stupa*— a hemispherical mound containing relics and effigies from which a central pillar rises bearing three discs. The design is heavily symbolic; the mound is the sacred mythical mountain Meru, the pillar is its axis, and the discs represent the Triple Refuge of the Buddhist faith— the Buddha, his doctrine, and his disciples.

Among the most important Buddhist sites excavated since World War II are at Ratnagiri, near Bhuvanecvar, and the jungle community at Sirpur, east of Raipur. Each revealed typical eighth-century Buddhist monasteries based on similar designs—a porch and inner hall surrounded by cells

left: *This stupa, c.400 AD, stands within the ruins of Mohra Korado Monastery, Taxila.*

with a shrine cavity in the middle of the rear wall. The monumental masonry at Ratnagiri is outstanding in its depiction of floral scrolls and images of gods while at Sirpur archeologists discovered bronzes which could only have been shaped through advanced technical skills. Another common Buddhist structure is the *chaitya* or worship hall, some of the finest examples of which can be found at Karli, south-east of Bombay. Here the *chaitya* has been hewn out of a cave; the natural rock formations shaped into pillars and vaults in imitation of more traditional wooden halls. This early second century AD site also contains many fine carvings and a small *stupa*.

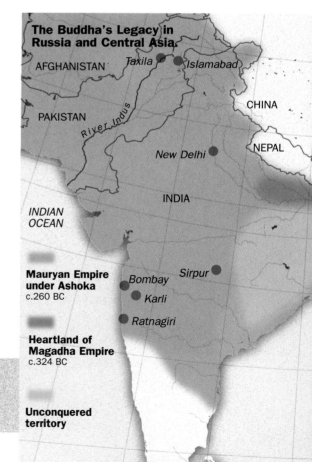

The Buddha's Legacy in Russia and Central Asia

AFGHANISTAN — Taxila — Islamabad

PAKISTAN

River Indus

CHINA

New Delhi

NEPAL

INDIA

INDIAN OCEAN

Mauryan Empire under Ashoka c.260 BC — Bombay — Sirpur — Karli — Ratnagiri

Heartland of Magadha Empire c.324 BC

Unconquered territory

CHAPTER NINE

THE FAR EAST

The geographical size of Eastern Asia makes it hard to establish a running theme for its archeological history. In any case archeology is not about a neat and ordered progression of events from one point in time to another. The reality is that widely differing cultural traditions evolve and expand at different rates; some achieving domination, others absorbed, still others lost forever. It is an easy mistake to assume that the "Iron Age" or the "Stone Age" occurred pretty well simultaneously across the world. In fact there are tribesmen in parts of Borneo's dense jungle interior who are living an "Iron Age" existence today! Similarly, the Celts of central Asia were producing superb bronzes at a time when China had never even heard of the metal.

Chinese culture is the most prominent in the Far East. Its innovative artwork, architecture, and reservoir of religious and philosophical thinking make it one of the truly great early civilizations. Archeological sites such as the Great Wall, the Shang tombs of Anyang, and the grave complex of the First Emperor Qin Shih Huang Ti illustrate how successive rulers were masters at ruthlessly marshaling vast numbers of people to a single cause. Considered alongside the region's definitive traditions of jade sculpture, statuary, and lavishly-decorated tombs, it is easy to see how early travelers must have viewed the Chinese with a sense of awe and mystery. The empire's influence, together with the rise of Hinduism and Buddhism, governed subsequent development in South East Asia and helped produce the continent's greatest single work of architecture— the temple of Angkor Wat in Cambodia.

This chapter, however, begins with the arrival of the first early humans in Eastern Asia. The details are still unfolding and fossils excavated from the Zhoukoudian cave complex continue to pose awkward questions for scholars about the prehistoric colonization of the world.

below: *Buddhism became a widespread influence throughout East Asia, culminating in some splendid temples in Indonesia, including the famous monument of Borobodur, Java. Along its topmost levels, Buddhas contemplate the cardinal points amid ranks of stupa.*

The Great Wall of China

MONGOLIA

JAPAN

■ Hongshan

The Great Wall of China

■ Ming Tombs

NORTH
KOREA

SOUTH
KOREA

■ Zhoukoudian Caves
■ Yungang

The   Great   Wall   of   China

■ Suez

■ Helan Mountains   ■ Anyong

■ Yaoshan

■ Luoyang
■ Longmen

NORTH
PACIFIC
OCEAN

■ Xi'an

Warriors and horses of the
Terracotta Army

Bronze ding of the Shang
dynasty, c.1300 BC.

INDIA
(ASSAM)

CHINA

BURMA

■ Zuojiang Cliffs

SOUTH
CHINA
SEA

The Angkor Wat
complex.

LAOS

THAILAND

VIETNAM

ANDAMAN
SEA

■ Angkor Wat

CAMBODIA

PEKING MAN
Evidence of mankind's origins in China

The Zhoukoudian caves south-west of Beijing (Peking) are a treasure trove of early human fossils. They contain the largest concentration of *homo erectus* ("upright man") remains anywhere in the world, with the bones of at least 40 hominids so far recovered. Some of these date back half a million years and it seems that for 250,000 years the caves were in continuous occupation. Among the 100,000 or so artifacts recovered there is the earliest evidence yet found of prehistoric use of fire.

Zhoukoudian, sometimes known by its old name Chou K'ou Tein, was the focus of intense activity by paleoanthropologists during the 1920s and 30s. The first hint of its importance came from a Swedish mining consultant called J. Gunnar Andersson, who turned up several human-like teeth while pursuing his hobby of fossil collecting. Andersson's finds attracted the attention of a Canadian anatomist called Davidson Black who in 1927 made a major advance by assembling teeth and fragments of skull into a previously unknown species which he dubbed *Sinanthropus pekinensis*, or "Peking Man."

Following Black's death the excavations were taken over by the German anatomist Franz Weidenreich, regarded as one of the world's greatest researchers on human evolution. As visiting Professor of Anatomy at the Beijing Union Medical College he threw himself into an intensive study of the Zhoukoudian site and his superbly precise

descriptions of the fossils found is still a model for students of biological anthropology. Weidenreich's dedication later proved crucially important. The outbreak of war and the occupation of China by the Japanese Imperial Army in 1937 forced him to secure the safety of the fossils by shipping them out of the country to the United States. The ship was captured by the Japanese, and the fossils lost. Only the plaster casts taken by Weidenreich remain, although excavations during the 1960s and 70s have since produced a number of new specimens.

In one sense, data from Zhoukoudian has vastly illuminated our understanding of prehistory. In another it has muddied the waters. We know from ash, seed, and bone analysis that the earliest cave occupants would have been vying with wild animals such as hyenas and leopards for security and shelter. Indeed, most of the animal bones found were probably left there by other animals—only a few carry tell-tale signs of butchery and roasting. We can also estimate from uranium series dating (measuring an object's decline in radioactivity over time) at the site that the climate swung from cold to warm and back to cold between 500,000 and 230,000 years ago.

left: *A skull belonging to Pithecanthropus erectus, discovered in Java in 1891, and belonging to the same period as Peking Man.*

c.2,000,000 BC	c.700,000 BC	c.460,000 BC	c.250,000 BC	c.100,000 BC	c.100,000–30,000 BC	c.30,000 BC	30,000 BC
Homo erectus humans begin to move out of Africa to colonize Asia.	*Homo erectus* people live north of 45° latitude.	Earliest confirmed use of fire, in China.	Some *Homo erectus* populations begin to develop *Homo sapiens* characteristics.	True *Homo sapiens* emerge in Middle East.	Anatomically modern people and Neanderthals co-exist.	Neanderthal people disappear completely after being slowly replaced by *Homo sapiens*.	Most of inhabitable world has been colonised.

Zhoukoudian fossils were smuggled out of China as the Japanese Imperial Army advanced.

above: *The reconstructed skull of Sinanthropus pekinensis, or Peking Man as christened by Davidson Black in 1927.*

Evolutionary questions

However, later work on the anatomical makeup of Peking Man has ignited an intense debate about human origins. The conventional line is that *homo erectus* originated in eastern Africa and moved rapidly into Asia once stone tools had been developed some two million years ago. Much later, probably between 200,000 and 120,000 years ago, our own species *homo sapiens* also emerged in Africa/south-west Asia and followed a similar pattern of colonizing Asia, eventually replacing *homo erectus* completely. This is a view generally supported by molecular biologists.

So far, so good. The difficulty comes with genetic studies suggesting that some of the features of *homo erectus* appear to have been carried forward into the modern-day population of Asia. In other words, Chinese *homo erectus* gradually evolved into Chinese *homo sapiens* without any input from a migrating African population. If this theory is correct, it means modern humans may have emerged simultaneously in many different parts of the world.

Mountain of Flowers

The biggest rock-art panel in the world is at Huashan—the "Mountain of Flowers"—beside the Zuojiang River near China's border with Vietnam. Here paintings dating back 4,000 years stretch across a 650-foot by 130-foot (200m by 40m) cliff face and include images of magicians, chiefs, and soldiers. Some of the Huashan paintings are as high as 400 feet (122m) and could not have been done without the aid of scaffolding, ladders, or some perilous prehistoric abseiling on ropes secured at the cliff edge.

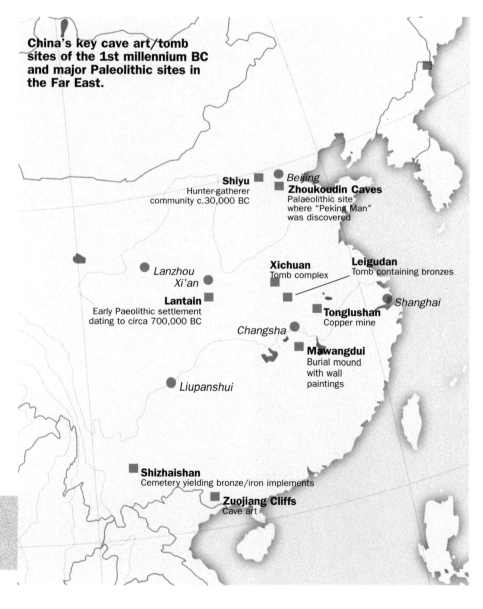

China's key cave art/tomb sites of the 1st millennium BC and major Paleolithic sites in the Far East.

Shiyu
Hunter-gatherer community c.30,000 BC

Beijing
Zhoukoudin Caves
Palaeolithic site where "Peking Man" was discovered

Lanzhou
Xi'an

Xichuan
Tomb complex

Leigudan
Tomb containing bronzes

Lantain
Early Paeolithic settlement dating to circa 700,000 BC

Tonglushan
Copper mine

Shanghai

Changsha

Mawangdui
Burial mound with wall paintings

Liupanshui

Shizhaishan
Cemetery yielding bronze/iron implements

Zuojiang Cliffs
Cave art

c.9000 BC	c.2000 BC
Beginning of civilization around the world following end of ice age.	Huashan rock panels created.

JADE IN CHINA
Ancient craftsmanship

A tradition of carving jade has persisted in China for perhaps 6,000 years. Early examples date from the Neolithic period (c.4000–c.2000 BC) and at first were mostly blades for either practical or ceremonial use. As the skill of the carvers developed, two regions in particular—Hongshan, north-east of Beijing, and Liangzhu, in the Shanghai delta region—acquired reputations for particularly high quality and technically sophisticated work. It is around Hongshan that the first figurative jade art appeared in the form of birds, turtles, and so-called "pig-dragons."

Hongshan pig-dragons are thought by some to be symbolic representations of Pig Mountain, near Niuheliang in Liaoning province. Many pieces were recovered from a burial complex of 13 separate hillside tombs that look down on a valley dominated in the south by this mountain. On the northern side of the valley archeologists have found a temple dug into the ground, complete with plastered walls and evidence of monumental sculpture, and it is possible that this formed the ritual focus of the entire 30-square-mile (80 sq km) necropolis.

Impressive finds near Shanghai

Among the most outstanding Liangzhu jades are those recovered from cemeteries at Yingpashan, Yaoshan, and Sidun, north of Shanghai. At Sidun, excavation of a 65-foot (20m) high mound revealed the body of a young man surrounded by more than a hundred jade objects crafted into distinctive geometric shapes such as perforated discs or square blocks with circular bores. Another intriguing Liangshu design is the "double face" motif in which the features of two faces—eyebrows, eyes, noses, and sometimes mouths—are imposed upon each other almost in an attempt to deceive the eye. They can be

above: *A vase or "zong" fashioned from jade between 2500 and 1500 BC.*

viewed as two separate faces, or as a single person wearing a head-dress decorated with a facial design. This motif, and the skills involved in producing it, were passed on into the later Shang period—the first Imperial dynasty of China, in which a succession of 28 or 29 emperors ruled between c.1480 and 1050 BC.

The most beautiful of the Shang jades were found in 1975 at the Anyang royal cemetery north of Yinxu. These included plaques depicting dragons, birds, human figures, mythical beasts, and an array of wild animals. Shang style was adopted, and advanced, during the Zhou dynasty (c.1027–256 BC), when craftsmen used technical innovations

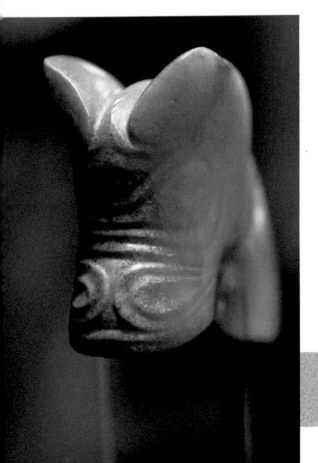

left: *A jade dragon head of the Hongshan figurative style. This piece dates to c.3500 BC.*

4236 BC	c.4000 BC	c.4000 BC	c.3700 BC	c.3500 BC
First date in Egyptian calendar.	First farmers in Britain.	Cities emerge in Euphrates valley, Mesopotamia.	Rock paintings in the Sahara reflect dessicating environment.	Alcoholic drinks being fermented in Middle East.

The invention of the iron drill resulted in ever more intricate designs.

such as the invention of iron drills to produce ever more intricate animal figures and exquisitely carved curling sculptures. In the subsequent Han dynasty (206 BC–AD 220) jade moved

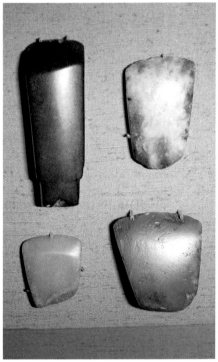

away from its traditional marketplace as a burial item toward fashionable, practical goods such as toilet boxes, drinking goblets, and desktop ornaments. That said, the most outstanding jade work of the period was produced in the form of burial suits for Prince Liu Sheng (d.113 BC) and his wife. When their tomb was uncovered at Mancheng, in Hebei province, they were each dressed in suits made of 2,500 jade plaques sewn together with gold thread—a labor of love that must have lasted a decade.

From the end of the Han period, right through to the close of the Qing dynasty in 1912 AD, the dating of jade is extremely difficult without a

left: These jade and stone axheads date from c.2500 BC, while the knife blade **right:** *was produced about 500 years later.*

definable archeological context. Overall, jade artifacts of all eras are a tribute to the patience and care of their makers—especially those made during the early Neolithic years. The material is notoriously difficult to work because it cannot be split or flaked like other stones and its smooth, rounded appearance could only have been achieved through long hours of graft using an abrasive material. In the case of the Hongshan and Liangzhu artists this probably involved rubbing away with a high-silicate bamboo mixed with sand.

Major finds of Hongshan and Liangzhu jades, 3rd—4th millennium BC.

MONGOLIA

CHINA

Hongshan
Temple complex (jades)

Niuheliang jade
Grave goods of Hongshan type

● Beijing

Mancheng rock
Tomb of Liu Sheng and Du Wan, buried in jade suits

Yaoshan
Liangzhu jades

Yingpashan
Early Liangzhu jades

● Lanzhou

● Xi'an

Shang jade phoenix ornament, 1300 BC.

● Shanghai

● Changsha

Fanshan
Liangzhu jades from ritual site

c.3500 BC	c.3372 BC	c.3300 BC
Copper in use in Thailand.	First date in Mayan calendar.	Sumerians start to use clay tokens in exchange for goods.

THE TERRACOTTA ARMY
Forever guarding China's First Emperor

In March 1974 a Chinese peasant named Yang Zhi-fa was sinking a well at Qin, near China's ancient capital of Xi'an, when he came across the mustachioed head of a clay soldier buried in the earth. Small clay human figures were not unusual in early Chinese royal graves but the enormity of this find became clear when further excavations revealed vast underground chambers containing life-size models of soldiers in full battle dress. This 7,000-strong "Terracotta Army" was arranged in traditional battle formation and equipped with 600 clay horses, 100 war chariots, and a breathtaking array of bows, arrows, spears, and swords crafted in an unusual alloy that had remained sharp and bright. The figures, all facing east, had been assembled to guard China's first emperor, Qin Shih Huang Ti, following his death in 210 BC. They are now one of China's main tourist attractions.

The awesome logistics operation that accompanied this burial probably involved hundreds of thousands of people over at least a decade. The underground chambers alone have an estimated floor space of 30,364 square yards (25,388 sq m) and necessitated the removal of 130,000 cubic yards (100,000 cubic meters) of earth. Floors were carefully laid with 250,000 fired clay bricks while the

roof required 10,500 cubic yards (8,000 cubic meters) of timber—mostly pine and cypress wood. Each warrior's head was individually modeled, probably as the portrait of a living person, and the collection incorporated a large range of facial features, expressions, ages, and even beards (25 different styles were recorded). Racial groups within the population were represented in immaculate detail down to the shape of their ear lobes. All these faces were then fitted to "mass-produced" body postures painted and modeled in the combat uniform of various ranks including generals, foot soldiers, cavalrymen, and kneeling archers. As a final touch, the name of the sculptor

responsible for each finished warrior was neatly etched and sealed beneath armpits or coat hems. Eighty five names have been discovered.

The precise high-temperature firing of the clay—around 1,472°F (800°C)—gave the models both their distinctive gray color and an extremely durable finish. Although they were buried for two thousand years, the intact figures emerged rock-hard and largely unaffected by damp. However many had been damaged by other means. Pit 1 for instance, which contained most of the figures, was severely blackened by fire and Pits 2 and 3 had suffered serious roof falls. Pit 3 was particularly interesting in that it seemed to be the army's command center. Here the generals are distinguishable by their increased height (around 5ins (13cm) taller than the average foot soldier), muscular bodies, and the presence of a personal guard.

The army seems a fittingly grand tribute to an emperor renowned for

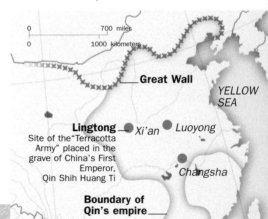

0   700 miles
0   1000 kilometers

Great Wall

YELLOW SEA

Lingtong — Xi'an   Luoyong
Site of the "Terracotta Army" placed in the grave of China's First Emperor, Qin Shih Huang Ti

Changsha

Boundary of Qin's empire

The empire of Qin Shih in 207 BC, three years after his death.

262 BC	221 BC	218 BC	206 BC	c.200 BC
Ashoka, Mauryan emperor, converts to Buddhism.	Ch'in dynasty unites China.	Hannibal of Carthage invades Italy.	Rome gains control of Spain..	Hopewell culture emerges in North American midwest.

The logistics operation to prepare the burial site involved hundreds of thousands of people.

thinking big. Shih Huang Ti can certainly be credited with unifying the warring kingdoms of China and for building much of the Great Wall. However, he was also a bloody tyrant who, in 213 BC, ordered that all books disagreeing with his view of history and philosophy should be burned. His tomb lies beneath a great burial mound roughly a mile from his clay guardians and, according to ancient Chinese writings, is the center of a vast underground palace protected by booby traps. It is rumored to contain a three-dimensional map of China under the Qin dynasty with rivers outlined in mercury. Whether or not this is true, excavation of the undisturbed tomb is likely to reveal untold treasures from Shih Huang Ti's reign.

Archeological treasures for the world

The worldwide furore created by the Terracotta Army find was such that Xi'an had to build a new airport to cope with the influx of tourists. During construction of a highway 12 miles

(19km) outside the city, workmen stumbled upon yet more subterranean soldiery—this time in the shape of 20in-high (50cm) solid clay statues of naked men. There are conflicting theories as to why these figures had no upper limbs. Some Chinese experts believe their arms were originally made of wood, which later rotted. Others think they were attached with rods of precious metal,

which were looted. The army was apparently linked to the tombs of the emperor Liu Qi and his wife, and was paraded in 24 separate chambers, set about 65 feet (20m) apart and aligned in 14 north-south rows. The chambers contained all manner of weapons, carts, coins, and jewelry—each piece manufactured to the same scale as the miniature warriors themselves.

opposite page: *Close-up of a kneeling terracotta archer unearthed near Emperor Qin Shih Huang Ti's tomb.*

right: *The massed ranks of the Terracotta Army, seen as they were found, in battle formation.*

THE GREAT WALL
One of mankind's most impressive achievements

China's Great Wall is said to be the only man-made structure visible from space. It once snaked unbroken across 1,500 miles (2,400km) of the barren northern frontier; from Jinwangdao in the east to Gaodai, Gansu Province, in the west. By any comparison, this makes it an extraordinary feat of engineering—even accepting that a virtually unlimited labor force was available. These pitiful workers—a combination of conscripts and slaves—suffered appalling privations and most died young from disease or malnutrition. Accounts of their misfortune still survive in modern-day folk songs and stories.

For 250 years prior to Qin Shih Huang Ti's accession as First Emperor in 221 BC, China was ravaged by internal warfare. This so-called "Warring States" period was heralded by the collapse of a feudal system during which the theoretical king of China, the grandly-titled "Son of Heaven," was reduced to little more than a puppet figurehead. He was forced to watch, impotent, as competing nobles squabbled for control of ever-more territory; building defensive walls to mark out their claims and to foil nomadic raiders from the northern steppes. The Qin dynasty's final victory over its great rival, the Chu, brought about unification under the totalitarian regime of Shih Huang Ti.

The need for security

The First Emperor viewed his northern boundary as the key to long-term security. Of course, he wanted to keep

above: *Detail from a gate at the center of the Juyangguan fortress.*

out the nomadic horsemen, but he also needed to prevent any drift north by his own farmers, many of whom might be tempted to forsake grain production for stock-rearing, so adding to the nomad population. Also, Shih Huang Ti needed a clear geographical divide to show where his laws, culture, and philosophies would be rigorously enforced. The Great Wall was a convenient solution to all three problems.

Shih Huang Ti began work almost immediately, appointing the Qin general Meng Tian to oversee the operation. This involved strengthening and connecting the existing rammed earth defenses erected during the Warring States period; river courses were followed rather than bridged and the contours of mountains and valleys

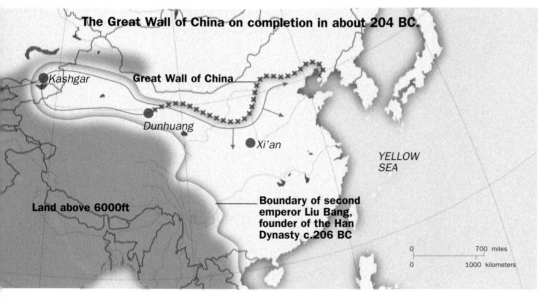

The Great Wall of China on completion in about 204 BC.

Kashgar

Great Wall of China

Dunhuang

Xi'an

YELLOW SEA

Land above 6000ft

Boundary of second emperor Liu Bang, founder of the Han Dynasty c.206 BC

| 0 | 700 miles |
| 0 | 1000 kilometers |

c.290 BC	224 BC	223 BC	c.214 BC	202 BC	200 BC	168 BC	100 BC
Alexandrian library founded.	Colossus of Rhodes, one of the Seven Wonders, destroyed in an earthquake.	Defeat of Chu dynasty.	Great Wall of China completed.	Han dynasty reunites China.	Etruria falls to the Romans.	Rome defeats Macedonia.	Camel first introduced into Sahara.

The Qin general Meng Tian built the wall—then committed suicide believing he had "cut the veins" of the earth.

above: *A view of the Jiayuguan fortress which marks the westernmost limit of the wall. Chinese generals later decided that outposts like this were impossible to maintain.*

were adapted as natural defenses. In the north Meng Tian created a substantially new line of defense, extending the wall to include the Ordos desert about 214 BC. Interestingly, he was full of remorse for what he had done. Shortly before being tricked into committing suicide (on forged orders supposedly from his dead emperor) Meng Tian wrote: "I have made walls and ditches over more than 10,000 li[†]. In this distance it is impossible not to have cut through the veins of the earth. I have a crime for which to die."

For most of its length the Great Wall is built of earth and stone, faced with fired clay bricks in eastern sections. It

The Great Wall as seen today. Thousands of slave workers died in appalling conditions during its construction.

is an average of 20 feet (6m) thick at the base, tapering to around 12 feet (3.7m) at the top. The height varies around 25 feet (7.6m), not counting the battlements, and the line is interspersed with watchtowers some 40 feet (12m) high every 600 feet (180m). Despite such formidable fortifications the problem—as the Romans discovered on the far smaller Hadrian's Wall in northern Britain— was to provide effective long-term manpower. The Chinese tackled this by setting up self-supporting agricultural garrisons, or *juntian*, in the far western reaches of the wall. Their brief was to hold any attack until reinforcements arrived but by the first century AD the Chinese military conceded that many were too remote to be of use.

† A unit of Chinese measurement. 4 li is roughly 1 mile or 1.6 km.

Final Victory of Qin Shih Huang Ti

The First Emperor's triumph over the Chu dynasty in 223 BC was achieved through the canniness of a veteran general, Wang Chien. Wang Chien followed some textbook Chinese military strategy, to the effect that enemies should be lured into a false sense of security. He ordered his 600,000-strong army to make camp, swim, sing, feast, and make merry. After weeks of this the Chu defenders began to look upon them with contempt and let their own discipline become lax. With this intelligence from his scouts, Wang Chien snapped his forces into fighting mode and secured a stunning victory.

YINXU
Capital of the Shang Dynasty

The discovery of Yinxu, the ancient seat of Shang kings near modern-day Anyang, was the result of a nifty piece of archeological detective work. Toward the end of the 19th century animal (and particularly turtle) bones inscribed with Chinese characters began appearing in backstreet stores across the north and east of the country. Buyers were informed that these old "oracle bones" could be ground up as ingredients for magical medicines. As it turned out, their history was indeed interwoven with ancient sorcery.

Curious, some historians began tracing the source of the bones and found they were regularly dug up by farmers north-east of Anyang. Translation of the inscriptions, along with other documentary evidence, indicated that they were used by high priests as a way of divining the future. Two opposite predictions were visualized and the priest would then insert a red-hot metal rod into a hole specially ground into a bone fragment. Depending on the way the bone cracked, a decision was made on whether the tidings were auspicious. Favorable pieces were inscribed with the words of the divination and stored away in underground archives. During the

20th century more than 100,000 of these have come to light, 4,500 of which bear text.

This divination process was apparently a key element in the religion of the Shang—the first known imperial dynasty of China, in which a succession of 29 kings ruled northern and central areas between about 1480 and 1050 BC. The kings were descended from Stone Age warrior chiefs who ruled through a potent combination of force, fear, tribal alliances, and a general belief that they were blessed with a sacred wisdom by Shang Di (the heavenly "Lord On High"). The priestly caste formed a social layer between the kings and the commoners, and the whole religious structure was based

on an afterlife, a multitude of gods and the powers of dead ancestors.

Human sacrifice

One particularly gruesome aspect of this religion was its unrestrained use of human sacrifice. During excavations at Anyang by China's doyen of archeology Li Chi, the Yinxu wooden palace complex was found to rest on a veritable "carpet" of human skulls. These had been scattered among the earthen foundations at the time of construction and were often sprinkled with red ocher (an iron oxide). Particular attention was paid to placing remains close to pillars and doors, as though the dead could act both as sentries and structural supports. The tombs of the kings

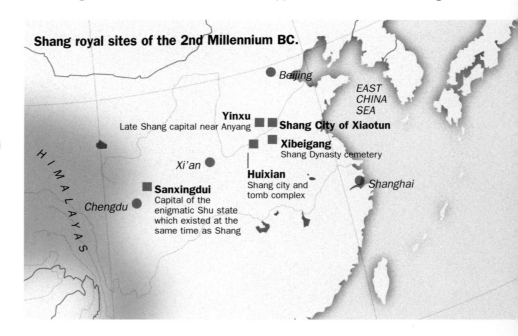

Shang royal sites of the 2nd Millennium BC.

Beijing

EAST CHINA SEA

Yinxu
Late Shang capital near Anyang

Shang City of Xiaotun

Xibeigang
Shang Dynasty cemetery

Xi'an

Huixian
Shang city and tomb complex

Shanghai

HIMALAYAS

Sanxingdui
Capital of the enigmatic Shu state which existed at the same time as Shang

Chengdu

1595 BC	c.1500 BC	c.1500 BC	c.1458 BC	c.1400 BC	c.1400 BC	c.1400–1100 BC	c.1240 BC
Hittites conquer Babylon.	Santorini in Aegean Sea is destroyed by a volcanic eruption.	Wood imported by sea from Lebanon to Egypt.	Hatshepsut, the only female pharaoh to rule Egypt, dies.	Syrians invent an early alphabet.	Horses are tamed in central Asia.	Mycenean civilization at its height.	Moses gives out the Ten Commandments.

Traditional Chinese sources demonized the last of the Shang kings as sadistic and bloodthirsty.

themselves were surrounded with hundreds more sacrificial burials and often grandly furnished with chariots (much-prized imports from the western steppelands), dead horses, bronze weapons, and jewel-encrusted artifacts. One of the richest graves, excavated by the Beijing Institute of Archeology in 1976, was that of Fu Hao, consort of the famous Shang ruler Wu Ding. It contained 440 bronzes, 590 jades, 560 artifacts fashioned in bone, and some 7,000 cowrie shells.

Studies of the Yinxu capital show that its art, craft, and food production were geared almost entirely to the needs of the nobility. Fashionable items included sophisticated stone and jade sculptures, bronze drinking vessels, linen and silk cloths, black and red pottery, and a crude white stoneware. The Shang had a highly-developed knowledge of bronze metalwork and knew how to smelt iron (though they did not apply this

to production of agricultural tools). Those peasants not employed as artisans or soldiers worked long hours in the fields to grow millet, barley, wheat, and perhaps rice. Meat took the form of domesticated pigs, dogs, sheep, and oxen, although hunting was also an important source of food.

Traditional Chinese accounts demonized the last of the Shang kings as particularly sadistic and bloodthirsty. Their rule was ultimately ended by the conquering Zhou dynasty, a semi-nomadic people from the north-west, who abandoned human sacrifice but embraced many other Shang ways to lay the foundations of Chinese civilization.

right: *A three-legged Ting vessel used to carry food during religious rituals.*

c.1200 BC	c.1200 BC	c.1150 BC	c.1100 BC	c.1120 BC	c.842 BC	753 BC	c.750 BC
Greeks destroy city of Troy.	Biblical exodus of Hebrews from Egypt.	The first topographical maps are produced in Egypt.	Phoenicians develop alphabetic script.	Mycenean civilization comes to an end.	Jehovah is adopted as Israel's only god.	Rome founded.	The *Iliad* (a poem about the siege of Troy) is written.

MING TOMBS, MURALS, AND MUMMIES
Diversity through the millennia

The Terracotta Army at Xi'an is just one example of Far Eastern burial traditions. Over thousands of years various unrelated pagan and spiritual beliefs, and an expanding Buddhist influence, have created an extraordinarily diverse archeological legacy. Examples include the austere stone-carved warriors forming the "spirit path" to Imperial Ming tombs (c.1368–1644 AD), the small dancing figurines found in Han Dynasty graves (c.206 BC–220 AD) and the golden splendor of the sixth-century "Heavenly Horse" burial (so named because of its birch-bark painting of a white horse) at Kyongju City, South Korea. Yet perhaps the most fascinating—and historically enlightening—fashion for honoring the dead takes the form of spectacular religious wall murals and carvings.

The Han period mural tombs are among the best known in China. There are good examples at Helingeer, in Inner Mongolia, Wangdu, and Luoyang—all involving the use of ink or paste-paint straight onto bricks.

Themes invariably focus on the perceived activities of the dead, their security and protection, and their rise into the "World of the Immortals." Yet within this framework there are also distinctive styles; Luoyang for instance portrays somewhat stunted scenes of a shaman (medium) with a bear-shaped head, surrounded by aides. At Helingeer the art is far more dynamic and dedicated to the interests of the rich, such as hunting, religious ceremony, and formal military processions.

Mother-goddess

Tang Dynasty tombs (c.seventh century AD) are different again. Many of these graves are found dotted among the hills surrounding the Wei River, near Xi'an, and reflect a far more complex approach to construction. The tomb of Prince Zhanghuai, who died before he could be crowned, consisted of a large earth pyramid above two underground chambers. These were accessed via long descending ramps decorated with wall murals depicting a procession of royal servants. Tang tombs celebrated mythological motifs such as the "Spirits of the Four Quarters"—the Black Warrior (actually a snake and turtle) of the North, the Red Phoenix of the South, the Green Dragon of the East, and the White Tiger of the West. The overall strategy was to fête the dead as though they were still living in a lavish royal court.

Lifesize and giant statues are a further impressive feature of Chinese religious artwork. At Yungang, west of Beijing, two huge Buddhist statues loom above caves inhabited by 5th-century monks—their facial features and background patterns carved with wonderful intricacy. Similarly, the pit-temple of Niuheliang, Liaoning Province, produced shattered pieces of seven different life-size clay statues—none of which had been fired. Some fragments appear to be of breasts, suggesting a mother-goddess idol, and at least one was fitted with jade eyes. How the simple Hongshan people who worshipped here in the third century BC managed to support skilled jade and clay

left: *The tomb of King Koryo and his queen at Kaesong, North Korea.*

c.1000 AD	c.1000 AD	1066 AD
Vikings land in North America.	Polynesians arrive in New Zealand.	Invasion of England by Norman French.

The dead were fêted as though they were still living in a royal court.

sculptors is open to question. The region relied on the most primitive forms of subsistence agriculture, and each day must have been a struggle to find food.

above: Stone sentinels guard the approach to the Koryo tomb. A similar "spirit path" can be found at the Imperial Ming tombs, Beijing.

Mummies of the Taklamakan Desert

In 1988 Victor Mair, a professor of Chinese Studies at the University of Pennsylvania, stumbled across an exhibit of mummified bodies at the Urumqi Museum in western China. These people, buried 4,000 years ago, had been preserved by salty sands at three sites in the Taklamakan Desert—Hami, Loulan, and Cherchen. Incredibly, their features were European rather than Chinese; with long limbs, high-bridged noses, and blond or red hair. Their discovery was sensitive because the official government line insisted that Chinese culture evolved without outside interference. In fact discreet studies have since shown that the mummies were Tokharians, a wave of migrants who unwittingly pioneered the Silk Road between Europe and China in the 2nd millennium BC. These people were working bronze before the Chinese had even heard of it. More remarkably, the weave and style of their clothes was unmistakeably Celtic—suggesting that this community, like the Celts, originated from the Indo-European family.

Mural and sculptured tombs and religious sites of China and Korea.

MONGOLIA

Dingling
Imperial Ming tomb built for Emperor Wan Li

NORTH KOREA

Beijing

SOUTH KOREA

Yungong
monumental Buddhist sculptures and wall carvings

Kyongju City
Site of the "Heavenly Horse" tomb, possibly of the Silla King

Luoyang
Mural tombs of the Han period c.AD25 onwards

EAST CHINA SEA

Lanzhou

Xi'an

CHINA

Longmen
Buddhist rock sculpture

Shanghai

The caves and Buddha statues in the hillside, Longmen.

c.1220 AD	c.1250 AD	c.1350 AD
Emergence of first Thai kingdom.	Expansion of Mongol Empire across Asia and Europe.	Renaissance begins in Italy.

TEMPLE OF ANGKOR WAT
Architectural feat of the Khmer rulers

Until 1860 Asia's greatest work of architecture was unknown to the West. Then French missionaries plowing through the central jungles of Cambodia, 200 miles north-west of the capital Phnom Penh, found themselves gazing at a lost temple; an almost unbelievably vast building entwined with trees, creepers, and dense bush. Several years later, French archeologists began the task of clearing vegetation, and documenting the superb stonework and statuary which marked almost every corner.

The temple of Angkor Wat remains the dominant feature of the city of Angkor (originally named Yasodharapura), the ancient capital of the Khmer kingdom. It was founded early in the ninth century and became the royal court of King Yasovarman I during his 11-year reign until 900 AD. By this time Khmer rulers had adopted southern Indian beliefs about god-kings and they each built their own temples as symbolic versions of Mount Meru—the mountain that according to Hindu tradition stands at the center of the world. Meru was said to be the home of the gods; ergo kings who lived in Meru-like temples could be seen as mini-gods. Religious belief aside, it was a handy way to keep the people in their place.

Work on Angkor Wat began c.1113 AD at the behest of the newly-crowned King Suryavarman II. Suryavarman, who reigned until 1150, wanted to portray himself as an incarnation of the god Vishnu—one of the three most revered deities of medieval Hinduism. Vishnu was (and is) said to possess universal wisdom, unchallenged power, and an ability to bring order out of chaos. To reflect this, Suryavarman embarked on an architectural *tour de force*, commissioning a structure 2,800 x 3,300 feet (850 x 1,000m) with three concentric walled enclosures encircled by moats to symbolize the oceans of the world. At the center was the temple itself with its five giant towers representing the five peaks of Meru (four of these have since crumbled). Inside, the walls bear some of history's most lavish stone carvings. These include the longest bas-relief decoration in the world—at one time lavishly painted and gilded—and pictorial translations of epic poems such as the Ramayana and the Mahabharata.

The economic demands of assembling such a vast structure was to be the Khmers' downfall. Building work continued for decades after Suryavarman's death—under the guidance of his successor Udayadityavarman—but it left the country vulnerable to invasion from the Champa kingdom based in what is now Vietnam. This in turn led to a general hemorrhaging of faith in the power of Hindu gods and late in the 12th century the Chams sacked Angkor. It was reclaimed by King Jayavarman VII, a Buddhist, and he quickly embarked on a monument to exceed Angkor Wat's grandeur—the temple of Angkor Thom. This stepped complex covers almost 5.5 square miles (15 sq km) within a square, moated enclosure. It centers on the Bayon temple with its huge stone effigies depicting the omnipresent Buddha and Jayavarman himself. Sadly, Angkor Thom was heavily defaced by later rulers who wanted their own images carved into immortality at the expense of existing ones. The temple also suffered from an inherent structural deficiency; the Khmer custom of lining up vertical masonry joints as a decorative feature left stonework suspect to erosion.

below: *A stone relief from Angkor Wat*

c.1000 AD	c.1000 AD	1066 AD	c.1220 AD	c.1250 AD
Vikings land in North America.	Polynesians arrive in New Zealand.	Invasion of England by Norman French.	Emergence of first Thai kingdom.	Expansion of Mongol Empire across Asia and Europe.

The demands of assembling such a vast structure was to be the Khmers' downfall.

above: *Even in ruination, Angkor Wat remains an impressive sight.*

The end of Angkor's era

By the 13th century Angkor had become one of the world's largest cities, with a total area of some 39 sq miles (100 sq km). Its glory was, however, short-lived. Faced with growing aggression from the neighboring Thai kingdom, Cambodians began a slow evacuation south and by 1431 they had insufficient resources to prevent the Thais from rampaging through Angkor. Thereafter, the city continued for a few years as a Buddhist pilgrimage center but by the beginning of the 16th century it had been largely abandoned to the jungle. Even so, Angkor Wat is today in a remarkably good state of repair having somehow avoided serious damage during the Cambodian conflicts of the late 20th century.

c.1350 AD	c.1409 AD	1492 AD
Renaissance begins in Italy.	Leipzig University is founded.	Columbus discovers America.

Key Buddhist and Hindu south-east Asia temple sites, 8th–13th centuries AD.

THAILAND

Angkor Wat Hindu/Buddhist temple complex

SOUTH CHINA SEA

Koh Ker Royal capital of Jayavarman IV

Bangkok

ANDAMAN SEA

CAMBODIA

Samber Prei Kuk Capital of Isanapura state and temple complex

Phnom Penh VIETNAM

Ho Chi Min City

Gunung Jerai Palace complex

Medan

M A L A Y S I A

Singapore

INDIAN OCEAN

I N D O N E S I A

BORNEO

SUMATRA

Dieng Ceremonial Hindu center

Borobodur Largest Buddhist monument in the world

Pugungraharjo Buddhist/Hindu standing stones

Jakarta JAVA

Prambanan Hindu and Buddhist temple complex

CHAPTER TEN

OCEANIA

N. KOREA

S. KOREA

JAPAN

CHINA

NORTH PACIFIC OCEAN

TAIWAN

Merging of peoples from different parts of Asia, pre 4th millennium BC

PHILIPPINE SEA

PHILIPPINES

Theory of the colonization of the Pacific.

It is a common misconception that Europeans first explored the major oceans of the world. In fact centuries before Columbus, Drake, or even the Vikings an incredibly resourceful people with advanced navigational techniques was spreading across the Pacific, colonizing new islands and establishing far-flung trade routes.

Some were descendants of the first aborigines (who themselves accomplished formidable journeys between south-east Asia and Australia 40,000 years previously). Others were Melanesian or Polynesian seafarers. Perhaps they were escaping tribal warfare or

BORNEO

INDONESIA

BISMARCK ARCHIPELAGO

NEW GUINEA

New Britain
(Lepita Culture)

SOLOMON ISLANDS

Tonga and Samoa become dispersal point for East Pacific

First Pacific explorers head out from Indonesia

c, 3000–1000 BC

SAMOA

Fiji

COOK ISLANDS

Tonga

Arnhem Land

NEW CALEDONIA

INDIAN OCEAN

SOUTH PACIFIC OCEAN

Carnarvon Gorge

AUSTRALIA

Purritjarra

Koonalda Cave

Lake Mungo

NEW ZEALAND

Wellington

Kow Swamp

Site of the Darwin meteorite crash

Kutikini Cave
20,000-year-old settlement in which tools made of glass (from the Darwin meteorite crash) have been found

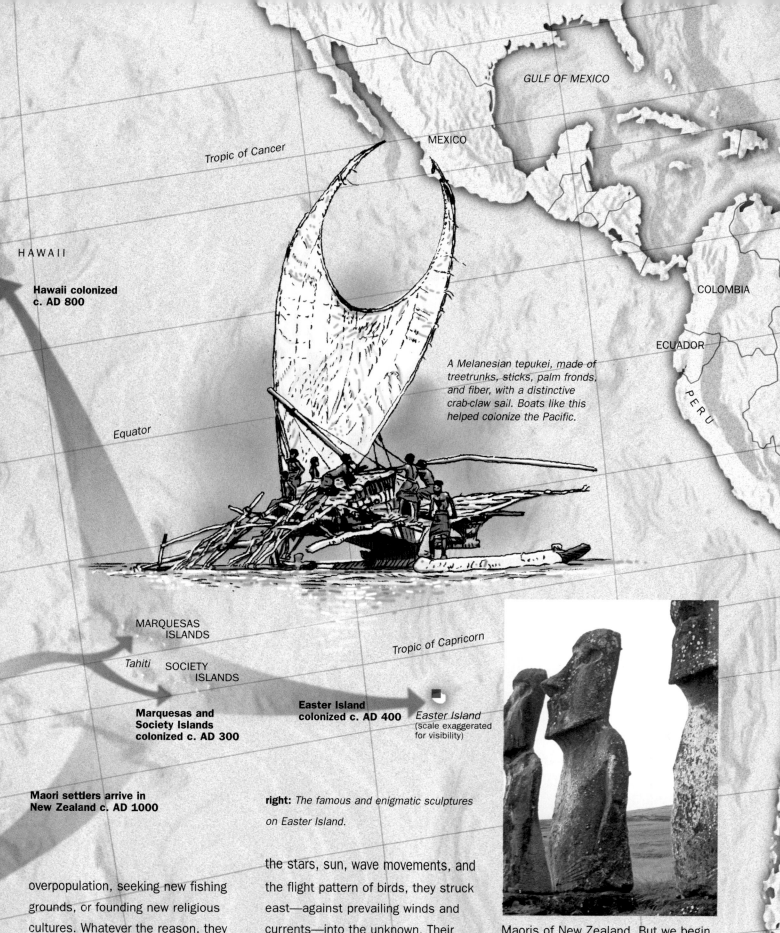

GULF OF MEXICO

MEXICO

Tropic of Cancer

HAWAII

**Hawaii colonized
c. AD 800**

COLOMBIA

ECUADOR

P E R U

Equator

*A Melanesian tepukei, made of
treetrunks, sticks, palm fronds,
and fiber, with a distinctive
crab-claw sail. Boats like this
helped colonize the Pacific.*

MARQUESAS
ISLANDS

Tropic of Capricorn

Tahiti SOCIETY
ISLANDS

**Marquesas and
Society Islands
colonized c. AD 300**

**Easter Island
colonized c. AD 400** *Easter Island*
(scale exaggerated
for visibility)

**Maori settlers arrive in
New Zealand c. AD 1000**

right: *The famous and enigmatic sculptures
on Easter Island.*

overpopulation, seeking new fishing grounds, or founding new religious cultures. Whatever the reason, they headed out in sturdy, double-hulled canoes up to 100 feet (30m) long and capable of carrying 140 people, together with domestic animals, supplies, and personal goods. Drawing on an advanced knowledge of the stars, sun, wave movements, and the flight pattern of birds, they struck east—against prevailing winds and currents—into the unknown. Their feat remains unparalleled

This chapter looks at the archeological evidence for this colonization; the legacy of the Lapita pottery makers, the bizarre ritualistic outpost of Easter Island, and the Maoris of New Zealand. But we begin with the story of prehistoric Australia where the lives of the first aborigines are being pieced together to reveal extraordinary details about the intelligence and reasoning power of early humans.

LAKE MUNGO
Riddle in the sands

Australia has a special part to play in boosting our knowledge of prehistoric man. Because it has never been joined to south-east Asia—even when sea levels were at their lowest—the first inhabitants of this vast continent must have traveled across at least 30 miles (50km) of ocean. The idea that early humans could build sturdy, sea-going craft 40,000 or possibly even 60,000 years ago is hard to credit. Yet, from the wealth of archeological data now emerging from Australia, we can be reasonably sure it happened.

Bowler's discovery

Lake Mungo, on the Willandra Lakes World Heritage site of western New South Wales, is a key geographical area in the continent's colonization. In 1968 Jim Bowler, a scientist studying the climatic history of the area, happened to glance at some burnt bones sticking out of a large, weathered, crescent-shaped dune beside the shores of Mungo. Under laboratory analysis it was established that these belonged to a young woman who died 25,000 years ago. Her bones had been cremated, smashed into minute fragments, and buried. Six years later, a second grave—this time dating from c.30,000 years ago—was found nearby. Here a man had been buried lying on his side and sprinkled

above: *Sand dunes along the east side of Lake Mungo. The effects of weathering have occasionally produced outstanding finds.*

with the iron oxide red ocher.

These finds instantly rewrote Australian prehistory. At a stroke, the timespan for early human presence had been almost doubled. But more important, the information posed difficult questions about the state of mind of these first aborigines. Did they have a concept of religion or spirituality? Had they begun to form views about an afterlife? What was the nature of their sexual relationships and their attitude to communal life? If they had the sophistication to cross oceans and carry out ritualistic cremations and burials what else could they do? Modern aborigines have their own myths, which may indeed be loosely based on real events. The coming of

their ancestors is explained in The Dreaming—a mythology in which the first colonists arrive in Australia to prepare the land for hunting and growing and to deposit the spirits of future children.

About 35,000 years ago Mungo was a freshwater lake. It is among 17 others at Willandra which dried up 14,000 years ago to leave a hostile, arid land in which vast sand dunes dominate a scene akin to a moonscape. It is rich in fossils and among the more exotic are remains of extinct creatures such as giant kangaroos, a type of oxen called a zygomaturus, and the Tasmanian tiger. The aborigines themselves seem to have feasted on freshwater mussels and fish such as golden perch. The typical meat diet consisted of wallabies and kangaroos and there is evidence that they also collected emu eggs. Much later, c.8000 BC, they developed

c.100,000 BC	c.50,000 BC	c.30,000 BC	c.30,000 BC	c.70,000–30,000 BC	c.24,000 BC	c.25,000–20,000 BC	c.10,000 BC
True *Homo sapiens* emerge in Middle East.	First known rock art, in Australia.	Neanderthal people disappear completely after being slowly replaced by *Homo sapiens*.	Most of inhabitable world has been colonised.	Temperatures drop globally.	Hunter-gatherers construct houses with roofs of clay in Europe.	Cave art flourishes in southern Europe.	Southern tip of South America is reached.

Excavations at Mungo
and Willandra rewrote Australian pre-history.

left: *Alice Kelly, a native Australian aborigine, views the shores of Lake Mungo.*

robust physical frame. The Kow Swamp bones are considerably younger—c.11,000 to 7500 BC—and some experts say they could not have evolved from the same genetic stock as the Mungo people. One idea is that there may have been at least two separate migrations to Australia; with the Kow people descending from an

a type of sandstone grinder with which they crushed wild seeds to make flour.

Comparisons between this site and others of a later date in Australia have produced confusing archeological findings. Foremost among these is the appearance of the bodies. The Lake Mungo people appear to have light, almost delicate, facial features which indicate significant differences from those in modern aborigines. Yet on the east shore of Kow Swamp, Victoria, the excavated remains from at least 40 burials suggest a more

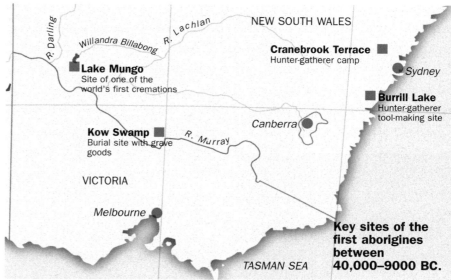

R. Darling

Willandra Billabong

R. Lachlan

NEW SOUTH WALES

Lake Mungo
Site of one of the
world's first cremations

Cranebrook Terrace
Hunter-gatherer camp

Sydney

Burrill Lake
Hunter-gatherer
tool-making site

Canberra

Kow Swamp
Burial site with grave
goods

R. Murray

VICTORIA

Melbourne

**Key sites of the
first aborigines
between
40,000–9000 BC.**

TASMAN SEA

ancient race in Java and the Mungo tribe evolving from Chinese stock. This remains a controversial view and some anthropologists suspect the differences in bone structure have been exaggerated.

below: *Sunrise over the dunes of Mungo Lake. The entire area is rich in fossils.*

ROCK ART AT CARNARVON GORGE
Australia's prehistoric artists

The countryside 250 miles (400km) west of Brisbane is a strikingly beautiful place. Here a huge sandstone massif rises out of the plains; cut into a maze of gorges by rivers and centuries of water erosion. As the Carnarvon National Park it is today the pride of Queensland, but it was a magnet for settlers long before any notions of tourism and conservation. Parts of the uplands were inhabited at least 19,000 years ago and by c.3000 BC it was the center of a major aboriginal community linked to the Bidjara tribe. Their staple diet was meat, such as the rock wallaby, and prepared seeds from the prolific zamia plant—rich in starch and protein, and still a common food in the tropics today.

From an archeological perspective, the most important feature of Carnarvon Gorge is its superb array of prehistoric stencils. These were produced using a primitive spraying technique in which the artist would take a mouthful of water mixed with ocher (a clay/iron oxide mineral) and blow it out in fine droplets against an object held against the rock. In this way flat items such as boomerangs appeared sharply-defined, while bulkier ones created a slightly blurred outline. Hands tend to be the most common stenciled images but there are also "lil-lils" (a type of club-cum-boomerang with a distinctive bump at one end), coolamons (shields), and stone tomahawks. Around a small hole in one rock face are the images of two lil-lils alongside adult hand stencils. It is thought these may be linked to a cremation or interment on the basis that a bark burial cylinder, containing the remains of a child, was found in a nearby hole. Indeed, almost all prehistoric aboriginal paintings appear to have some sort of religious function.

Much of the Carnarvon Gorge art dates from around 1500 BC, although at the nearby Kennif Cave there are examples thought to be at least 18,000 years old. The main colors used are red and mauve (ocher containing hematite and magnesium), yellow (limonite and hydrated iron oxide), and white (kaolin clay). White appears to have been a later fashion and is often daubed over older, colored stencils. Protected from light, there is no sign that any of the pigments have faded.

left: *Yagjagbula and Yabiringl, the spectacular "Lightning Brothers" of Ingaladdi waterhole in the Victoria River District are two characters from aboriginal mythology.*

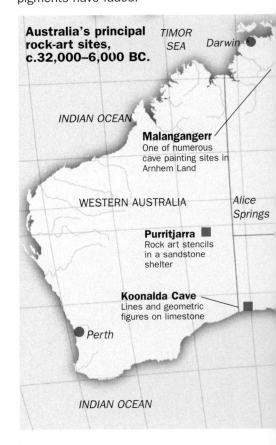

Australia's principal rock-art sites, c.32,000–6,000 BC.

TIMOR SEA

Darwin

INDIAN OCEAN

Malangangerr
One of numerous cave painting sites in Arnhem Land

WESTERN AUSTRALIA

Alice Springs

Purritjarra ■
Rock art stencils in a sandstone shelter

Koonalda Cave
Lines and geometric figures on limestone

Perth

INDIAN OCEAN

c.50,000 BC	c.50,000–40,000 BC	c.35,000 BC	c.30,000 BC	c.25,000 BC	c.17,000 BC	c.3000 BC	c.3000 BC
Beginning of colonisation of Australia.	First Australian rock art.	First colonists cross to Tasmania from Australia.	Last of the Neanderthals die out, in Europe.	Cave art is created in Europe.	First settlers in area of present Carnarvon National Park.	Newgrange stone building in Ireland built.	Bidjara tribe settle in area of present Carnarvon National Park.

Almost all early aboriginal paintings appear to have a religious function.

above: *Hands tend to be the most common stencils among Carnarvon Gorge rock art.*

The world's oldest art

New scientific techniques are now securing even older dates for rock art in the southern Australian deserts. Here stone engravings have become encased in "desert varnish," a dark, polished veneer caused by bacterial chemicals. Tiny organisms trapped under this chemical crust can be subjected to a form of radio carbon analysis to give a minimum age for the engravings they cover. In this way, some Australian rock art has been dated to c.40,000—50,000 years old, making it the oldest in the world.

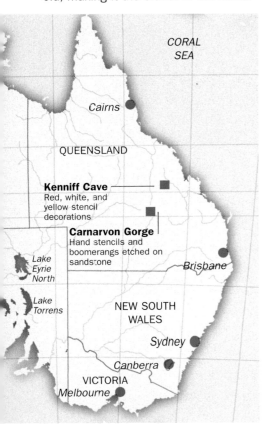

Paradoxically, it is also the last great global art movement of the 20th century with the work of some contemporary aborigine painters fetching tens of thousands of pounds at international auction houses.

The days when aboriginal art was considered irrelevant have long since gone. Discovering and interpreting these paintings is now anthropologically fashionable and clear regional and tribal variations have emerged. In Arnhem Land early artists painted "X-ray style" fish in which bones and intestines were combined with external features such as fins and tails to create a semi-abstract image. Koonalda Cave and the Mount Gambier caves contain galleries with geometric shapes and long, winding lines, while the Ingaladdi waterhole in the Victoria River District has the spectacular "Lightning Brothers"—two characters from aboriginal mythology. The older brother, Yagjagbula, is 9' 7" (2.9m) tall. Yabiringl, slightly to the fore, is 10' 5" (3.1m) tall. Both have disproportionately long penises (an art fertility feature common in many prehistoric cultures), elaborate headdresses with a central plume, and are carrying stone axes in their right hands.

c.2800 BC	c.2000 BC	c.1900 BC	c.1840 BC	c.1750 BC	c.1500 BC	c.1200 BC	c.1100 BC
First phase of work on Stonehenge is begun.	Inuit people living in Arctic.	Irrigation technology improves in Mesopotamia to nurture expanding population.	Lower Nubia is annexed by Egypt.	Hammurabi founds Babylonian Empire.	Most prolific time of rock art painting at Carnarvon N.P.	Greeks destroy city of Troy.	Phoenicians develop alphabetic script.

THE LAPITA MAKERS
Cultural clues from pottery

Since it was first identified on New Caledonia in 1952, Lapita pottery has become a lively subject within archeological circles. Fragments of these ornate, distinctive vessels can be found from Aitape, on the Sepik coast of New Guinea and as far east as Tonga, Fiji, and Samoa—providing clear pointers to the ambitious trading network of a people who became prehistoric nomads of the sea. The earliest Lapita-ware is about 4,000 years old and was made by self-sufficient communities who survived through a mixture of hunting, fishing, and the gathering of wild plants. As their contacts increased, their desire for commerce grew and soon Lapita goods were part of a flourishing inter-island market that also traded stone tools, obsidian glass, shells, and food.

Archaeological complexity

The geography of Oceania is daunting enough in itself. Add in the ethnic and racial groups, the pattern of settlement, and a 40,000 year chronology, and we are all entitled to be confused. In essence though, the region has produced three ethnic groupings: Micronesia (some 2,000 tiny islands east of the Philippines and mainly north of the equator); Polynesia (which encompasses islands in a triangular area of the central, eastern, and southern Pacific, including New Zealand and Easter Island); and Melanesia (most of the western Pacific islands south of the equator). Micronesia was first settled about 1500 BC, and its people have a blood type that sets them apart from Australian, Asiatic, and Polynesian people. Central Polynesia was occupied about the same time, although some outlying islands—including New Zealand—were not explored until as late as 1000 AD.

Melanesia seems likely to have

above: *A small carved ivory tiki figure. This one was probably used as a pendant.*

been the springboard for the push east. It was settled in two distinct waves—first c.40,000 BC with the spread of dark-skinned Papuans (cousins of the aborigines) across what is now New Guinea and the Bismarck Archipelago. Much later, c.2,000 BC, a South-east Asian culture arrived in the same area and expanded into the Solomon Islands,

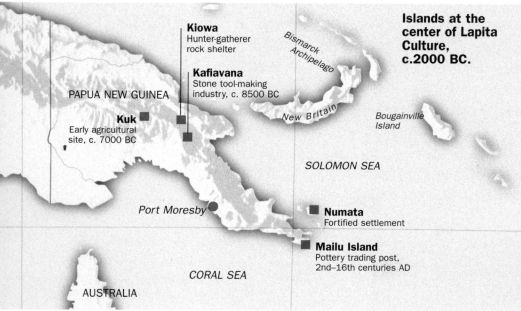

Kiowa
Hunter-gatherer rock shelter

Kafiavana
Stone tool-making industry, c. 8500 BC

PAPUA NEW GUINEA

Kuk
Early agricultural site, c. 7000 BC

Bismarck Archipelago

New Britain

Bougainville Island

Islands at the center of Lapita Culture, c.2000 BC.

SOLOMON SEA

Port Moresby

Numata
Fortified settlement

Mailu Island
Pottery trading post, 2nd–16th centuries AD

CORAL SEA

AUSTRALIA

c.40,000 BC	c.2000 BC	c.2000 BC
First settlers in Melanesia.	South-east Asian culture colonises Melanesia.	First metal-working in Peru.

right: *An ivory ear bolt decorated with tiki figures. The tiki is a common theme in Polynesian art and is thought to represent humans in primeval form.*

below: *This grotesque figure is a moai kavakava (emaciated man). It would have served as an ancestral heirloom and been worn as a giant pendant by its owner on feast days.*

Vanuatu, Fiji, New Caledonia, and Polynesia. It is these people who provide a credible explanation for the rise of Lapita culture. We can assume they found a few pockets of habitation—descendants of the early peoples who drifted out of Asia—and quickly imposed their own ways, religion, and technology.

However, some archeologists within the Pacific Rim are starting to question the validity of this hypotheses. For one thing, they say, there is very little evidence to suggest that Lapita was an invading empire. Neither is it clear that this pottery, styled using intricate stamps, was the symbol of some all-embracing cultural movement. It could just as easily be the case that it developed internally, perhaps centered on the Bismarck Archipelago, and was copied by hundreds of island potters keen to adopt a new pottery style. Part of the problem is that there are plenty of experts willing to offer interpretations of the Lapita phenomenon, yet comparatively few suitable sites for them to study.

Some scholars doubt whether it matters a jot either way. They suspect a hint of politically-correct parochialism in the rush to show that Lapitians and their Polynesian descendants have an inbred cultural lineage. However, the debate does raise some important questions. Can we really draw clear-cut conclusions about the colonization of an area as vast as Oceania on the basis of individual case studies, however thorough and academically proper these may be? To understand the expansion of prehistoric people around the world may require unusual and unconventional theories which still elude anthropologists and historians. Too many assumptions make unreliable science.

Understanding the expansion of prehistoric civilisations may require unusual and unconventional theories.

c.2000 BC	c.2000 BC	c.2000 BC	c.1900 BC	c.1840 BC	c.1800 BC	c.1750 BC	c.1500 BC
Use of sail on seagoing vessels in Aegean.	Inuit people living in Arctic.	Minoans produce painted pottery.	Irrigation technology improve in Mesopotamia to nurture expanding population.	Lower Nubia is annexed by Egypt.	Shamshi-Adad founds Assyrian state.	Hammurabi founds Babylonian Empire.	Micronesia settled.

MAORI FORTRESSES
The colonization of New Zealand

According to Maori legend New Zealand was colonized by a gifted navigator named Kupe, who led his people south from an unidentified Polynesian island called Hawaiki about a thousand years ago. Kupe is said to have first sighted the new land while it was covered in mist. He promptly named it Aotearoa or "Land of the Long, White Cloud," a name still used by Maoris today.

For those first settlers the new homeland must have seemed like paradise—unlimited fishing, unrestricted territory, and a comparatively secure environment. But within a few centuries a new wave of colonists arrived, fleeing the perils of overpopulation and famine on Hawaiki. They tried to carve out territories of their own, leading to bitter disputes with the established communities. This created a society locked in perpetual inter-tribal warfare, with the losers often ending up either as slaves or, worse, as food. Eating your enemies was considered to be a way of taking away their body energy, or *mana*.

Inevitably, status was paramount. Maoris adopted a sharply-defined class structure made up of chiefs, the nobility, priests, commoners, and slaves. No written records were kept of an individual's background (though Maoris did have a written language) but a verbal genealogy, known as Whakapapa, ensured it was never forgotten. In the same way, history was recorded through long, structured chants and songs while etiquette was preserved through complex and elaborate greeting rituals such as the *haka* war chant (these days ably demonstrated by New Zealand's All Blacks rugby team before the start of international matches), and the *wero* challenge. Respected leaders could be identified by their heavily-tattooed bodies—sometimes literally from head to toe—whereas women were permitted only a small single tattoo, or *moko*, on their chins. Clothing was largely fur and feather, while ornaments were bone or jade.

In times of peace land was held communally. However each tribe and sub-group had a sacred spot known as a *marae* where ancestral spirits could reside and be worshiped. This also served as a meeting place for elders to debate and judge important matters within the tribe. Living quarters were built inside a *pa*, a kind of earth-and-timber village fortress, examples of which which can still be found today dotted across the New Zealand landscape. The hills and coastline around the capital Wellington

below: *The peak of the pa on Onawe Peninsula, with fortification remains. This is the first example of a trench defense designed for use with muskets,*

c.1000 AD	c.1000 AD	c.1200–1250	c.1220 AD	c.1250 AD	1337–1453	c.1350 AD	1492 AD
Vikings land in North America.	Polynesians arrive in New Zealand.	Dwellings carved into Cliff Canyon, Colorado, North America.	Emergence of first Thai kingdom.	Expansion of Mongol Empire across Asia and Europe.	England and France fight the Hundred Years' War.	Renaissance begins in Italy.	Columbus discovers America.

The macabre European demand for severed heads ensured the Maori had a thriving export market.

contain some *pa* sites which remained occupied well into the 20th century. However most fell in to rapid decline with the coming of the Europeans in the late 18th century and the ceding of overall sovereignty to Britain under the 1840 Treaty of Waitangi.

The end of traditional culture

In 1850 one European traveler, Tacy Kemp, described a visit to Ohaua *pa*, north of Ohau Point: "The greater part of it is secured to the natives as a reserve, but nearly deserted, there being only five individuals in the *pa*. The *pa* and many of the huts are in a state of decay and in a few months will be probably quite deserted. There is no cultivation, the soil is poor, and the country hilly and badly timbered." Other writers told how the population of some *pa*s had been halved inside a decade because of disease. One native teacher at Ohariu, near Wellington, claimed to personally have buried 100 adults in the space of 10 years.

above: *Te Porere Redoubt, south of Lake Taupo, was built by visionary Maori leader Te Kooti Rikirangi Te Turiki for his last battle against government forces.*

Faced with this kind of catastrophe it is little wonder that Maoris embraced the "reforms" of civilization. Prostitution and disease, and a burgeoning trade in firearms precipitated ever more bloody internal conflicts. Such was the macabre European demand for preserved, severed heads that Maori chiefs found they had a thriving export market… as long as they had enough slaves to decapitate. In less severe forms, the culture clash in New Zealand continues today over land rights and the militancy of young Maoris facing long-term unemployment.

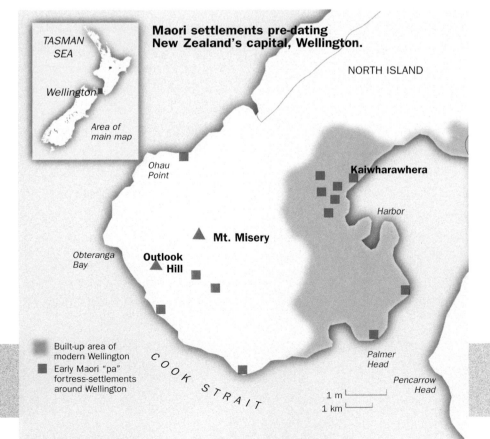

Maori settlements pre-dating New Zealand's capital, Wellington.

TASMAN SEA

Wellington

Area of main map

NORTH ISLAND

Ohau Point

Kaiwharawhera

Harbor

▲ Mt. Misery

Obteranga Bay

Outlook ▲ **Hill**

COOK STRAIT

Palmer Head

Pencarrow Head

■ Built-up area of modern Wellington
■ Early Maori "pa" fortress-settlements around Wellington

1 m
1 km

c.1500 AD

Culture of Easter Island begins to die out.

c.1800 AD

Beginning of colonization of New Zealand by Europeans.

STATUES OF EASTER ISLAND
Ominous monuments to an isolated people

The history of Easter Island reads like some bizarre science fiction experiment in mass imprisonment. It is an extraordinary story of courage, excess, isolation, and desperation, and is unparalleled anywhere else in the world. To walk on the island today, among its somber stone-carved giants and the rock carvings recording strange and dangerous rituals, is to wonder at a civilization cut off from outside influence for perhaps 1,500 years. In failing to create a sustainable economy and environment its people doomed themselves to slow destruction. Those who today preach an apocalyptic future for Planet Earth need look no further for an historical example.

The first settlers on Easter Island probably arrived in the early centuries AD from eastern Polynesia. There were perhaps several dozen, huddled together in the double-hulled canoes which had proved their seaworthiness so admirably over previous centuries. With them they brought live chickens, dogs, pigs, and rats, plants such as

More than 800 hillside statues were erected—each bearing distinctive, angular facial features.

sweet potatoes, bananas, and breadfruit, and various grain crops. Not all of these would survive on the island, but in the early years there were plenty of additional food sources such as forest birds and unlimited supplies of fish. Soon the newcomers were carving huge swathes out of dense rainforest to establish their farms.

The island's geographical position, and its archeological legacy, suggests there was only ever one influx of colonists. The 66 square miles (171 sq km) of volcanic outcrop lies 2,328 miles (3,622 km) from the South American coast and 2,250 miles from Pitcairn, to the north-west, and it seems unlikely in the extreme that anyone would have contemplated a return journey to spread word of its existence. Gradually the population

increased to the point that by c.1400 AD it probably exceeded 10,000 people—the culture's so-called Golden Age. With this growth came an advanced social and religious structure of which the statues, thought to represent the spirits of ancestors, were an integral part. More than 800 of them were erected; all following a similar design with angular facial features, truncated lower limbs, arms pressed to sides, and hands folded in front to merge with a loincloth. Many were erected on stone platforms and at least 230 were laboriously hauled by sledge and rollers from the main quarry to coastal venues where they were positioned facing away from the sea to watch over villages below. Typically, these figures range in size from 6' 7" to 33'

Primary sites of Easter Island.

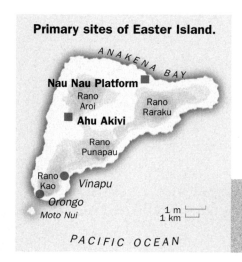

ANAKENA BAY

Nau Nau Platform

Rano Aroi

Rano Raraku

Ahu Akivi

Rano Punapau

Rano Kao   Vinapu

Orongo
Moto Nui

1 m
1 km

PACIFIC OCEAN

410 AD	c.630 AD	c.1000 AD	c.1000 AD	1066 AD
The Roman Empire is invaded and collapses.	Mohammed founds Islam.	Vikings land in North America.	Polynesians arrive in New Zealand.	Invasion of England by Norman French.

Easter Island people became poverty-stricken—trapped in a prison of their own making.

The Bird Man Cult

In September each year Easter Island's finest young men would gather above a rocky beach near the southern ceremonial village of Orongo. Each would represent a tribal elder—warriors competing to be the following year's chief or "birdman." Together the unenviable contestants would attempt a terrifying 300' (100m) descent down the cliffside, swim across half a mile (0.8 km) of water frequented by sharks, climb the nearby islet of Moto Nui, hunt out the nest of a frigate bird, steal an egg, and transport it unbroken back across the water to his sponsor. The winning warrior would then be declared the earthly incarnation of the god Makemake and would lead nature rituals throughout the year ahead.

(2m—10m) but one, such as the unfinished "El Gigante," is 66' (20m) high and weighed about 270 tons.

Catastrophe looms

Sometime after 1500 AD this essentially peaceful community erupted into internecine warfare. Statues were attacked and toppled, large quantities of obsidian volcanic glass was quarried for use as spearheads, and the priests who had presided over a centuries-old ancestor cult were toppled in favor of a new warrior caste. The precise reasons behind this revolution are unclear but it does not take a genius to see that the islanders were committing economic suicide. Their population increase meant extra food was required, yet economically worthless activities such as stone carving were continued, reducing the numbers of farmers and fishermen available to feed the burgeoning population. Worse still, there was deforestation on a catastrophic scale to meet the demands of shack-building, statue-rolling, and canoe-making. When the trees finally disappeared canoes could not be rebuilt; deep sea fishing was abandoned and the island's protein-rich fish diet was lost forever.

By the time the first European explorers arrived in 1722 Easter Island was a dying culture, its last 2,000 people living in abject poverty—trapped in a prison of their own making.

The altar of Ahu Akivi. Stone platforms like this support many of the statues.

CHAPTER ELEVEN

SOUTH AND CENTRAL AMERICA

When the Spanish conquistadors began looting Inca treasures they were amazed to find how easy it all was. After tricking warriors into believing they were returning sacred religious artifacts they promptly made the emperor Atahualpa their prisoner and puppet king. Such was the centralized nature of the state that there was no effective protest. In this way the vast Inca empire was held to ransom by a force of just 180 Spaniards.

But then the Americas are full of surprises. Archeologists have been forced into a drastic reassessment of the date humans first walked these lands following excavations of the site at Monte Verde in Southern Chile. Here, fragments of charcoal dating back 33,000 years seriously question the established idea that colonization took place relatively recently (c.12,000 BC) across the last Ice Age land bridge between Asia and America. Were there prehistoric inter-continental sailors of previously unimagined skill? Or did the push into the New World from Asia occur much earlier. The jury is still out on these issues.

Whatever the truth of its history, South and Central America have no shortage of fascinating cultures. In this chapter we consider the rise of the mysterious Nasca people and their strange desert markings, the immeasurably rich pyramid tomb of the Lord of Sipán, the "Pompeii-style" destruction of the El Salvadorean village of El Cerén, and the secret Mayan cave rituals at Naj Tunich, Guatemala. One thing is clear. In their knowledge of the natural world, their superb artwork, and their ability to organize millions of people, these native peoples were a far cry from their 16th-century European portrayal as heathen savages.

This Peruvian head c.100 BC—600 AD, the Early Intermediate Period of Moche culture, is made from gold with encrustations of turqouise.

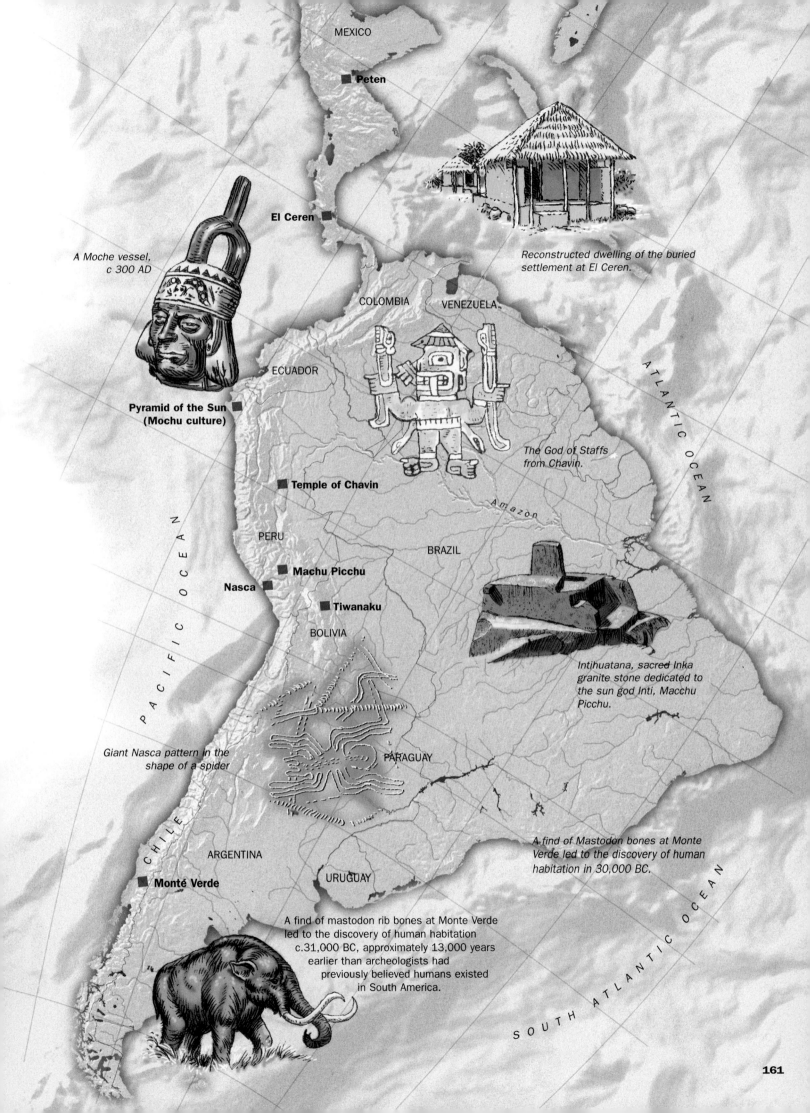

MEXICO

■ **Peten**

Reconstructed dwelling of the buried settlement at El Ceren.

■ **El Ceren**

*A Moche vessel,
c 300 AD*

COLOMBIA   VENEZUELA

ECUADOR

The God of Staffs
from Chavin.

**Pyramid of the Sun
(Mochu culture)** ■

■ **Temple of Chavin**

A m a z o n

PERU   BRAZIL

Machu Picchu ■

Nasca ■

■ **Tiwanaku**

BOLIVIA

Intihuatana, sacred Inka
granite stone dedicated to
the sun god Inti, Macchu
Picchu.

PACIFIC OCEAN

ATLANTIC OCEAN

*Giant Nasca pattern in the
shape of a spider*

PARAGUAY

A find of Mastodon bones at Monte
Verde led to the discovery of human
habitation in 30,000 BC.

CHILE

ARGENTINA

URUGUAY

■ **Monté Verde**

A find of mastodon rib bones at Monte Verde
led to the discovery of human habitation
c.31,000 BC, approximately 13,000 years
earlier than archeologists had
previously believed humans existed
in South America.

SOUTH ATLANTIC OCEAN

TIWANAKU AND THE PRE-INCAS
The political center of South America

When the Spanish conquistadors subjugated the Inca Empire in 1532 they were eager to learn what other great civilizations—and therefore potential treasures—existed in western South America. Inca chiefs insisted that there were no others; that they had blessed the Andes with civilization and all previous occupants had been mere jungle barbarians. The Spanish weren't so sure.

Soon travelers such as Pedro Cieza de Leon were documenting the great Inca buildings and noticed others, of a distinctly different style, in ruins among them. De Leon became particularly interested in two sites—Tiwanaku, on a plateau near Lake Titicaca, and Wari in central Peru—and wrote: "I venture to say that it could have been that before the Incas ruled there must have been another people of wisdom in these realms, who came from some unknown place,

who made this things."

Centuries later he was proved right. Studies of artistic themes on pottery and ornamental weapons showed that Tiwanaku and Wari were centers of similar though separate cultures that existed long before the Incas.

Wari seems to have been a military empire that flourished briefly between the eighth and 11th centuries AD. But Tiwanaku is probably far older—at least as early as the third century AD—and was an important pilgrimage

center. It included a large paved area to accommodate the masses and elaborate monumental masonry which, despite the determination of the Spanish to destroy idolatry, still retains something of its magnificence.

The Gate of the Sun, with its god-like figure standing on a raised dais, flanked by rows of strange birds, was carved from a single block of stone, while the 650-foot (200m) long Akapana mound was designed to allow a stream to flow over and around it; perhaps a shrine acknowledging the life-giving properties of water. The andesite stone used to face this mound was quarried more than 62 miles (100 km) away.

left: *A plaster model of the Gate Of The Sun, one of Tiwanaku's most celebrated monuments.*

MODEL OF THE MONOLITHIC GATEWAY

c.2000 BC	c.200 AD	410 AD
First Nasca lines made.	Tiwanaku founded.	In Europe, the Roman Empire is invaded and collapses.

The city's decline began around 1000 AD when lower rainfall reduced the effectiveness of irrigation.

Frost-free agriculture techniques

Akapana is one of the highlights of Tiwanaku's so-called "monuments precinct," a series of manmade platforms set across 50 acres (20 ha). Many of the structures—such as the Kalasaya mound, with its walls of alternating megaliths and infilled rubble, and the Sunken Courtyard, of similar design but with carved stone heads set into the wall—date from 200–600 AD. In the following four centuries this ingenious stonework

Pre-Inca culture at Tiwanaku

left: The Sunken Courtyard with the Kalasaya enclosure in the background. At its height Tiwanaku had an urban population of more than 25,000.

dominated architectural thought across the southern and central Andes and influenced the decoration of ceramics and the style of sculpture. Many of the outstanding statues found at Tiwanaku are now on display at an archeological park in the Bolivian capital of La Paz.

The growth of Tiwanaku was probably linked to great agricultural prosperity around the shores of Lake Titicaca, which then covered a much larger area. Here, 12,600 feet (4580m) above sea level, farmers developed a network of raised-bed and shoreline canals to extend their growing season. The warmth retained by the canals during the day was enough to allay frosts at night, drastically improving food production.

At its height, Tiwanaku supported an urban population of between 25,000 and 40,000 people and wielded political control in much of what is now Bolivia, Argentina, Chile, and Peru. The state's decline seems to have begun around 1000 AD, at a time when lower rainfall diminished the effectiveness of the canal beds and resulted in the drastic retreat of Titicaca. By then, Tiwanaku had

The Cloud People

One of the great unsolved riddles of South American archeology centers on the legend of a "lost white tribe" whose heartland lay in cloud forest around the Lake of the Condors in north-eastern Peru. The Incas knew this civilization as the Chachapoya, or Cloud People, and described them to the invading Spanish as tall and blond. The staggering implication is that somehow an invading tribe of outsiders—potentially Europeans—somehow ended up living an isolated existence in a remote corner of Peru around 1000 AD. It is hoped DNA analysis on mummies from a supposed Chachapoyan tomb will at least establish whether the dead were white-skinned.

established the roots of an Andean civilization and tradition.

Its modern-day manifestation can be seen in the Quechua language, which is spoken by ten million people from Ecuador to Argentina, most of them living in a mountain landscape of between 3000 and 11,000 feet (900–3450m). It is possible that the Tiwanaku state unified Quechua tribes with those of the other main language group, the Aymara.

c.630 AD	c.700–1100 AD	c.1000 AD	c.1000 AD	c.1500 AD
Mohammed founds Islam.	Wari flourishes.	Vikings land in North America.	Polynesians arrive in New Zealand.	Last Nasca lines made.

THE LINES OF NASCA
Oversized art or astronomical calendar?

The Nasca plateau in southern Peru is one of the driest places on earth. It gets perhaps an inch of rain every two years and the surface is shielded from wind erosion by a buffer of warm, still air caused by heat radiation from dark rocks covering the desert floor. These are ideal conditions for the preservation of ancient structures, as shown by the earth drawings of Nasca. This gigantic complex of lines, geometric shapes, and animal images was formed by removing sun-blackened stones to reveal pale yellow soil.

It is thought that most of the straight lines were made over a long period between 2000 BC and 1500 AD, while the animal figures—which include monkeys, spiders, and snakes—were drawn by a specific Nasca culture that emerged between 100 and 500 AD. It is possible that these were used in a religious procession or they pointed toward sacred mountains or cemeteries. They may even have formed part of an irrigation system; perhaps a symbolic offering to the gods who sent rain.

Among the first scholars to tackle the Nasca lines were American historian Paul Kosok and his wife Rose. In 1941 they began studying old Peruvian irrigation systems but spent most of their time mapping the apparently chaotic collection of lines that stretched across the desert. On one occasion they stopped at the center of a spider's web stone pattern to watch a dramatic sunset. "We suddenly noticed," Paul Kosok wrote later, "that it was setting almost exactly over the end of one of the long single lines. A moment later we recalled that it was June 22, the day of the winter solstice in the Southern Hemisphere—the shortest day of the year and the day when the sun sets farthest north of due west. With a great thrill we realized at once that we had apparently found the key to the riddle."

Plotting and measuring the Nascan lines

Unfortunately it wasn't that simple. Kosok's conclusion that the lines were a prehistoric guide to the movements of the stars was controversial and he had to return to his Long Island University lecturing job before he completed a methodical

above: *This aerial view of part of the Nasca Lines shows a representation of a bird. The Lines are best seen from the air.*

study. He persuaded 36-year-old German mathematician Maria Reiche to continue the investigation. She had fled the rise of the Nazi party in 1932 to take up a governess's job in Peru, but from that moment Nasca dominated her life.

Reiche spent weeks camping alone in the desert, waking at dawn to map

The Influence of Nasca Culture

BRAZIL

ANDES MOUNTAINS

Lima

Machu Picchu
(lost city of the Inkas)

Ico

Nasca

Lake Titicaca

LaPaz

BOLIVIA

Nasca Lines

Tiwanaku

CHILE

PACIFIC OCEAN

American airline executive Jim Woodman sought to prove that the Nascans could have been the world's first balloonists.

2000 BC	c.1800 BC	1674 BC	c.1600 BC	c.1550 BC	c.1500 BC	c.1500 BC	c.1460 BC
First Nasca lines made.	Advanced mathematics is used for accounting in Egypt.	Memphis, the Egyptian capital, falls to the Hyksos.	Shang dynasty in China creates the first urban civilization in that region.	Pharaohs begin to be interred in the Valley of the Kings.	Demise of the Minoan civilization.	People living near the Great Lakes of North America discover metallurgy.	Thutmose III extends Egypt's empire to Mesopotamia.

the rising points of the sun and planets. She spent hours sweeping the markings of debris and bought so many brooms that local townsfolk suspected she was a witch! She later recalled sweeping a spiral shape for days and laughing out loud when she realized it was the tail of a vast monkey. Reiche concluded that the lines were laid by stretching twine between wooden posts (keeping three in sight ensured a straight course, even when crossing a skyline). Curves were produced by a similar process, in which twine helped shape interlinking arcs.

Reiche's observations backed Kosok's astronomical theories and shed new light on the line-makers' techniques and influences. She logged similarities between the drawings and the design of Nasca pottery and showed how the earth artists had prepared miniature ground plans, around 6 feet (2m) square, before embarking on larger-scale projects. She discovered that the most common Nascan units of measurement were equivalent to ten inches (25cm) and 4.5 feet (1.37m), although there was also a unit of 5.95 feet (1.8m). A famous image known as the "Candelabra," drawn on a hillside at Pisco Bay 130 miles north of the desert, is exactly 595 feet long.

The lack of hard facts about the Nasca people has spawned some weird theories. Hotel manager and amateur archeologist Erik von Däniken was demonized by scholars for suggesting that the markings were made for alien spacecraft. His argument that the lines were meant to be viewed from the air so captivated American airline executive Jim

Woodman that in 1975 he sought to prove that the Nascans could have been the world's first balloonists. Encouraged by Inca legends about flying people, he launched a balloon made entirely of materials available in the fifth century AD. It reached an altitude of 1,200 feet (365m) and flew for 14 minutes—long enough, argued Woodman, to substantiate his theory.

c.1450 BC	c.1400 BC	c.1390 BC	c.1350 BC	c.200 AD	100–500 AD	1500 AD	1500 AD
The earliest Indian *Vedas* are written.	Horses are used as transport in central Asia.	Writing begins in China.	A new Egyptian religion is established, based on a solar cult.	Roman Empire is at its height in Europe.	Drawings of Nasca animals made.	Spanish begin conquest of South America.	Last of the Nasca lines drawn.

JAGUARS OF CHAVÍN DE HUANTAR
Remains of a lost civilization in the Peruvian Andes

In the 1920s the "father" of Peruvian archeology, Julio C. Tello, began excavations at the mountain village of Chavín de Huantar in northern Peru. Tello, a native Peruvian Indian whose abilities had secured him a scholarship to Harvard University, was convinced that the origins of his country's civilization lay not among the ancient ceremonial sites of the coastal plain but instead high in the Andes. Gradually, he built up a picture of a widespread religious cult characterized by jaguar motifs on masonry, metalwork, cloth, and pottery.

The existence of Chavín had been known for centuries. Spanish missionaries spoke of huge structures built of massive stone blocks to which Indian pilgrims would deliver sacrifices and offerings, and receive their "oracles from the Devil." But it was Tello who established the real importance of the site; uncovering the old temples with their intricate stone carvings of grotesque, snarling humans, mythological creatures, and jungle species such as jaguars, crocodiles, and parrots. He realised these bore close similarities to stone reliefs he had documented in other parts of the Andes, and the image of a so-called "staff deity"—a god depicted with a staff in each hand—was adapted in later cultures such as Wari and Tiwanaku.

It is thought construction of the Chavín temples began c.900 BC with modifications continuing over the ensuing 700 years. The main building was U-shaped and arranged around a sunken plaza, presumably the spot where worshippers gathered. Close by, a covered gallery contained the remains of deliberately broken pottery presented as offerings to stone idols such as the Lanzon, or

The New Temple at Chavin de Huantar.

c.900 BC	c.750 BC	c.600 BC	539 BC	510 BC	505 BC	c.500 BC	c.500 BC
Construction of the Chavín temples begins.	The *Iliad* is written in Greece.	The Celtic Hallstatt civilization thrives in Europe.	Persian Empire founded under Cyrus the Great.	Foundation of Roman republic.	Democracy established in Athens.	First European towns established.	Paracus culture flourishes in Peru.

Looters began squabbling over their booty and one of them contacted police.

"Smiling God"—a human-like creature with a cat's fangs and snakes for hair whose central position indicates that the entire temple was built around him. Studies of the broken vessels confirmed

above: *An anthropomorphic storage jar of Chavin-type design.*

Tello's belief that Chavín united many isolated villages and settlements behind a single religious cult.

Some 200 years after Chavín a new religion emerged—this time from the dry desert plain that stretches across Peru's north coast. Until relatively recently this Moche culture had been notable mainly for its massive mudbrick pyramids such as the Huaca del Sol (Pyramid of the Sun)—at 1,115' by 130' (340m by 40m) the largest anywhere in the Americas—and beautiful ceramic work with themes of hunting, fishing, and eroticism. Moche tombs were known to be particularly rich in gold and silverware and had been targets for robbers ever since the arrival of the conquistadors. But it wasn't until February 1987, when a group of looters tunnelled into a small and apparently unexceptional pyramid at Sipán, that archeologists were to appreciate the true power and influence of the Moche ruling classes. The looters began squabbling over their booty and one of them contacted police. Within days the site was sealed off for a major excavation.

A Sentry for Eternity

The chamber penetrated by the gang had been virtually ransacked. But during a close external inspection of the rest of the pyramid the

above: *An Inca poncho with interlocking designs. Inca art was heavily influenced by earlier cultures.*

archeological team noticed an area where mud bricks had at one time been removed to make an entrance passage. They began digging and soon came across the remains of a man interred with his feet hacked off. The obvious conclusion was that he was a spirit guard—mutilated to ensure he stayed at his post for eternity—and that further treasures lay within. The team was not disappointed. In another chamber they discovered the corpse of the Lord of Sipán, aged about 40 when he died, his coffin crammed with some of the finest artifacts ever recovered from a South American site. These included gold and feather head-dresses, clothing decorated with metal ornaments, finely-worked jewelry of gold, silver, and precious gems, and various shell and bead artifacts. Around the Lord's coffin lay the bodies of two other men (one of whom was buried with a dog) and three women; wives and servants who would tend to him in the afterlife.

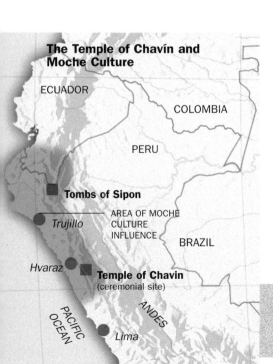

The Temple of Chavín and Moche Culture

ECUADOR

COLOMBIA

PERU

■ Tombs of Sipon

Trujillo — AREA OF MOCHE CULTURE INFLUENCE

BRAZIL

Hvaraz

■ Temple of Chavin (ceremonial site)

PACIFIC OCEAN

ANDES

Lima

c.325 BC	221 BC	218 BC	c.200 BC	c.200 BC
Alexander the Great creates a huge empire for Macedonia.	Ch'in dynasty unites China.	Hannibal of Carthage invades Italy.	Hopewell culture emerges in North American midwest.	Adena culture thrives in the Ohio region.

MACHU PICCHU
Mountain retreat of the Incas' emperor

above: *A view of Machu Picchu in its stunning Andean setting.*

High above the Urubamba river in the heart of the Peruvian Andes lies Machu Picchu, one of the world's most spectacular fortress palaces. Nestling on a high ridge between two rugged mountain peaks it was built by the emperor Pachacuti Inca Yupanqui as a country retreat, a sacred place where he could escape the demands of dictatorial duty in the capital Cuzco 50 miles (80km) to the south-east. Machu Picchu got its "lost city" tag from the American historian and explorer Hiram Bingham who, as director of the 1911 Yale University Peruvian Expedition, found its ruins hidden beneath dense upland scrub. The following year he returned equipped for a major excavation and discovered the true glory of the city; its shrines and temples, ornamental streams and baths, and magnificent architecture.

Machu Picchu covers an area of about five square miles (13 sq km) and is designed in a series of terraces, linked by stairways, which radiate from a central courtyard. Apart from the royal quarters, and some larger structures apparently used for religious ceremonies, most of the buildings are simple, one-roomed stone houses arranged around small paved courts. The masonry work demonstrates a high level of engineering skill and technical knowledge; resulting in a palace truly fit for a leader regarded as one of the world's inspirational conquerors. However, despite Bingham's beliefs, it is not the site of Tampu Tocco—the mythological "cave with three windows" from which Inca ancestors supposedly emerged. Neither is it Vilcabamba, where they made their last stand against the invading

left: *This gold mask was made by Chimu people, rivals of the Inca, sometime between the 12th and 16th centuries AD.*

Spanish. Current thinking places both sites elsewhere in the Inca empire.

For centuries Inca warriors contented themselves with being big fish in a small pond. Their heartland was in the southern upland region of Peru's Cordillera region and right up until the mid-15th century they remained entrenched within a 20-mile (32km) radius of Cuzco. Their eighth ruler Viracocha began extending the boundaries in 1437 but it was his son Pachacuti, grandson Topa, and great-grandson Huayna Capac who systematically annexed territory with conquering zeal. By the time Huayna died in 1525 the empire stretched from what is now southern Colombia, through Ecuador and Peru, and on to Bolivia, northern Argentina, and Chile.

c.1000 AD	1099 AD	c.1113–1500 AD	1215 AD	c.1350 AD
Polynesians arrive in New Zealand.	The Crusaders invade Jerusalem.	Angkor Wat flourishes in Cambodia.	Mongol armies capture Beijing.	Renaissance begins in Italy.

As Inca warriors gathered gold for the Spanish their leader Atahualpa was ruthlessly strangled.

Maintaining a vast empire

At first sight it is hard to see how Inca leaders could possibly maintain control over a mountainous, heavily-forested territory that stretched 2,175 miles (3,500 km) north to south, 500 miles (800 km) east to west, and encompassed a population of varied cultures and tribes totalling up to 16 million people. The fact that they did maintain such a solid grip is testament to their superb organizational abilities. The people regarded their Inca (emperor) as a god within his lifetime and established an impressive communications system to ensure he was kept informed of events throughout the four administrative regions which made up his kingdom. This involved a network of stone roads patrolled by state-trained relay runners who were capable of delivering messages at rates of 250 miles (400km) per day. Such was the centralized nature of Inca society that food production was organized almost on communist lines, with government experts supervizing crop selection, irrigation, terracing, and fertilization. The state also took a share of each harvest to store for times of need.

Unfortunately for the Incas, their unquestioning obedience was instrumental in their downfall. When Huayna died in 1525 he failed to appoint a successor and two of his sons—the half-brothers Huáscar and Atahualpa—began a bitter civil war ending in Huáscar's imprisonment. At

Stairs from a street in Machu Picchu lead to the circular "Torreon," an astronomical observatory.

this point fate intervened in the shape of the Spanish conquistador Francisco Pizarro, whose meagre 180-strong band of armed explorers first convinced the Incas that they were returning religious artifacts, then cooly seized control of the entire empire by keeping Atahualpa under house arrest. Fearful that his rival would assume power Atahualpa ordered Huáscar's execution and offered the Spaniards chests full of gold in return for freedom. Pizarro accepted, but even as the Incas dutifully gathered gold from across the empire he ordered Atahualpa to be strangled. Within a few decades, the once great empire lay in ruins.

Machu Picchu (Lost City of the Incas) and Cuzco

BRAZIL

ANDES MOUNTAINS

PERU

River Urubamba

Lima

■ Machu Picchu

Cuzco

Lake Titicaca

PACIFIC OCEAN

1433 AD	c.1437 AD	1497 AD	1519	c.1520 AD
Chinese ships explore as far as East Africa.	Viracocha begins extending Inca boundaries.	John Cabot discovers Labrador	The Spanish subdue the Aztecs in Mexico.	Portugal is the richest nation in Europe.

DISASTER AT EL CERÉN
The demise of a New World Pompeii

Around 175 AD a catastrophic eruption of the Ilopongo volcano devastated most of El Salvador and depopulated the western Zapotitán Valley. It took almost three centuries before farming communities regained a tenuous foothold there, replanting crops such as cotton, corn, tomatoes, beans, cacao, manioc, and chillies, and building sturdy thatched shelters of timber-reinforced adobe (mudbrick). These people had close links with the native Mayan Indians to the north-west, although ethnically they were probably of a different tribe. It is unclear why they migrated to the Zapotitán area; the most obvious reason is that their former lands were becoming too crowded, creating pressure on food production. Whatever the truth, El Cerén became one of their first settlements and for a century or so it flourished.

In many ways the lifestyle of sixth century El Cerén peasants was superior to that of their 20th century counterparts. The people were efficient storers of grain, skilled vegetable gardeners, and generally well-organized. The village had a central communal plaza surrounded by public assembly rooms and a rare type of steam-bath with a distinctive domed ceiling. At home the citizens adopted the Mayan custom of using separate huts for specialized functions—kitchens, living rooms, workshops, and storage areas were split up rather than housed together under one roof. They ate from brightly-decorated pots, slept on mat-covered benches tucked away at the back of living quarters, kept domestic animals such as dogs and ducks, and used cutting tools made of Obsidian glass—the blades carefully stored amidst thatched roofs to prevent domestic accidents. How do we know all this? Because sometime around the end of the sixth century AD another volcano, the Laguna Caldera, erupted and buried the village in

Reconstruction of a typical dwelling unearthed at El Cerén. The walls are of mudbrick and the roof is thatch.

79 AD	100–500 AD	c.100 AD	c.150 AD	165 AD	c.200 BC–550 AD	220 AD	410 AD
Destruction of Pompeii.	Drawings of Nasca animals made.	Chinese and Roman empires almost meet near Caspian Sea.	Nok culture in West Africa produces terracotta sculpture.	Smallpox epidemic in Roman Empire.	Hopewell culture flourishes in North American midwest.	Han dynasty collapses in China.	The Roman Empire is invaded and collapses.

Within a few days there was no remaining sign of human habitation.

volcanic ash. Just like Pompeii in 79 AD, an entire culture was blanketed and immaculately preserved.

Fleeing the effects of the volcano

Fortunately for the inhabitants there was some warning. The first explosion came early one August evening when farm laborers had returned home and finished eating their evening meal with their families. No one, not even the children, had yet gone to bed and there was time for a hurried evacuation before the volcanic fall-out began to rain down. Within a few days there was no remaining sign of human habitation. Every last structure was buried beneath a 16-foot (5m) layer of ash and may have remained untouched forever had it not been for

a chance discovery in 1976 when a bulldozer working on a building site clearance partially uncovered an old El Cerén structure. Since then some 11 buildings have been excavated and radiocarbon dating of roof thatch by the University of Colorado suggests the eruption occurred c.AD 590. Archeological investigations were severely disrupted by the bloody civil war in El Salvador throughout the 1980s, but in the years ahead it is hoped that El Cerén can be completely reconstructed to reveal further secrets of Mayan domestic life.

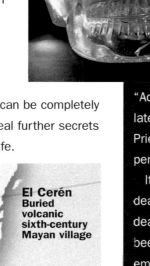

GULF OF MEXICO

El Cerén
Buried volcanic sixth-century Mayan village

MEXICO

BELIZE

Acapulco

SIERRA MADRE MOUNTAINS

GUATEMALA

HONDURAS

Guatemala City

PACIFIC OCEAN

San Salvador

Cihautan Mayan City

El Cerén

EL SALVADOR

NICARAGUA

418 AD	439 AD	451 AD	c.500 AD	c.500 AD	552 AD	c.630 AD	c.1000 AD
A barbarian Visigoth state is set up within the decimated Roman Empire.	Vandals capture the Roman city of Carthage.	An alliance of Romans and barbarians defeats the Huns.	Persia and India are attacked by the Huns.	Teotihuacán in Mexico is largest city in the world, with population of 200,000.	Buddhism is introduced into Japan.	Mohammed founds Islam.	Adena mound-builders flourish in North American mid-west.

CAVE RITUALS AT NAJ TUNICH
Mayan art and hieroglyphics

One of the deepest caves in central America can be found in Peten, the south-east region of Guatemala. Here, on the edge of the Maya mountain range, the cave of Naj Tunich drops almost 1.25 miles (2km) beneath the earth in a fantastic series of passages and chambers. To the Mayans it was a center of supernatural power, an entrance to the spirit world, and a sacred place for worship. They placed bones and pottery grave goods in its deepest recesses, decorated the sides with vibrant paintings, and made hieroglyphic wall inscriptions referring to individuals by name, place of origin, and date.

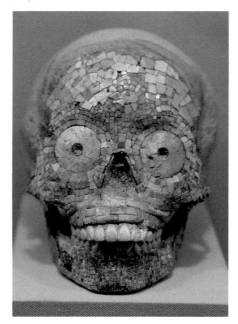

above: *A mosaic skull sculpture c.15th century. Skulls of this kind were perceived as sources of great religious power.*

above: *An Aztec Quexalott head formed from mosaic, with mussel shells for the teeth.*

Their function

These inscriptions were not necessarily tributes to the dead. Maya tradition encouraged pilgrimages to caves and conducting private, magical rites to awaken the spirits lurking within. This involved incense-burning and, on occasions, use of the pilgrim's own blood. Some of the hundred or so Naj Tunich paintings were probably painted during these introspective moments of personal reflection and their legacy offers a unique glimpse into a previously hidden aspect of the Mayan lifestyle. It seems the cave, with its internal stone buildings and walled alcoves (probably serving as

c.900 BC	814 BC	c.750 BC	c.700 BC	609 BC	c.600 BC	581 BC	539 BC
Construction of the Chavín temples begins.	City of Carthage is founded.	The *Iliad* is written in Greece.	Naj Tunich ceramics produced in abundance.	End of Assyrian Empire.	The Celtic Hallstatt civilization thrives in Europe.	Burning of Jerusalem by Nebuchadrezzar II	Greeks defeat Carthage.

Pilgrims visiting the caves would conduct private rituals, sometimes using drops of their own blood.

above: *This Mayan lintel stone from Yaxchilan, Mexico, lists nine generations of rulers.*

tombs) provided a shared place of worship for several different states such as the Sacul, Ixtutz, and Ixkun. It would have been regarded as complementing, rather than rivaling, other great Mayan religious centers like Palenque, Uxmal, Mayapán, Copán, Tikal, Uaxactún, and Chichén Itzá.

Some of the Naj Tunich paintings are simple portraits; bold sweeping lines almost akin to graffiti. Others though are far more complex and continue to puzzle archeologists. One painting shows a man with semi-erect penis embracing a lover who, anatomically, appears to be female. However, closer inspection shows that the "woman" has clear male facial characteristics and wears hair tied into a long pigtail. In Mayan eyes pigtails were synonymous with a woman's sexuality which suggests that this scene is either a straightforward piece of homosexual erotic art, or a more light-hearted depiction of a female impersonator. Naj Tunich is full of similar artistic enigmas.

The beautifully precise calligraphy is easier to interpret. Much of this was produced about the eighth century BC at a time when Mayan ceramics were at their best. It seems likely that pot artists also tried their hand at rock painting, given the obvious similarities in style. One of the clearest inscriptions, written above a natural alcove in the cave, measures some 5' (1.5m) across and features so-called emblem glyphs (part pictures; part letters) which faithfully record the

Living by Mayan Time

Fearsomely complicated it may be, but the Mayan calendar was the most accurate developed by humankind until the appearance of the Gregorian version in the 16th century. Essentially it worked like this: The year started on July 16 when the sun reached its highest point in the sky; there were 365 days, 364 of which were divided into 28 13-day weeks; the New Year began on the 365th day. Running independently and concurrently with this were 18 20-day months. It meant that once every 260 days (13 x 20) the week and the month began on the same day. A fundamental belief of Mayan nature-worship was that the gods could be trusted to control certain units of time and the behavior of everyone during these periods.

identities of people from different locations participating in a joint ritual. From this it is reasonable to conclude that Naj Tunich was bound up in a sophisticated political structure in which religious beliefs occasionally took precedence over inter-tribal rivalry.

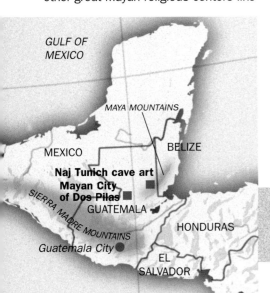

GULF OF MEXICO

MAYA MOUNTAINS

MEXICO

BELIZE

Naj Tunich cave art
Mayan City
of Dos Pilas

SIERRA MADRE MOUNTAINS

GUATEMALA

HONDURAS

Guatemala City

EL SALVADOR

517 BC	509 BC	490 BC	c.325 BC	c.200 BC
A canal is constructed from the Nile to the Red Sea.	Roman Republic is founded.	The Athenian shrine at Delphi is the first marble building in Greece.	Alexander the Great creates a huge empire for Macedonia.	Adena culture thrives in the Ohio region.

CHAPTER TWELVE

MEXICO AND NORTH AMERICA

There is a myth, probably invented in Europe, that North Americans are fascinated by history because they have none of their own. The reality is very different. If certain anthropological theories are right, prehistoric Ice Age explorers were venturing across the Bering Straits land-bridge from c.30,000 BC onward. They began a drift south that produced resourceful and successful cultures such as the Indians of the Great Plains, the stone age Olmec and Toltec peoples, the artistic Mayans, and the militaristic Aztecs.

While it is true that North America has relatively few surviving examples of early art and architecture this is not necessarily a yardstick by which to judge the continent's archeological worth. The nomadic tradition of the Plains Indians—which remained substantially unchanged for millennia up until the European invasion of the 17th and 18th centuries—gives many pointers to the lifestyle of hunter-gatherer communities across the world. Equally intriguing are the moundbuilders, with their mysterious devotion to earth animal effigies, and the strange, abandoned villages of the south-western deserts.

In the final pages of this chapter we look at the riddle of the Viking colonists, the hazards they faced as America's first European settlers, and their decision to return home following confrontations with the native inhabitants.

The enigmatic face of an Olmec basalt statue glares with haughty belligerence.

SASKATCHEWAN

**Moose Mountain
Medicine Wheel** ■

MANITOBA

ONTARIO

QUEBEC

L'Anse aux Meadows ■

MONTANA

NORTH DAKOTA

MINNESOTA

MAINE.

■ **Bighorn
Medicine Wheel**

SOUTH DAKOTA

WISCONSIN

MICHIGAN

VM

NH

MASS.

WYOMING

NEBRASKA

IOWA

NEW YORK

COLORADO

ILLINOIS

INDIANA

Hopewell

PENNSYLVANIA

Grave Creek

OHIO

■ **Mesa Verde**

Chaco Canyon

KANSAS

MISSOURI

KENTUCKY

N. CAROLINA

*Hopewell culture
artifacts: a bronze bird
with stone eye, and a
mound pipe in the
shape of a frog.*

— **Snaketown**

OKLAHOMA

ARKANSAS

TENNESSEE

S. CAROLINA

*Anasazi drinking
vessel.*

NEW MEXICO

TEXAS

LOUISIANA

MISSISSIPPI

ALABAMA

GEORGIA

FLORIDA

ATLANTIC OCEAN

MEXICO

GULF OF MEXICO

*The Great Temple at
Tenochtitlan as it looked
around 1520 AD.*

*Reconstruction of the palace
at Kabah, Yucatan.*

Tenochtitlan ■ ■ **Teotihuacan**

Tres Zapotes
San Lorenzo ■ ■ **La Venta**
Monte Alban ■

Palenque

PACIFIC OCEAN

*Bas-relief of a priest
smoking, from
Palenque.*

175

RISE OF THE OLMEC
Ancient empire of Mexico

above: *One of the largest Olmec basalt statues. The square head and thick lips are typical features and this piece may have represented a star or planet god.*

The invention of Carbon 14 dating by the American chemist Willard F. Libby in 1947 created the most valuable archeological tool in history. Libby established that the radioactivity of organic material (such as human, animal, or plant remains) declines at a known rate once the organism concerned has died. In this way the age of artifacts up to 50,000 years old can be estimated with reasonable accuracy, although the older the material the greater the degree of uncertainty. A stone axehead, for instance, can be dated using organic material found in the soil around it.

One of the first controversies resolved by C14 dating centered on the age of artifacts produced by the Olmec people of Mexico. This civilization was not discovered until 1862 when a sugar-cane worker tending a plantation at Tres Zapotes found a huge, carved basalt head sticking out of the ground. Seven years later the Mexican archeologist José Melgar published his analysis of the find, noting that the wide nose and exaggerated, thick lips bore comparison with classic Ethiopian art. However, no further artifacts turned up until 1925 when excavations at the ancient Olmec city of La Venta, Tabasco, and the San Martín Pajapan volcano, Veracruz, produced a second large stone head and a basalt sculpture of a contorted face.

The German historian Hermann Beyer named these items "olmecan," after 16th century references to an Olmec people reportedly indigenous to the area, but it was not until the late 1930s that the real breakthrough came courtesy of Matthew Stirling, director of the Bureau of American Ethnology. His discovery at Tres Zapotes of a second colossal stone head, this time inscribed with datable hieroglyphics, showed that the Olmec civilization was older than the Mayan. For a time this theory was denigrated by Mayan experts but in 1957 the first C14 analysis on La Venta material forced them to recognize their mistake. Further work at the San Lorenzo site

above: *A jade figurine of a jaguar spirit. Olmec art was gradually absorbed into Mayan culture from 900 BC.*

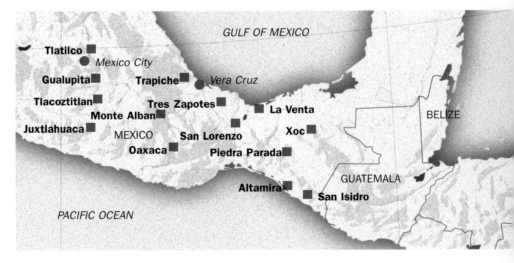

GULF OF MEXICO

Tlatilco
● Mexico City
Gualupita
Trapiche ■ ● Vera Cruz
Tlacoztitlan ■
Tres Zapotes ■
Monte Alban ■ La Venta ■
BELIZE
Juxtlahuaca ■ MEXICO
San Lorenzo ■ Xoc ■
Oaxaca ■
Piedra Parada ■
GUATEMALA
Altamira ■ San Isidro ■
PACIFIC OCEAN

c.2000 BC	c.1900 BC	c.1840 BC	c.1750 BC	c.1200 BC	c.1100 BC	c.1120 BC	753 BC
Inuit people living in Arctic.	Irrigation technology improves in Mesopotamia to nurture expanding population.	Lower Nubia annexed by Egypt.	Hammurabi founds Babylonian Empire.	Greeks destroy city of Troy.	Phoenicians develop alphabetic script.	Mycenean civilization comes to an end.	Rome founded.

Players defeated in the ritualistic Ball Game sometimes paid the ultimate price.

placed the rise of Olmec culture firmly in the 12th century BC and more recent work dates it even earlier—c.1500 BC. From 900 BC it seems to gradually have become absorbed into the more widespread Mayan tradition.

The Olmec empire

The Olmec people were based west of Mexico's Yucatán peninsula, an area of swampy river valleys and dense jungle. Although their first settlements were concentrated near this Gulf coast their influence spread through the central highlands, on to Oaxaca, and from there across southern and western Mexico. Examples of highly-

below: *Detail from a stone relief. The rounded shapes and images show clear Olmec influences.*

distinctive carvings (the facial characteristics in Olmecan art typically include a snarling mouth, a squarish head with central cleft, and enormous flaring eyebrows) have turned up in large numbers at sites 600 miles apart. The Olmec were the first Central American people to experiment with stone sculpture and architecture, and their artwork ranges in size from 9' (2.7m) high basalt heads to hand-held jade figurines. The axial street plan at La Venta—the city that replaced San Lorenzo as their cultural hub c.900BC—was copied for centuries by other urban centers, and their writing undoubtedly formed the basics of Mayan hieroglyphics. Yet although they flourished for more than six centuries, there remain significant gaps in our knowledge of their way of life.

Rules of the Ball Game

Invented by Olmec priests, the Ball Game was a cross between Spanish pelota, basketball, and volleyball. It was played on a H-shaped pitch in which two high-sided walls were separated by a central line. The idea was to volley a rubber ball so that it bounced into the opposition half, striking it only with hips, elbows, or knees. To spice up the rules a team could score an outright victory by directing the ball through either of a pair of stone rings suspended some 20' above the ground (a rare feat since the rings were only slightly bigger than the circumference of the ball. The player who managed to pull this off was entitled to take all the worldly goods, including the clothes, of any spectator he could catch. The game was later adopted by the Aztecs, who believed the pattern of play could predict the future, and the Mayans whose sense of competitive spirit meant the losers were occasionally ritually slaughtered.

TEMPLE OF THE INSCRIPTIONS
Royal resting place

above: *The jade burial mask of King Pacal the Great found in Palenque's Temple of the Inscriptions.*

The city of Palenque, in what is now Chiapas State, Mexico, showed Mayan architecture at its classical best. Dating from the fourth to the 10th century AD, the city was centered around great stone pyramids set on basalt bases and topped by temples or sanctuaries. Unlike the Egyptian pyramids these structures were not generally designed as funeral chambers for royalty. Instead their function seemed to be mainly esthetic; supporting monumental wall reliefs and hieroglyphic etchings which extolled great moments in Mayan history. One of the pyramids however hid a deeper secret— a riddle that would remain unlocked for more than 1200 years.

For years the Temple of the Inscriptions was thought to be just another Mayan religious monument, albeit with great emphasis on hieroglyphics. It takes its name from two large stone tablets set into the rear wall of its portico and a third plastered onto an interior chamber. Together, these contain more than 600 hieroglyphs, forming the second-longest Mayan inscription yet discovered. Their existence was thoroughly documented in 1840 by the American lawyer and historian John Lloyd Stephens, but in 1949 Alberto Ruz Lhuillier, a Mexican archeologist, decided he wanted a closer look. He was curious to discover why the sanctuary's stone floor was formed of large, precisely-chiselled slabs when rougher-cut floors predominated elsewhere at Palenque. More intriguing still, one particular slab in the rear chamber bore a double row of circular holes filled with stone plugs— as though designed to be lifted by some special tool. Nearby, Ruz observed, the rear wall of the chamber disappeared beneath the floor. He became convinced that the holed slab was the doorway to a secret underground passage.

right: *Stairway to the Temple. A secret passageway was found beneath a stone floor.*

A difficult excavation

He was right. When the slab was lifted laborers found a steep stairway filled with rubble—presenting an awkward and labor-intensive clearance job. It was a further three years before Ruz reached the bottom of the stairs and discovered a stone box filled with decorated bowls, jade, bead jewelry, shells containing a red dye, and a pearl. This was the first clear indication of an undisturbed tomb and by the time Ruz's team broke into another chamber to discover the skeletons of six human sacrifices he knew he was on the verge of an extraordinary discovery. A massive triangular slab blocking the main passageway was then removed and Ruz found himself gazing at an open door through which a short flight of stairs led to a 13' x 33' (4 x 10m) crypt at the heart of the pyramid. Its walls, crusted over with centuries of

410 AD	c.500 AD	552 AD	542-594 AD	c.597 AD	604 AD	c.625 AD	c.630 AD
Roman Empire is invaded and collapses.	Teotihuacán in Mexico is largest city in the world, with population of 200,000.	Buddhism introduced into Japan.	Plague halves population of Europe.	St. Augustine arrives in Britain to convert population to Christianity.	First written constitution in Japan.	Burial of Saxon chieftain at Sutton Hoo in East Anglia, England.	Mohammed founds Islam.

Treasure surrounding Pacal's body was an unequivocal testament to his standing in Mayan society.

above: *The Temple of the Inscriptions had a built-in "psychoduct" linking Pacal's spirit to his people*

water-borne calcium deposits, bore the images of nine guardian figures carved from plaster. In the center of the chamber, some 82 feet (25m) below the Temple of the Inscriptions, lay a sarcophagus borne on six stone pillars—the final resting place of Palenque's King Pacal the Great.

The treasure surrounding his body was an unequivocal testament to Pacal's standing in Mayan society. There was a heavy bias toward jade in the form of necklaces, bracelets, pectoral ornaments, rings, and ear jewelry. The king had been buried in a mosaic jade mask and jade ornaments had been placed into each of his hands and left lying at his feet; there was even a jade belt lying on the limestone lid of the sarcophagus. Other grave goods included ceramic pots, for food,

and two life-size plaster heads. Perhaps most remarkable of all was the 13-foot (4m) long lid itself, carved with one of the best-known and most evocative scenes in Mayan art— Pacal's descent into the underworld. The dead ruler, curled into the fetal position, is pictured with a "tree of life" sprouting from his falling body and a fearsome mythological bird above a two-headed serpent. His ancestors are shown emerging from caves at the top and bottom, and his dynasty is assured by the placing of descendants apparently rising from the ground. To maintain his spirit's links with the people a so-called "psychoduct"—a mortar tube—led from the sarcophagus to a stone tube in the main entrance passage. This rose up 67 stairs to

emerge beneath the sanctuary floor.

Although the hieroglyphs record that Pacal ruled between 615 AD and 683 there remains uncertainty about the age he died. Anatomists suggest he must have been only about 40 but the glyphs insist that he was 80. In common with other global religious traditions it is possible that the ages of great leaders were exaggerated in order to imbue them with supernatural powers.

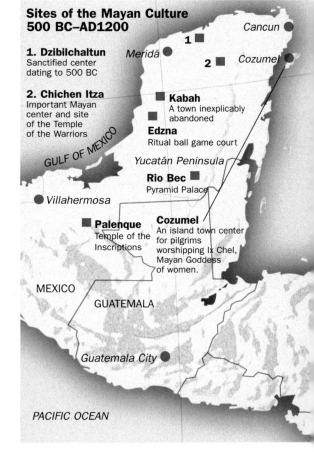

**Sites of the Mayan Culture
500 BC–AD1200**

1. Dzibilchaltun
Sanctified center dating to 500 BC

2. Chichen Itza
Important Mayan center and site of the Temple of the Warriors

Cancun

Merida

Cozumel

Kabah
A town inexplicably abandoned

Edzna
Ritual ball game court

GULF OF MEXICO

Yucatán Peninsula

Rio Bec
Pyramid Palace

Villahermosa

Palenque
Temple of the Inscriptions

Cozumel
An island town center for pilgrims worshipping Ix Chel, Mayan Goddess of women.

MEXICO

GUATEMALA

Guatemala City

PACIFIC OCEAN

c.650 AD	c.795 AD	794 AD	775 AD	800 AD	c.800 AD	982 AD	c.1100 AD
The Tang Empire is most successful Chinese dynasty to date.	First large-scale plundering of British Isles by Vikings.	Capital of Japan is moved to Kyoto.	The kingdom of Srijaya conquers Malaysia.	Charlemagne becomes Holy Roman Emperor.	Abbasid culture reaches its height in Mesopotamia.	Erik the Red discovers Greenland.	Mesa Verde Anasazi cliff dwellings flourish.

TEMPLE OF THE FEATHERED SERPENT, TEOTIHUACÁN
An unfolding archeological story

Teotihuacán is the most enigmatic of cities. By the sixth century AD it had a population of perhaps 200,000 and covered almost eight square miles— far larger and more advanced than any European urban center of the age. Its phenomenal Pyramid of the Sun (where religious worship included gruesome human sacrifices) was the largest ever built in Central America, and its Temple of the Feathered Serpent, boasting a magnificent western facade, is arguably Mexico's most important ancient structure. This building, with its fearsome, brightly-painted stone serpents became the focus of a military cult which heavily influenced the later Toltec and Aztec civilizations. In fact

The Pyramid of the Sun was used for human sacrifice.

the Aztecs were so impressed that they dubbed Teotihuacán the "Place of the Gods" and believed it was the spot on which the world was created.

For all this, the ruins of the city have yielded very little information about its original inhabitants. No writing has been found and it is unclear what language was spoken. The clearest picture so far has emerged from an excavation of the Temple site in the early 1980s when archeologists from Mexico's National Institute of Anthropology and History discovered several mass-burial pits in front of the entrance. In total they recovered 120 bodies, laid out in groups of 20, together with hundreds of valuable offerings such as shell and greenstone ornaments and obsidian (a sharp volcanic glass). Many wore carved shell necklaces designed to look like

above: *A stone feathered serpent, part of the Teotihuacán temple's superb western facade.*

human jaws or teeth and some had crude, circular mirrors made of fool's gold (pyrite) and slate fastened to the small of their back. These are tell-tale symbols of a warrior class. Aztec fighters used similar back mirrors— which they called tezcacuitlapilli.

The Institute's finds demanded a major rethink on the purposes of the Temple. Previously it was considered

Ultimate honor could be attained only through dying on the battlefield or volunteering for sacrificial ceremonies.

to be a purely religious site but the presence of so many sacrificed warriors suggests it was probably the focal point of a powerful, dictatorial military regime that exerted huge psychological control over the masses from c.200 AD. This cult may have been the historical root of Aztec sacrifice rituals, in which warriors were encouraged to believe that ultimate honor could only be attained through being slaughtered on the battlefield or volunteering for death at the hands of the priests. It must be said that warrior sacrifices were reserved only for the most important Aztec religious ceremonies. A somewhat more common sight was that of unfortunate prisoners being manhandled up the steps of a pyramid and stretched across the High Priest's convex stone to have their hearts cut out with a knife.

The feathered serpent

Many links between Teotihuacán and later cultures lie in the ubiquitous Feathered Serpent image. It appears in the art and architecture of the Toltecs, who established their own military state in nearby Tula after the sacking and burning of Teotihuacán c.750 AD. It is represented in a particular type of head-dress worn by Mayan warriors during times when the position of the planet Venus summoned them to war. Similarly the Aztecs, whose culture dominated Mexico between the 12th and 15th

above: *This skull rack was probably a symbol of power for the Teotihuacan militaristic regime and its successors.*

centuries, closely identified it with Venus and military conquest. In this way, a combination of astrology, mythology, and symbolism combined to create a Venus "war cult" that spread across Central America in the course of the millennium.

In October 1998 Professor George Cowgill of the Arizona State University reported a new breakthrough in Teotihuacán archeology with the location of a possible royal grave beneath the Pyramid of the Moon, the city's second largest pyramid. The body had been buried seated and surrounded by obsidian and greenstone offerings (similar to those found in the mass burials). The tomb is thought to date from about 100 AD—a time when the civilization was in its infancy—and experts believe it could be the first of many royal burials waiting to be discovered on the same site.

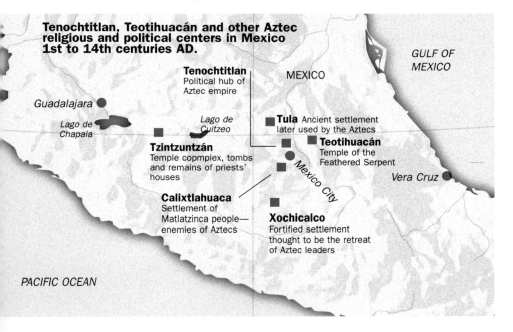

Tenochtitlan, Teotihuacán and other Aztec religious and political centers in Mexico 1st to 14th centuries AD.

GULF OF MEXICO

MEXICO

Tenochtitlan
Political hub of Aztec empire

Guadalajara

Lago de Chapala

Lago de Cuitzeo

Tula Ancient settlement later used by the Aztecs

Teotihuacán
Temple of the Feathered Serpent

Mexico City

Vera Cruz

Tzintzuntzán
Temple copmplex, tombs and remains of priests' houses

Calixtlahuaca
Settlement of Matlatzinca people— enemies of Aztecs

Xochicalco
Fortified settlement thought to be the retreat of Aztec leaders

PACIFIC OCEAN

74 AD	135 AD	c.400 AD	c.500 AD	c.500 AD	542-594 AD	604 AD	790 AD
Silk trade between China and Rome begins.	Unsuccessful Jewish revolt in Israel against Romans.	Inca settle along much of South American Pacific coast.	African Ghanaian Empire is most powerful in West following collapse of Rome.	Teotihuacán in Mexico is largest city in the world, with population of 200,000.	Plague halves the population of Europe.	First written constitution in Japan.	First large-scale Viking invasion of Britain.

MOUNDBUILDERS OF NORTH AMERICA
Enigma of America's midwest

When in the 1780s the first white pioneers began exploring the Ohio valley they were astounded to find dozens of man-made earthworks shaped like animals. Most impressive of these was the Great Serpent Mound, a 1200' (366m) snake fashioned so that an oval tomb lay partly in its open mouth. Soon the settlers were discovering earth effigies beside the banks of the Mississippi and further afield into eastern areas of North America. East of St Louis they came across an odd-looking artificial hill in the shape of a 108' (33m)-high truncated pyramid. This was later misleadingly named Monks Mound (after a group of Trappist monks who set up home there at the end of the 19th century) but it was actually part of a much earlier 2,000-acre (800 ha) religious complex known to native Indians as Cahokia.

The attitude of the settlers to the earth shapes was perhaps predictable. They could see no way that ancestors of primitive woodland Indians were responsible so they instead came up with visions of an advanced, ancient race whose culture had been destroyed by a barbarian horde. Some theories suggested the earth animals were constructed by survivors of the Biblical Flood; others that they were built by—in no particular order—migrants from Atlantis, Welshmen, a "lost tribe" from Israel, a bunch of wandering Hindu shepherds traveling from India to Mexico, early explorers from the likes of Greece, Rome, Egypt, Tuscany, and Denmark and, most imaginatively of all, a race of American giants. It was a mythical melting pot that attracted dreamers, cranks, pseudo-archeologists, romantic antiquaries, and amateur historians—all with their own particular spin to put on the story. Into this motley assortment stepped an itinerant trader of Indian art and craftwork—William Pidgeon.

A "lost" civilization?

Pidgeon was a passionate believer in the "lost civilization" theory, and in 1840 he began logging previously

below: *North American soapstone sculpture, of uncertain date, thought to depict a warrior beheading his victim.*

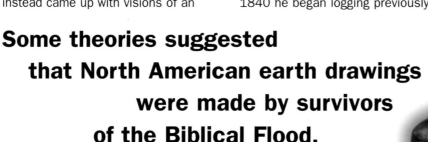

Some theories suggested that North American earth drawings were made by survivors of the Biblical Flood.

c.1000 BC	c.200 BC	c.200 AD	c.550 AD	c.600 AD	c.1500–1600 AD	c.1610 AD	1776 AD
Adena culture begins in upper mid-west.	Hopewell culture starts producing earthworks.	End of Adena culture.	End of Hopewell culture.	Mississippian tradition begins.	Mississippian tradition destroyed by Spanish conquistadors.	English colonisation of North America begins.	American revolution ends with large expansion westward.

Heartland of America's Moundbuilding Culture

MICHIGAN
Lake Michigan
Chicago
Detroit
Lake Erie
PENN.
Pittsburgh
INDIANA
OHIO
Columbus
Newark Mounds
Hopewell Culture, 2000 BC–400 AD
ILLINOIS
R. Illinois
R. Mississippee
Wabash
Indianapolis
Great Serpent Mound
Hopewell Culture, 2000 BC–400 AD
Grave Creek
Center of Adena Culture, 3rd–2nd centuries BC
W. VIRGINIA
St. Louis
Cahokia
Ceremonial center of Mississippian mound builders, 8th–15th centuries AD
MISSOURI
R. Ohio
KENTUCKY
Appalachians
Indian Knoll
4th millennium BC settlement with shell mound

unknown earthwork monuments west of the Great Lakes. Within a few months he had located a menagerie of creature-effigies, many of them hidden in forests, including lizards, falcons, turtles, panthers and, on a ridge in Iowa, a procession of bears. He later told how he befriended a medicine man called De-coo-dah, who claimed that the effigies were built by a vanquished tribe forced by their conquerors to acknowledge astronomical bodies and constellations as gods, instead of animal idols. De-coo-dah explained: "When the worshippers of reptiles were reduced by the fortunes of war, and compelled to recognize the sun, moon, and heavenly bodies as the only objects worthy of adoration, they secretly entombed their gods in the earthwork symbols which represented the heavenly bodies."

Pidgeon remained unconvinced but his mystical theories were, in any case, soon torn apart. In the 1880s a government-backed ethnologist named Cyrus Thomas began an exhaustive study of more than 2,000 old Indian sites deploying methodical archeological fieldwork, rigorous archive assessment, and the close physical examination of 4,000 ancient artifacts. His conclusions meant there could no longer be any doubt.

The earthworks and mounds could be demonstrably linked to native Indian culture. The question was no longer who built them, but why.

In the wake of Thomas's study archeologists were able to categorize the mound-building in three phases. The first, the Adena, was named after a site in Ohio and flourished in the upper mid-west between about 1000 BC and 200 AD. During this period burial chambers and animal shapes were constructed—including the Great Serpent Mound. The Adena builders were seamlessly succeeded by the Hopewell people, skilled artists and

merchants who between 200 BC and 550 AD produced some of the larger earthworks, including those which so fazed Pidgeon. Finally, around 600 AD, came the Mississippian tradition with its huge and elaborate religious centers exemplified by Cahokia. These people remained for nearly a thousand years until they were gradually annihilated by Spanish conquistadors in the 16th century. Sadly, they represented our last chance to know the true motives of the moundbuilders.

below: *A view of the Great Serpent Mound. An oval tomb lies partly in its mouth.*

c.1780 AD

Discovery of earthworks by US settlers.

1840 AD

Pidgeon begins logging earthwork monuments.

THE ANASAZI
Desert farmers of Mesa Verde

The deserts of the American south-west are unforgiving places. Even today, as technology invades every aspect of farming, they remain largely untamed, their vast rock-strewn landscapes broken only by the occasional river gorge or steep flat-topped "mesas." Native Indians living 2,500 years ago should have had no chance of squeezing a living from these drought-stricken lands. Yet resourceful tribes such as the Anasazi, who occupied the "four corners" territory where the states of New Mexico, Colorado, Utah, and Arizona now meet, not only survived life on the edge of starvation but for centuries thrived upon it. Ironically it was this arid, hostile environment that preserved the remnants of their culture so well.

Plants such as corn, beans, and squash had been grown in central America for thousands of years and by c.500 BC these crops were spreading further and further north. Soon cotton and tobacco plantations were established and within the span of a few centuries farmers had switched from a system geared to small amounts of rainfall to a sophisticated network of irrigation ditches and huge storage dams. Knowledge was shared openly between the Anasazi and their neighbors—the Hohokam (of modern-day southern Arizona) and the Mogollon (who occupied eastern Arizona and western New Mexico)—although each tribe also maintained distinctive architectural and artistic traditions.

Rewards of stability

As food production grew more stable, so increased effort was put into constructing extensive stone-built towns and an improved roads network. Chaco Canyon in New Mexico was first settled by farmers living in cramped, single-room houses built partly underground. However by c.AD 1000 this core had expanded into a rural sprawl of 13 separate Anasazi villages one of which, Pueblo Bonito, boasted more than 700 separate rooms and some 34 pit-houses or *kivas*—a kind of cross between a community center and a temple. The religious background of these people is unclear, although the sun and stars seem to have figured prominently. The supernova (exploding star) that created the Crab Nebula was faithfully recorded in one building sometime after its occurrence in July 1054.

Another spectacular village is the Cliff Palace of the Mesa Verde National Park in Colorado. Here early stone and timber pit-dwellings stand alongside a sophisticated Anasazi village built snugly beneath an overhanging section of cliff. Steps cut into the sheer rock face gave farm laborers a short cut to the fields above and, in the years between the 11th and 13th centuries AD, their crops became the

left: *The dramatic setting of the Cliff Palace at Mesa Verde. This settlement was the hub of a Colorado-based chiefdom between the 11th and 13th centuries AD.*

c.500 BC	c.500 AD	c.1000 AD
Central American crops grown in present-day Arizona and New Mexico.	Increasingly sophisticated irrigation makes desert agriculture possible.	Chaco Canyon occupied, with 13 separate Anasazi villages.

European explorers who rediscovered Mesa Verde believed it had only recently been abandoned.

above: *A view of the Cliff Palace illustrating circular kivas - buildings which served a dual role as temples and community centers.*

cornerstone of a vibrant and economically robust urban community. Their nemesis took the form of a great drought that devastated farms across the northern half of the region in the 13th century. So hurriedly did they

leave that the European explorers who rediscovered the village in the 16th century suspected that it had only recently been abandoned. Timber structures were intact, ceramic pots stood half-filled with corn and shoes made from yucca plants still lay undisturbed on the floors.

The Blythe Giant

The development of manned flight opened exciting possibilities for archeology. Buildings, earth-drawings, and field systems disturb topsoil sufficiently to create a permanent impression which, though sometimes undetectable on the ground, becomes clear from the air. In 1923 Colonel Jerry Phillips of the United States Army Air Service was flying his open-cockpit biplane 5,000' (1,500m) above the Mojave Desert near the town of Blythe, California, when he glanced down to see the figure of a huge giant and long-tailed animal spreading across the landscape. Since then more than 275 symbols and hieroglyphs have been identified along the lower Colorado River valley. They are thought to have been made by the Mojave Indians and date back to c.3000 BC.

The Blythe Giant stone alignment and other earth drawings of the American south-west.

Calico Mountains
200,000-year-old hunter-gatherer community—arguably the oldest known archeological site in North America

Mesa Verde and the Anasazi heartland

Denver

UTAH

COLORADO

NEVADA

Chaco Canyon
Sophisticated Pueblo Indian center
c. 10th–13th centuries AD

Mesa Verde National Park
Center of Anasazi Culture
c. 11th–13th centuries AD

Las Vegas

Grand Canyon

Pecos
Pueblo village

NEW MEXICO

Mojave Desert

CALIFORNIA

Broken K Pueblo
Pueblo Indian center with underground ritual rooms

Bandelier
4000 BC–AD 1500. A National Monument comprising of thousands of ancient sites. Occupied by the Anasazi between 11th and 15th centuries AD.

Los Angeles

R. Colorado

ARIZONA

Blythe Giant

Phoenix

Snaketown
Hohokam Indian settlement with platform mounds and rock alignments

MEXICO

PACIFIC OCEAN

Ventana Cave
Linked to Hohokam Indians

1054 AD	c.1100 AD	1200s
Supernova occurs—recorded by Anasazi.	Mesa Verde Anasazi cliff dwellings flourish.	Drought seriously threatens cliff dwellings.

NATIVE AMERICANS
Hunters of the Great Plains

Until the coming of Europeans in the 17th century, the lives of native Americans on North America's central plains had continued essentially unchanged for thousands of years. This huge region, extending from the Canadian border in the north to Texas in the south, and from the spine of the Rockies across to the Great Lakes, once provided hunter-gatherer people with virtually unlimited sources of meat from animals such as mammoth, buffalo, and antelope. With more than a million square miles (2.6m sq km) of grassland to share—and a nomadic tribal culture linked to seasonal migration—there was little chance of any one area becoming over-hunted. The fact that mammoth effectively

below: Stone medicine wheels can be found right across the North American Plains.

became extinct here and in Asia about 10,000 BC may be due to a combination of factors, including climatic change, and not solely due to over-enthusiastic spearmen!

So sparse was the population that by the time invading Europeans arrived it is thought only ten million people lived in the whole of North America—roughly one-eighth of the combined total for Central and South America. With so much available the Plains Indians inevitably became expert hunters and their religious and social life was heavily influenced by communal kill techniques. There is clear evidence of mass mammoth slaughter and butchery at places like Blackwater Draw in New Mexico, while at the imaginatively-named Head-Smashed-In site near Alberta, Canada, fourth millennium BC hunters herded dozens of buffalo together and stampeded them over a cliff. A

variation on this theme can be found at Casper, Wyoming, where 75 beasts were driven into an encircling sand dune and speared to death. Elsewhere herds were cornered in canyons or specially-built wooden compounds.

Planning the hunt

Communal kills were usually held in the Fall to build up a store of meat for the harsh winter months. These events involved laborious planning—often hundreds of men and women would be involved—but the risk of failure still remained high. The danger for kill organizers was that a large herd could scatter without warning, ruining days or even weeks of work in which numbers had been patiently built up by merging small groups of buffalo. A cliff stampede, for example, involved marking out a

Bighorn Mountains medecine wheel and other stone wheel structures of North America

ALBERTA   SASKATCHEWAN

● Calgary   C   A   N

South Saskatchewan

Regina ●

Majorville ■
Medecine wheel
c. 2500 BC

Moose Mountain ■
6th-century BC
medecine wheel

Head-Smashed-In
c. 3500 BC, site where
ancient hunters would
drive bison over cliffs to
their deaths

Missouri

MONTANA

U N I T E D S T A T E S

■ **Bighorn Mountains**
Indian stone circle, or
"medicine wheel"

IDAHO   WYOMING

The danger for kill organizers was that a large buffalo herd could scatter without warning.

funnel-shaped drive route in which the thinnest section ended at the cliff edge. It took only a few hunters to lose their nerve, or a gap to open in the drive boundaries, for the stampede to change course and the animals to retain freedom.

Unsurprisingly, tribal leaders would get very edgy in the days before a major kill. There would be a ban on individual hunting for fear that the buffalo would sense impending doom and start to drift away. Elaborate religious ceremonies would be planned for days in advance and various nature omens consulted to ensure perfect timing. There also seems to have been great spiritual significance attached to stone spearheads, many of which were flaked to a precision well beyond that needed for them to be accurately thrown. By about 500 BC the development of bows and arrows significantly increased the efficiency of hunting parties, although there is no evidence to suggest that this seriously threatened the buffalo population. Rather, it was the advance of European settlers from the 1830s onwards that drove the species to the verge of extinction.

Plains Indians had no tradition of permanent buildings but they did leave their mark in the form of stone "medicine wheels." There are about 50 of these still surviving but among the best known are the Canadian examples at Majorville, Alberta, and Moose Mountain, Saskatchewan, and the Bighorn Wheel in Wyoming's Bighorn Mountains. They are simple structures with a hub, outer rim, and numerous spokes, and are sometimes linked to small cairns. There is clear evidence that Bighorn was used as an astronomical observatory but the wheels may also have been aids to spiritual healing.

MANITOBA
Lake Winnipeg
ONTARIO
A   D   A
Lake Manitoba
Bannock Point
500 BC–AD 800
Indian rock carvings, mostly of animals
NORTH DAKOTA
Lake Superior
MINNESOTA
O F   A M E R I C A
SOUTH DAKOTA
Minneapolis
IOWA

c.50,000–10,000 BC	c.10,000 BC	c.9000 BC	c.4000 BC	c.1500 BC
Humans cross from Asia into Americas.	Mammoths become extinct.	End of ice age allows first towns, like Jericho, to be built.	Clear evidence of complex herding and hunting of Buffalo by Native Americans.	Olmec culture emerges in present-day Mexico.

VIKING OUTPOSTS
The first Europeans in the New World

The story of Viking landings in North America begins in 982 AD when an outlaw Norwegian called Erik the Red discovered Greenland and founded a settlement near the modern town of Julianehåb. About this time Iceland had suffered a terrible famine, and when Erik traveled there four years later in search of fellow emigrants he filled 25 ships. At this time the climate was warmer than today and the empty expanse of Greenland offered plenty of opportunity to farm and hunt. Soon the Viking pioneers were trading in fur, hides, ropes, animal oils, wool, and walrus ivory, and importing—mainly from Norway—grain, iron, timber, and European clothing.

Onward to unknown lands

The Greenland settlements could not, however, support a large population and Erik's son—Leif Eriksson—took responsibility for exploring further west. He knew from accounts of other seafarers blown off-course that something lay out there; the question was whether the land could offer a sustainable living. Around 1002 his scouting expedition put ashore in three places he named Helluland, Markland, and Vinland. Helluland is generally acknowledged as the southern part of Baffin Island, Markland is thought to be part of Labrador, south of Nain, but the geographical position of Vinland remains a hotly-contested scholarly debate. One possible candidate is the settlement of L'Anse aux Meadows on the Newfoundland Coast.

Excavations at this site by Helge and Anne Ingstad have unearthed the remains of eight turf-roofed houses, some stone fireplaces, a smithy, smelted iron, and around 120 other artifacts. The comparatively small number of items recovered is indicative of the transient nature of the village. The settlers made no obvious attempt at expansion or rebuilding and their quarters were very basic, with simple bench-beds and holes in the roof to act as chimneys. The largest house had five rooms with an attached workshed, and was probably shared accommodation for several families.

The Vinland mentioned in the Viking sagas was under the overall leadership of an Icelander called Thorfinn Karlsefni, who married Erik the Red's

above: *Viking monument at the Brattahlid settlement, Eiriksfjord, Eastern Greenland. Norse colonies on Greenland provided a springboard to the west.*

The Vikings—first European settlers of North America.

ICELAND

GREENLAND

Estimated route from Scandanavia

LABRADOR SEA

Viking longboat.

ATLANTIC OCEAN

CANADA

■ **L'Anse Aux Meadows**
Viking settlement

NEWFOUNDLAND

NEW BRUNSWICK

USA

MAINE

Halifax
NOVA SCOTIA

c.400–800 AD	c.795 AD	c.840–850 AD	c.860 AD	c.900 AD
Dark Ages in Europe results in Barbarian (including Viking) raids.	First large-scale plundering of British Isles by Vikings.	Vikings attack many settlements on western European coasts.	Iceland discovered by Vikings, and later colonized.	Vikings trade as far afield as Black Sea.

Karlsefni's diplomacy ensured that hostile natives bought milk rather than weapons.

A ruined Viking settlement at Qagsslarssuk on the coast of Greenland.

daughter-in-law Gudrid. Karlsefni had been so impressed with Leif Eriksson's account of Vinland—its wild grapes, plentiful salmon, temperate climate, wide grasslands, and unlimited timber supply—that he resolved to establish a permanent colony. Several of his men took their wives with them on the voyage, together with seed, breeding cattle, and a good supply of weapons. But they soon ran into problems with the natives, whom they called Skrælingar (it possibly means "screechers" or "uglies").

According to the Grœnlending Saga the first attempt at trade between Norse and native was a confusing affair that could have turned nasty without some subtle diplomacy from Karlsefni. It states: "Neither party could understand the other's language. Then the Skrælings unslung

their bales, untied them, and proffered their wares, and above all wanted weapons in exchange. Karlsefni, though, forbade them the sale of weapons. And now he hit on this idea; he told the women to carry out milk to them and the moment they saw the milk that was the one thing they wanted to buy, nothing else." Sadly for the colonists this uneasy peace did not last. With hostility increasing, no superiority of weapons or manpower, and an unfeasibly long supply line from Greenland, the Vinland settlement was abandoned after just three winters. By 1020 colonizing voyages west had largely ended to be replaced purely by trading missions.

Vinland's location remains tantalizingly unclear. There are arguments for placing it anywhere

between Newfoundland and Florida but the discovery of a single, genuine, Viking settlement along North America's east coast will undoubtedly revise all current theories. As things stand, all we can say is that Karlsefni and his successors probably got no further than southern Maine.

above: Reconstructed Norse houses at L'Anse aux Meadows on the Newfoundland coast.

982 AD	c.1002 AD	c.1014 AD	c.1020 AD	c.1100 AD	1492 AD	c.1520–1800 AD	c.1600–1800 AD
Erik the Red discovers Greenland.	Leif Eriksson lands at three North American sites.	Irish kingdoms weaken Viking hold on Ireland.	Colonizing voyages to North America end; replaced by trading missions.	Development of nation states in Europe ends Viking era.	Columbus credited with discovery of America.	Spanish and Portuguese colonize North and South America.	British, French, Dutch, and others join colonization.

SUMMARY

The distinguished French archeologist Professor Gilbert Charles-Picard of the Sorbonne, Paris, once teasingly wrote that the aims of archeology were fundamentally absurd. "It's entire purpose," he suggested, "is to restore dead things to life. Nature, hostile to all waste, tirelessly reabsorbs the smallest remnants of anything which once lived and uses them again to produce more life. Archeology, in attempting to preserve fossils and corpses, is working against nature."

While this is demonstrably true, the same could be said of NASA's defiance of gravity and doctors who attempt to cure "natural" diseases with drugs. There is nothing absurd about working against nature; indeed it could be argued that by equipping humankind with an insatiable curiosity, nature requires us to try! Having said that, archeology is beset with absurdities.

The rush to embrace academic innovation is one example. Time and again in this book there are references to new techniques advancing the frontiers of archeological knowledge, like rafts of certainty in a sea of doubt. Unfortunately, the rafts occasionally capsize.

Linear regression technique (LRT) is a good illustration. For decades, archeologists calculated the age a person died by taking a large sample of bones of known dates and plotting on a graph how typical characteristics (such as worn joints) change over time. This produced a "line of best fit" used to determine the age of the bones being studied. The system has, however, resulted in puzzling inconsistencies. For example, when anthropologists dated the bones of the seventh century Mayan king Hanab Pakal, they concluded that he

died in his 40s. Yet the inscription on his tombstone insisted he was 80.

In March 1999, however, a joint study at the universities of Leeds and Bradford showed that LRT methodology is fundamentally flawed. It "tends to underestimate the ages of the oldest people in the population you are studying," sometimes by as much as 30 years. It seems that relying too heavily on a tried-and-trusted formula can make a mockery of the most exhaustive excavation.

Clearing away the past

Professional archeologists are painfully aware of the hazards of their craft. Some even argue that there are no such things as "facts" in their business, given that it is impossible to make truly accurate deductions about ancient buildings and artifacts cut adrift from time and social context. Even written history—which dates back a mere 5,000 years—is far from an exact science.

Another absurdity lies in the way we perceive archeology. Only in the last few centuries has humankind given much thought to preserving its roots. Roman and Greek architects habitually cleared sites of ancient buildings to make way for their own structures. Christianity, the Reformation, the French and Russian revolutions, and the Chinese Cultural Revolution are just a few examples of political and religious movements that have trashed treasures of the past. Artifacts have been preserved and illegally traded at least since the first century AD (the Greeks were among the first antique dealers), although the motivation was financial rather than cultural.

In 1996, with the above very much in mind, the author interviewed one of the world's leading restorers of Egyptian artifacts, who was awaiting

trial on charges of handling items looted from Egyptian tombs (he later received a six-year sentence). He spoke with venom about the "scandalous" persecution of collectors and how "much of the stuff stored away in museums is of little interest." Academics may be outraged by his attitude but the great Western museums can hardly claim the moral high ground. What proportion of their collections, one wonders, should technically be regarded as stolen goods?

For all the arguments that rage through archeology, it is worth reminding ourselves that in essence it is a fantastically enriching, uplifting, and fascinating subject that within a few hundred years has transformed our knowledge of the human race. Leaf back through the pages of this book and you are struck by the breathtaking ingenuity of the people who shaped our past. This book has no scholarly pretenses, other than offering concise and accurate summaries of the most spectacular archeological sites and pinpointing them on the world map. If it leaves readers with a sense of wonder, it has done its job.

"Archeology, in attempting to preserve fossils and corpses, is working against nature." But human curiosity makes us want to know what happened to this Viking...

INDEX